Jungmann/Santoro

German GmbH Law
Das Deutsche GmbH-Recht

German GmbH Law
Das deutsche GmbH-Recht

A Guide to the German Company with Limited Liability
Including Bilingual Versions of the Relevant Statutes

von

Prof. Dr. Carsten Jungmann

LL.M. (Yale), M.Sc. in Finance (Leicester)
Honorarprofessor und Programmdirektor an der Bucerius Law School in Hamburg
Rechtsanwalt/Syndikusrechtsanwalt

und

David Santoro

J.D., Attorney-at-Law (New York)
Frankfurt am Main

2. Auflage 2020

C.H.BECK

Zitiervorschlag: *Jungmann/Santoro* German GmbH Law, S.

www.beck.de

ISBN 978 3 406 75036 6

Wilhelmstraße 9, 80801 München

Druck und Bindung: Druckhaus Nomos
In den Lissen 12, 76547 Sinzheim

Satz: DTP-Vorlagen der Autoren
Umschlaggestaltung: Druckerei C.H. Beck Nördlingen

CO_2 neutral
chbeck.de/nachhaltig

Gedruckt auf säurefreiem, alterungsbeständigem Papier
(hergestellt aus chlorfrei gebleichtem Zellstoff)

Preface

In Germany, there are more than 1,000,000 companies with limited liability (*Gesellschaften mit beschränkter Haftung*), in addition to the roughly 18,000 stock corporations (*Aktiengesellschaften*). The company with limited liability (commonly referred to with its German abbreviation, "GmbH") is therefore the most frequently used kind of legal entity in Germany. This holds especially true with regard to start-ups.

The growing importance of this legal entity in the world's fourth largest economy has been accompanied by the globalization of business. As barriers to international commerce have receded and the mobility of capital has increased, more and more of these companies have been owned and/or managed by English-speaking entrepreneurs. Of course, in recent years the broad trends toward free trade and free movement of capital have come under pressure in some parts. In particular, it remains to be seen what impact the United Kingdom's exit from the European Union will have on how U.K. companies conduct business in the European Union, and one possible outcome is increased consideration of the GmbH as an alternative to the British Limited. Irrespective of such possible developments, German GmbHs often have business relationships to suppliers, customers and other creditors abroad. All of these parties have a vested interest in the rules governing this legal entity.

In light of these circumstances, it is not surprising that practitioners as well as students and academics from all over the world want to know more about the German Act pertaining to Companies with Limited Liability (*Gesetz betreffend die Gesellschaften mit beschränkter Haftung*), which we refer to as the "GmbH Act" in this book. However, not everyone interested in the German GmbH can receive the necessary information from the GmbH Act itself and from textbooks or commentaries on the GmbH Act that are in German. Especially since the GmbH Act underwent a major reform in 2008, there was a strong demand for a sound and up-to-date translation of the GmbH Act into English. In light of the fact that English is the commonly used language in the German start-up scene, this demand has grown further.

This book aspires to satisfy this demand. It is addressed to both lawyers and entrepreneurs, on the one hand, and students and academics, on the other. Lawyers and entrepreneurs will find the translation of the GmbH Act useful when doing business in Germany and/or giving or getting advice on German company law or when writing memos in English. In order to further facilitate such tasks, our book contains a dictionary-like list of vocabulary as well as a glossary, which, like an encyclopedia, explains phrases, principles and key features in an alphabetical order. Particularly given the current uncertainty surrounding the future relationship between the European Union and the United Kingdom, moreover, we hope the concise and user-friendly format of this book will help entrepreneurs and in-house counsel who need to consider whether the GmbH is an appropriate legal form for their businesses. In addition, there are students who dedicate a part of their legal education to German company law or who participate in comparative legal studies, and there are foreign academics and researchers who have a keen interest in the German GmbH. In our book, these users will find a textbook-like part illustrating the fundamentals of GmbH law in a systematic and comprehensive way. The focus is on the illustration of the system of

GmbH law and its particularities, as well on topics that are of special interest from a comparative perspective, rather than on technical details.

Parts of our book originally emerged from lectures and speeches given at numerous institutions of higher education around the world. For this second edition, all parts of our book have been completely revised and updated; accordingly, all translations are accurate as of the beginning of the year 2020. To reflect, inter alia, the rather recent reforms of the statutes pertaining to corporate reorganization procedures, we have added translations of numerous further provisions.

As in the first edition, we strived to translate the GmbH Act as literally as possible in order to supply a translation that can indeed be used as the basis for an interpretation of the German GmbH Act by foreign legal academics and practitioners. Accordingly, we refrained from an interpretative approach to translation and we did not fill gaps in the German text. We also did not try to modernize the sometimes old-fashioned style of the GmbH Act or to enhance the quality of the GmbH Act with regard to its clarity and consistency. Ambiguity in the translation therefore basically resembles the ambiguity in the German version of the GmbH Act.

In addition, in order to prevent misunderstandings, we avoided translating German terms of the GmbH Act with established English phrases that evoke certain associations in foreign jurisdictions, not necessarily corresponding to the German meaning. Prominent and obvious examples are the translations of "*Geschäftsanteil*" and "*Gesellschafter*" to "membership interest" and "member" rather than to "share" and "shareholder". Readers that are, at a first glance, surprised (or even confused) by such translations might refer to the list of vocabulary and the glossary to find an explanation and to understand the system and the logic of our approach.

In this second edition, we gave tribute to feedback from the readers of our book and made a few changes in our translation. For example, in instances where the English translation would either deviate from the requirements of the GmbH Act or might not identify the designated institutions, etc. clearly enough, we retained the German terms in brackets in most of these instances. Often found examples are "Commercial Code" (*Handelsgesetzbuch*) and "commercial register" (*Handelsregister*). Again, the glossary provides further clarification of these phrases.

Company law closely interacts with accounting principles, disclosure requirements and insolvency-related duties. Therefore, our translation of the GmbH Act is accompanied by a translation of selected provisions of the Commercial Code (*Handelsgesetzbuch*), the Stock Corporation Act (*Aktiengesetz*) and the Insolvency Code (*Insolvenzordnung*). Their relevance to GmbH law as well as the impact of the law of groups of companies (*Konzernrecht*) and the increasing practical importance of corporate reorganization were the criteria for choosing these provisions.

We hope that this book will contribute to the understanding of the law pertaining to German GmbHs among (foreign) legal experts, entrepreneurs and investors as well as law students and academics – at least by reducing the language barrier. Of course, any translation leaves room for conflicting views, and this also holds true with regard to our literal translation approach. As stated in our first edition, readers are invited to submit their opinions and experiences regarding our translation.

The publication of this book would not have been possible without the generous support of a donor who preferred to remain anonymous but to whom we owe a special debt of gratitude.

Hamburg/Frankfurt, March 2020

Carsten Jungmann
David P. Santoro

Contents

Bibliography

Altgen, Christian, The Acquisition of GmbH Shares in Good Faith, 9 German Law Journal 1141 (2008).

Armour, John, Legal Capital: An Outdated Concept?, 7 European Business Organization Law Review (EBOR) 5 (2006).

Armour, John/Hansmann, Henry/Kraakman, Reinier/Pargendler, Marianna, What Is Corporate Law?, in The Anatomy of Corporate Law – A Comparative and Functional Approach, 1 (Reinier Kraakman et al. eds., 3rd ed. 2017).

Bachmann, Gregor, Introductory Editorial: Renovating the German Private Limited Company, 9 German Law Journal 1063 (2008).

Beurskens, Michael/Noack, Ulrich, The Reform of German Private Limited Company: Is the GmbH Ready for the 21st Century?, 9 German Law Journal 1069 (2008).

Bork, Reinhard, Debt Restructuring in Germany, 15 European Company and Financial Law Review (ECFR) 503 (2018).

Cahn, Andreas/Donald, David C., Comparative Company Law – Text and Cases on the Laws Governing Corporations in Germany, the UK and the USA (2nd ed. 2018).

Casper, Matthias, Liability of the Managing Director and the Shareholder in the GmbH (Private Limited Company) in Crisis, 9 German Law Journal 1125 (2008).

Deipenbrock, Gudula, The 'Business Judgment Rule' and the Problem of Hindsight Bias – Observations from a German Company Law Perspective, 27 European Business Law Review 197 (2016).

Ferran, Eilís, Revisiting Legal Capital, 20 European Business Organization Law Review (EBOR) 521 (2019).

Fleischer, Holger, A Guide to German Company Law for International Lawyers – Distinctive Features, Particularities, Idiosyncrasies, in German and Nordic Perspectives on Company Law and Capital Markets Law, 3 (Holger Fleischer et al. eds., 2015).

Gelter, Martin, The Subordination of Shareholder Loans in Bankruptcy, 26 International Review of Law and Economics 478 (2006).

Gelter, Martin/Roth, Jürg, Subordination of Shareholder Loans from a Legal and Economic Perspective, 5 Journal for Institutional Comparisons 40 (2007).

Harbarth, Stephan, From SPE to SMC: The German Political Debate on the Reform of the "Small Company", 12 European Company and Financial Law Review (ECFR) 230 (2015).

Hirte, Heribert/Lanzius, Tim/Mock, Sebastian, Directors' disqualification and creditor protection, in Legal Capital in Europe, 254 (Marcus Lutter ed., 2006).

Huber, Ulrich/Habersack, Mathias, Special Rules for Shareholder Loans: Which Consequences Would Arise for Shareholders if the System of Legal Capital Should be Abolished?, in Legal Capital in Europe, 308 (Marcus Lutter ed., 2006).

Jungmann, Carsten, The Effectiveness of Corporate Governance in One-Tier and Two-Tier Board Systems, 3 European Company and Financial Law Review (ECFR) 426 (2006).

Kalss, Susanne/Adensamer, Nikolaus/Oelkers, Janine, Director's Duties in the Vicinity of Insolvency – A Comparative Analysis with Reports from Germany, Austria, Belgium, Denmark, England, Finland, France, Italy, the Netherlands, Norway, Spain and Sweden, in Legal Capital in Europe, 112 (Marcus Lutter ed., 2006).

Ladiges, Manuel, Criminal Liability of Directors of a Private Limited Company Seated in Germany, 24 Criminal Law Forum 87 (2013).

Miola, Massimo, Legal Capital and Limited Liability Companies: the European Perspective, 2 European Company and Financial Law Review (ECFR) 413 (2005).

Müller, Klaus J., The GmbH – A Guide to the German Limited Liability Company (3rd ed. 2016).

Nacke, Reinhard, The Law of Insolvency and Security Interests, in Key Aspects of German Business Law, 127 (Michael Wendler et al. eds., 2008).

Rickford, Jonathan, Legal Approaches to Restricting Distributions to Shareholders: Balance Sheet Tests and Solvency Tests, 7 European Business Organization Law Review (EBOR) 135 (2006).

Rosengarten, Joachim/Burmeister, Frank/Klein, Martin, Mergers and Acquisitions in Germany (2nd ed., 2016).

Rosengarten, Joachim/Burmeister, Frank/Klein, Martin, The German Limited Liability Company (8th ed. 2015).

Roth, Frank, Arbitration and Company Law in Germany, 12 European Company Law 151 (2015).

Sandrock, Otto, The Colossus of German Supervisory Codetermination: An Institution in Crisis, 16 European Business Law Review 83 (2005).

Schaper, Martin, Hybrid Legal Forms at the Gates: The Transition from Combined Legal Forms to Hybrid Corporations and its Consequences for Creditor Protection, 10 European Company and Financial Law Review (ECFR) 75 (2013).

*Scheuch, Alexande*r, Konzernrecht: An Overview of the German Regulation of Corporate Groups and Resulting Liability Issues, 13 European Company Law 191 (2016).

Schillig, Michael, The Transition from Corporate Governance to Bankruptcy Governance – Convergence of German and US law?, 7 European Company and Financial Law Review (ECFR) 116 (2010).

Schmidt, Jessica, The New Unternehmergesellschaft (Entrepreneurial Company) and the Limited – A Comparison, 9 German Law Journal 1093 (2008).

Schmidt, Karsten, Grounds for Insolvency and Liability for Delays in Filing for Insolvency Proceedings – Necessary Supplement to Capital Protection, in Legal Capital in Europe, 144 (Marcus Lutter ed., 2006).

Schmolke, Klaus Ulrich, Expulsion and Valuation Clauses – Freedom of Contract vs. Legal Paternalism in German Partnership and Close Corporation Law, 9 European Company and Financial Law Review (ECFR) 380 (2012).

Teichmann, Christoph, Modernizing the GmbH: Germany's Move in Regulatory Competition, 7 European Company Law Volume 20 (2010).

Veil, Rüdiger, Capital Maintenance – The regime of the Capital Directive versus Alternative Systems, in Legal Capital in Europe, 75 (Marcus Lutter ed., 2006).

Verse, Dirk, Shareholder Loans in Corporate Insolvency – A New Approach to an Old Problem, 9 German Law Journal 1109 (2008).

Vetter, Jochen/Schwandtner, Christian, Cash Pooling Under the Revised German Private Limited Companies Act (GmbHG), 9 German Law Journal 1155 (2008).

Wagner, Gerhard, Officers' and Directors' Liability Under German Law — A Potemkin Village, 16 Theoretical Inquiries in Law 69 (2015).

Wedemann, Frauke, Reforming the Law of Limited Liability Companies in Germany, in German and Nordic Perspectives on Company Law and Capital Markets Law, 41 (Holger Fleischer et al. eds., 2015).

Wirth, Gerhard/Arnold, Michael/Morshäuser, Ralf/Carl, Peter Steffen/Greene, Mark, Corporate Law in Germany (3rd ed. 2017).

Wymeersch, Eddy, Comparative Study on Company Types in Selected EU States, 6 European Company and Financial Law Review (ECFR) 71 (2009).

Chapter 1. The German GmbH Law

A. Introduction

1 Today, most countries of the world, through a variety of devices, seek to extend the benefits of limited liability to smaller businesses, while still allowing a degree of flexibility not granted to larger corporations. Some countries have accomplished this feat by creating through statute new legal entities that fall somewhere between partnerships and stock corporations on the business organization continuum. Others, by contrast, have declined to create a distinct legal entity, with the stock corporation being the sole provider of limited liability; but even many of these jurisdictions have developed special statutory provisions or case law that adapt the existing stock corporation to address the specific needs of smaller or medium-sized businesses.[1]

Germany belongs to the first group of jurisdictions. German company law provides, in addition to the Stock Corporation Act (*Aktiengesetz*), another act for a smaller form of incorporated legal entity (*Kapitalgesellschaft*). This business legal entity is called "*Gesellschaft mit beschränkter Haftung*", which means "company with limited liability", and is abbreviated "*GmbH*".

In addition to civil partnerships (*BGB-Gesellschaften* or *Gesellschaften bürgerlichen Rechts*), German law acknowledges commercial companies (*Handelsgesellschaften*) and incorporated legal entities (*Kapitalgesellschaften*). The legal framework attributable to these entities is not contained in one comprehensive "Company Act" but rather a multitude of statutory acts.[2] The statutory provisions on the GmbH are set forth in the Act pertaining to Companies with Limited Liability (*Gesetz betreffend die Gesellschaften mit beschränkter Haftung*), which in German is frequently referred to as the "*GmbH-Gesetz*" or the abbreviation "*GmbHG*", and to which we refer in this book as the "GmbH Act".

2 German GmbHs share the five core structural characteristics generally accepted to be typical for incorporated legal entities.[3] That means that a GmbH has a separate legal personality, its members are shielded from personal liability, the membership interests are transferable, management tasks are delegated by the members to the managing directors with a board structure and the GmbH follows the principle of investor ownership. German GmbHs are, in general, the predominant legal entity for smaller, local or regional businesses. They are typically controlled by only a few members. For example, family businesses are often incorporated in the form of a GmbH. However, some of the German GmbHs have a large number of members

---

[1] For a comprehensive overview of different types of incorporated legal entities in selected Member States of the European Union, see *Wymeersch,* Comparative Study on Company Types in Selected EU States, 6 European Company and Financial Law Review (ECFR) 71 et seq. (2009).

[2] Cf. *Fleischer,* A Guide to German Company Law for International Lawyers – Distinctive Features, Particularities, Idiosyncrasies, in German and Nordic Perspectives on Company Law and Capital Markets Law, 3, 5 et seq. (Holger Fleischer et al. eds., 2015).

[3] *Armour/Hansmann/Kraakman/Pargendler,* What Is Corporate Law?, in The Anatomy of Corporate Law – A Comparative and Functional Approach, 1, 5 et seq. (Reinier Kraakman et al. eds., 2017).

and/or a very large capital stock. GmbHs cannot be listed on stock exchanges, i.e., membership interests cannot be traded publicly.

The advantages of the GmbH as the corporate form for smaller or medium-sized businesses are obvious. The GmbH combines the already mentioned members' privilege of not being liable for the debts of the GmbH with quite flexible statutory rules and moderate disclosure requirements. Contrary to partnership law, the GmbH Act does not require that at least one of the members serves as a managing partner, and contrary to stock corporation law, the members' ability to influence the actions of the managing directors is far-reaching.

3 It is a general principle of German company law to counterbalance the members' privilege of limited liability with the interests of creditors. As a result, German company law is, with regard to stock corporations as well as with regard to GmbHs, heavily aimed at creditor protection. Contrary to partnership law where (general) partners are personally liable for the commitments of the partnership, German company law protects creditors through the so-called legal capital system with its capital maintenance rules (*Kapitalerhaltungsregeln*). These rules are, first of all, designed to preclude distributions of the capital stock to shareholders/members so that at least some assets are available to creditors in the case of insolvency. With respect to the stock corporation, creditor protection through the capital maintenance rules is even stricter than with respect to the GmbH.[4]

I. Historical Background

4 It is true to say that the company with limited liability is a "German invention". This form of commercial company dates back to the late 19th century. Industrial life in Germany and Europe at that time had already broadly accepted the stock corporation as an alternative to the pre-existing types of commercial partnerships. The general idea was that commercial partnerships were convenient for smaller and medium-sized family businesses, whereas bigger ones took the form of the stock corporation, which effectively organized and managed large sums of capital contributed by a great number of rather passive investors.

Over the years, however, it became apparent that the business world needed something in between: a form of commercial organization that was more flexible than a stock corporation (and therefore, like a commercial partnership, convenient for smaller businesses), but that also offered limited liability to the shareholders/members (like a stock corporation). The result was the GmbH: a new incorporated legal entity with close relationships between its members and quite flexible statutory provisions.

5 The GmbH Act came into force in 1892. The new legal entity became a remarkable success: In Germany, there are about one million GmbHs today, and many countries (especially western countries) adopted versions of this legal entity. At the same time, however, there are numerous countries in the world in which the company with limited liability is less accepted in business life. In these countries small, or even family-run, stock corporations are much more prominent.

---

[4] For consequences of Member States leaving the European Union on possibilities for moving away from legal capital rules, see *Ferran,* 20 European Business Organization Law Review (EBOR) 521 et seq. (2019).

II. Legislative Innovation in the Recent Past

The impact of case law on the law pertaining to companies with limited liability is greater than one might think with regard to a civil law jurisdiction, in which the law is largely statute-based. Indeed, there are some landmark rulings of the Federal Court of Justice (*Bundesgerichtshof*) that shaped this area of the law significantly.[5] Nevertheless, it is true to say that the legislator has the even greater influence. Since 1892, the GmbH Act has been amended several times. More recently, such amendments were predominantly the result of European legislative acts and, in most instances, aimed to increase the level of creditor protection. However, in nearly 130 years of GmbH history, there have been only two epochal reforms: in 1980 and, with an even more significant impact, in 2008. **6**

The 2008 reform act had far-reaching implications for GmbH law (and also for German insolvency law) indeed.[6] The reform was not a reaction to changes on the European level, but rather a purely national initiative. As indicated by its name, the underlying idea of the Act on the Modernization of GmbH Law and on the Combating of Abuses (*Gesetz zur Modernisierung des GmbH-Rechts und zur Bekämpfung von Missbräuchen*) attempted to achieve two somewhat conflicting objectives: first, to make the GmbH more attractive to businesses, especially relative to foreign limited liability companies (such as the British private limited company, i.e., the "limited" or "ltd."), which had gained ground against the German GmbH as the entity of choice, and, second, to enhance creditor protection. **7**

The amendments were designed to promote and facilitate the incorporation of GmbHs in Germany. The flexibility in transferring membership interests of a GmbH was enhanced, and it became easier to register companies for entry in the commercial register (*Handelsregister*). Some minor changes were related to the recognition of a GmbH after its transfer into another Member State of the European Union. The central topics of the reform, however, concerned the German system of legal capital. It is now less formalistic, and the former rules concerning member loans in lieu of equity (*eigenkapitalersetzende Gesellschafterdarlehen*) were replaced by an approach based on insolvency law.

Contrary to some reform proposals,[7] the GmbH's minimum capital stock amount of 25,000 euros was not changed by the 2008 reform act. However, the reform act introduced the entrepreneurial company (limited liability) (*Unternehmergesellschaft (haftungsbeschränkt)*) and thereby the possibility of incorporating a GmbH with a capital stock amount of less than 25,000 euros.[8] In this case, however, the company may not be called "*Gesellschaft mit beschränkter Haftung*" or "*GmbH*". Rather, the phrase "*Unternehmergesellschaft (haftungsbeschränkt)*" or the short form "*UG (haftungs-*

---

[5] Cf. *Fleischer,* A Guide to German Company Law for International Lawyers – Distinctive Features, Particularities, Idiosyncrasies, in German and Nordic Perspectives on Company Law and Capital Markets Law, 3, 14 et seq. (Holger Fleischer et al. eds., 2015).

[6] For an overview, see *Bachmann*, Introductory Special: Renovating the German Private Limited Company, 9 German Law Journal 1063 et seq. (2008) and *Teichmann,* Modernizing the GmbH: Germany's Move in Regulatory Competition, 7 European Company Law Volume 20 et seq. (2010).

[7] There was even a Governmental Draft proposing a minimum capital stock in the amount of 10,000 euros (see *Beurskens/Noack,* The Reform of German Private Limited Company: Is the GmbH Ready for the 21st Century?, 9 German Law Journal 1069, 1072 (2008)).

[8] For more details see *Schmidt,* The New Unternehmergesellschaft (Entrepreneurial Company) and the Limited – A Comparison, 9 German Law Journal 1093 et seq. (2008).

beschränkt)" must be part of the company name to put potential creditors on notice of the company's lower capitalization.

8 Most of the provisions of the GmbH Act are applicable to an entrepreneurial company (limited liability). However, the incorporation process is more efficient and simpler. For example, in order to avert costly valuation requirements, in-kind contributions are not permitted. At the same time, however, the distribution of profits is limited. The company is obligated to save at least one fourth of its annual profit until the total equity resources meet the requirements of a GmbH (i.e., until the total equity resources meet or exceed the threshold of 25,000 euros). The idea behind the introduction of the entrepreneurial company (limited liability) was to provide better access to limited liability companies for small businesses. Today, the entrepreneurial company (limited liability) has gained quite some practical importance: Roughly 150,000 entrepreneurial companies (limited liability) have meanwhile been established.[9] Nevertheless, even more than ten years after the 2008 reform act, the purported advantages and disadvantages of the new form of a GmbH and the underlying legislative intention are controversial.

The amendments of the GmbH Act after the 2008 reform act had a less substantive impact on the law pertaining to companies with limited liability. Mostly, they were the consequence of legislative innovation on the EU level, for example with the aim of modernizing accounting law, reforming audit rules or improving anti-money laundering and transparency mechanisms. In addition, the German legislator amended the GmbH Act in order to foster equal participation of women and men in leadership positions.

B. Incorporating a Company with Limited Liability

I. Purpose of a GmbH and Eligible Members

9 According to § 1 of the GmbH Act, GmbHs may be incorporated for any lawful purpose, as long as the provisions of the GmbH Act are observed. It is necessary to register the GmbH for entry in the commercial register (*Handelsregister*) at the court of registry (*Registergericht*) in the district in which it has its registered office.

Although the GmbH is a commercial company, the entry of the company in the commercial register (*Handelsregister*) does not depend on whether the company will serve a commercial purpose. Thus, a GmbH could be used for any business purpose, e.g., to offer professional services (such as running a clinic or a law firm), or even for non-profit purposes. Since 2013, a GmbH may use the abbreviation "gGmbH" (where the "g" stands for "*gemeinnützig*", i.e. for non-profit making purposes) as part of its firm name when it exclusively and directly pursues non-profit purposes.

The necessity to state the business purpose in the articles of association notwithstanding, German company law, contrary to other jurisdictions, does not adhere to the ultra vires doctrine. Accordingly, acts of the managing directors not promoting the company purpose are not void, but rather binding on the GmbH.

[9] Research Project "Entrepreneurial Company" of the Faculty of Law at the University of Jena (www.rewi.unijena.de/Fakultät/Institute/Institut+für+Rechtstatsachenforschung/Forschungsprojekt+Unternehmergesellschaft.html (last accessed March 26, 2020)); for slightly older statistical data (also on other legal entities) see *Fleischer,* A Guide to German Company Law for International Lawyers – Distinctive Features, Particularities, Idiosyncrasies, in German and Nordic Perspectives on Company Law and Capital Markets Law, 3, 7 et seq. (Holger Fleischer et al. eds., 2015).

Quite often in practice, GmbHs have a special business purpose: A GmbH can be 10
incorporated with the only purpose of serving as the (sole) general partner of a limited commercial partnership (*Kommanditgesellschaft*). The often observed abbreviation "*GmbH & Co. KG*" indicates that the business is run in the form of a limited commercial partnership (*Kommanditgesellschaft*), but that this limited commercial partnership does not have a natural person, but rather a GmbH, as its general partner.[10]

The Commercial Code (*Handelsgesetzbuch*) distinguishes between two kinds of commercial companies (*Handelsgesellschaften*), namely between general commercial partnerships (*offene Handelsgesellschaften*) and limited commercial partnerships (*Kommanditgesellschaften*). While, in the former, all partners are jointly and severally liable to creditors for the obligations of the partnership in the same way, there are two kinds of partners in the latter: general partner(s) and limited partner(s). A limited partner is excluded from the management and the representation of the partnership, and his liability for obligations of the partnership is limited by a certain sum that needs to be registered in the commercial register (*Handelsregister*). Once the limited partner has rendered a contribution to the partnership, the value of which equals or exceeds the registered sum, and as long as there is no repayment of the contribution, the liability of a limited partner is finite.

The general partner, by contrast, has the rights and the liabilities of a partner in a general partnership. Accordingly, he represents the company, and his liability is unlimited. Incorporated legal entities (*Kapitalgesellschaften*) such as the GmbH can also be a general partner. If, however, there is no general partner that is a natural person but only a legal person, e.g., GmbH(s), then the limited commercial partnership needs to have the abbreviation "*GmbH & Co. KG*" as part of its company name. In addition, a GmbH & Co. KG is governed by rules that more or less resemble the provisions of the GmbH Act addressing the protection of creditors. These rules, however, simply modify the legal system of a limited commercial partnership governed by the Commercial Code (*Handelsgesetzbuch*). They do not constitute a framework for a genuine hybrid legal entity.[11] However, the Insolvency Code (*Insolvenzordnung*) expressly acknowledges a GmbH & Co. KG as a group of undertakings and, consequently, applies the special rules concerning insolvent groups of companies.

Commercial companies, governed by the Commercial Code (*Handelsgesetzbuch*), have to be distinguished from civil partnerships (*BGB-Gesellschaften* or *Gesellschaften bürgerlichen Rechts*) which are governed by the Civil Code. These are non-registered, non-commercial partnerships, which can be organized either as a disclosed partnership (*Außengesellschaft*) or as an undisclosed partnership (*Innengesellschaft*). Only the disclosed partnership has legal personality. That means that the partnership itself is bound by its debts and obligations, and that transactions can be made and civil actions can be initiated in the name of such a disclosed partnership. In addition, every partner is jointly and severally liable. An undisclosed partnership, by contrast, lacks legal personality. Any civil action must be initiated or responded to in the name of a partner, but not in the name of the partnership (which would not be possible) and not in the name of all partners (which is not necessary).

§ 1 of the GmbH Act also states that there may be one or more members in a 11
GmbH. Thus, the law expressly acknowledges incorporated legal entities with only one sole member. Accordingly, it is possible for a single person to incorporate a GmbH. This member can be a natural person, but also a commercial company (partnership or incorporated legal entity), and it is indeed rather common in practice that, e.g., a parent company establishes a subsidiary (which, in German, is oftentimes referred to as a "daughter company" ("*Tochtergesellschaft*")) for a division of its business. Consequently, a group of companies (*Konzern*) can consist of a parent

---

[10] For more details on GmbH & Co. KGs see *Müller*, The GmbH – A Guide to the German Limited Liability Company, 177 et seq.

[11] See *Schaper,* Hybrid Legal Forms at the Gates: The Transition from Combined Legal Forms to Hybrid Corporations and its Consequences for Creditor Protection, 10 European Company and Financial Law Review (ECFR) 75, 92 et seq. (2013).

company (e.g., a stock corporation) that owns one or several GmbHs (on the suitability of GmbHs as daughter companies in groups of companies see para. 57).

II. Content of the Articles of Association

12 § 3 of the GmbH Act provides the mandatory minimum requirements of the articles of association (*Gesellschaftsvertrag* or *Satzung*). In the GmbH Act, the articles of association are described imprecisely as a kind of contract among the members. Instead, the description "statute of the legal entity" seems to be more accurate. The articles of association are obligatory and binding on all members, including future members. With regard to the specific GmbH and its members, they have basically the same effect as statutory law.

German company law does not explicitly recognize additional corporate statutes such as by-laws. Nonetheless, such contractual side-agreements (*schuldrechtliche Nebenabreden*) are frequently used in practice, especially because they are not registered in the commercial register (*Handelsregister*) and thus not disclosed. Contractual side-agreements are governed by the law of obligations. To what extent they are of a binding character, however, is subject to a controversial debate in Germany.

In addition to the company name and the registered office, the articles of association must contain, inter alia, the capital stock amount and the par values of the membership interests that each member receives/accepts in exchange for his contribution to the capital stock (§ 3 of the GmbH Act). With the exception of an entrepreneurial company (limited liability), the capital stock of the company must amount to at least 25,000 euros.

13 The company will not be registered in the commercial register (*Handelsregister*) if the articles of association do not comply with the mandatory minimum content requirements. In practice, however, the articles will be far more comprehensive than the minimum statutory requirements, as the purpose is to regulate the details that the members intend to agree upon for the future. Contrary to German stock corporation law, GmbH law is very flexible. That means that the articles of association may contain provisions that deviate from the rules of the GmbH Act. Nevertheless, this flexibility has its limits. In particular, the articles of association may not deviate from provisions of the GmbH Act that govern the rights of third persons or that protect the interests of creditors.

If certain requirements imposed by case law are observed, it is possible to include arbitration clauses in the articles of association of a GmbH.[12] In such an instance, all disputes arising among the members and/or between the GmbH and its members in connection with the articles of association or their validity can be finally settled in an arbitration proceeding. The German Arbitration Institute (*Deutsche Institution für Schiedsgerichtsbarkeit e. V.*), a registered civil association for the promotion of national and international arbitration, for example, provides sample arbitration clauses meeting the requirements set up by the Federal Court of Justice (*Bundesgerichtshof*) on its website.

14 Generally, the articles of association require notarial form (*notarielle Form*) and must be signed by all members. However, the involvement of a notary (*Notar*) may be reduced to a minimum. According to § 2(1a) of the GmbH Act, a company can be incorporated following a simplified procedure along the lines of a model protocol

---

[12] Cf. *Roth,* Arbitration and Company Law in Germany, 12 European Company Law, 151 et seq. (2015).

(found in the appendix to the GmbH Act) if there are no more than three members and only one managing director.[13]

III. Entry of the GmbH in the Commercial Register (*Handelsregister*) and Beginning of the GmbH's Existence as Such

The company with limited liability must be registered for entry in the commercial register (*Handelsregister*) at the local court (*Amtsgericht*) where the company has its registered office (§ 7 of the GmbH Act). 15

The registration may first be effected when, with regard to the membership interests, certain minimum amounts have been rendered (see below para. 32). In addition, § 8 of the GmbH Act contains the (minimum) contents of the registration. For example, not only the articles of association must be appended to the registration, but also a list stating the names of the (founding) members of the GmbH, the legitimating documents of the managing directors if the managing directors are not appointed in the articles of association, the report on the incorporation using in-kind contributions (if applicable), etc.

It is not until after the entry in the commercial register that the GmbH as a legal entity with the privilege of limited liability exists. Hence, the existence of a legal person (*juristische Person*) prior to the entry in the commercial register (*Handelsregister*) needs to be considered for cases in which actions are taken on behalf of the not yet existent GmbH. 16

In practice, this problem does not occur in every instance, as many new GmbHs are incorporated in connection with the transformation of a non-GmbH legal entity under the rules of the Transformation Act (*Umwandlungsgesetz*). Also, GmbHs have often been incorporated, e.g., by law firms or audit firms, as "shelf companies" (*Vorratsgesellschaften*). Such companies have typically never engaged in business. They are then acquired by means of a share purchase by persons who want to incorporate a company without going through the incorporation process. They simply have to change the business purpose of such a shelf company and adapt the articles of association to the needs of their business.

"Shelf companies" can also be companies that were already used to run a business, but which became inactive. According to case law, this is, from an economic perspective, comparable to the incorporation of a GmbH (*wirtschaftliche Neugründung*) and, consequently, the rules relating to the incorporation of a GmbH must also be observed when the membership interests of a "shelf company" are acquired.[14] Therefore, the managing directors must issue a declaration that the assets of the "shelf company" equal or exceed the capital subscribed. This made the use of "shelf companies" that were already engaged in business before rather uncommon.

However, whenever a GmbH is created as a new legal entity, i.e., as a legal entity that did not exist before, one has to identify the moment in which the law recognizes the company as a new legal entity. The wording of the GmbH Act is at least confus-

[13] For the modernization of the process of incorporation by the 2008 reform of the GmbH Act see *Beurskens/Noack,* The Reform of German Private Limited Company: Is the GmbH Ready for the 21st Century?, 9 German Law Journal 1069, 1074 et seq. (2008).

[14] Federal Court of Justice (*Bundesgerichtshof*), Judgment of December 9, 2002, Case II ZB 12/02 (published in BGHZ 153, 158 [Vol. 153, page 158 et seq. of the Official Collection of Decisions in Civil Matters]).

ing, if not misleading: § 11 of the GmbH Act states that the company with limited liability does not exist as such before its entry in the commercial register (*Handelsregister*); but, in reality, this does not mean that the company does not exist until that point in time.

1. The So-called Company in Formation

17 After execution of the articles of association (in notarial form), the company is to be registered for entry in the commercial register (*Handelsregister*). Even after registration, however, it may take weeks before the actual entry is effected by the court of registry (*Registergericht*). Oftentimes, this gives rise to a problem because the incorporating members cannot afford to wait that long to start the business activities of the GmbH.

To address this problem, German courts acknowledge the existence of a legal entity even prior to the entry of the GmbH in the commercial register (*Handelsregister*). The so-called company in formation (*Vorgesellschaft*) exists as soon as the articles of association are signed by all members (in notarial form).

There might even exist, depending on the circumstances of the individual case, a legal entity prior to the founding of the company in formation and prior to the execution of the articles of association. If the incorporating members formed a contract with the common purpose to found a GmbH, then this contract might form a pre-formation company (*Vorgründungsgesellschaft*). Such a pre-formation company is typically a partnership. Depending on the nature of the activities of this partnership, it is either a civil partnership (which is the rule) or a (general) commercial partnership (which is the exception to the rule). The existence of the pre-formation company comes to an end once its objectives are achieved, i.e., normally upon the execution of the articles of association. With regard to the liability of the incorporating members that are also partners of the pre-formation company, the usual partnership law rules apply. This means the joint and several liability of the partners (see above para. 10).

It is important to keep in mind that the pre-formation company is not identical to the company in formation or to the GmbH entered in the commercial register (*Handelsregister*). As a consequence, assets etc. of the pre-formation company do not automatically become assets of the GmbH (neither of the GmbH as the company in formation nor of the GmbH entered into the commercial register (*Handelsregister*)). The resulting necessity to transfer assets might be disadvantageous with regard to taxes, while the transfer of liabilities and contractual relationships might be dependent on the consent of creditors, etc.

18 The company in formation's purpose is to effectuate the entry of the GmbH in the commercial register (*Handelsregister*). However, other legal acts in the name of the company in formation are not void or "ultra vires". On the contrary, contracts can be entered into and claims can be established in the name of the company in formation. GmbH law is applicable to the company in formation with the exception of provisions that necessitate the entry of the GmbH in the commercial register (*Handelsregister*). Consequently, for practical purposes, it can be stated that, in contrast to the wording of § 11 of the GmbH Act, the "birth" of the GmbH occurs when the articles of association are executed (in notarial form), rather than when the company is entered in the commercial register (*Handelsregister*).

18a To grant the incorporating members the privilege of limited liability before entry of the company in the commercial register (*Handelsregister*) appears to be risky; this is because it is only afterwards that the court has ensured that the company is properly incorporated and registered, that in-kind contributions have been correctly valued, etc. From the point of view of the creditors of the company in formation, this gives rise to legitimate concern. Thus, to protect the creditors, § 11(2) of the GmbH Act imposes personal and joint and several liability on the "acting persons" (i.e., the managing directors or other persons acting as managing directors for the GmbH) for acts carried out in the name of the GmbH before entry of the company in the commercial register (*Handelsregister*).

In addition to the "acting persons", the Federal Court of Justice (*Bundesgerichtshof*) 19
has held that the incorporating members are liable without limitation for all commitments of the GmbH in formation arising in the period prior to the entry in the commercial register (*Handelsregister*). This liability is called "liability for the covering of losses" (*Verlustdeckungshaftung*).[15] However, as a rule, the incorporating members are not directly liable to the creditors of the GmbH. Rather, they must reimburse the GmbH for the total amount of its debts and losses. The justification for this concept of liability is based on the principle that only the assets of the GmbH are subject to the claims of the company's creditors (§ 13(2) of the GmbH Act). The courts have, however, recognized exceptions to the rule: For example, if there is only one incorporating member, if the GmbH becomes insolvent, or if it is never entered in the commercial register (*Handelsregister*), the incorporating members may be held directly liable by the GmbH's creditors.

Accordingly, the combination of early recognition of the company in formation as a legal entity and the applicable liability rules can be summarized as follows: The incorporating members are allowed to begin the business activities of the GmbH before it is entered in the commercial register (*Handelsregister*). However, any activity of the company in formation will be accompanied by the risk of personal liability of the incorporating members (and of the "acting persons" in the sense of § 11(2) of the GmbH Act).

In the future, the process of incorporating a GmbH will become faster and simpler. According to Directive (EU) 2019/1151 of June 20, 2019, amending Directive (EU) 2017/1132 as regards the use of digital tools and processes in company law, EU Member States have to ensure that it is possible to incorporate a GmbH online, and that the incorporation process is – when a company is formed exclusively by a natural person and when there are no contributions in-kind – completed within five working days. Due to this directive, the GmbH Act must be amended by August 2021 at the latest.

2. The Effect of the Entry of the GmbH in the Commercial Register (*Handelsregister*)

Upon its entry in the commercial register (*Handelsregister*), the GmbH as such is 20
acknowledged as a legal entity with the privilege of limited liability (see § 11(2) of the GmbH Act). The GmbH entered in the commercial register (*Handelsregister*) is identical to the company in formation. Assets and liabilities of the company in formation automatically become assets and liabilities of the company entered in the commercial register.

After entry of the GmbH in the commercial register (*Handelsregister*), only the company assets are subject to the claims of the company's creditors for its liabilities (§ 13(2) of the GmbH Act). The liability of the acting persons according to § 11(2) of the GmbH Act, as well as the liability of the incorporating members, for the liabilities of the company in formation are extinguished.

---

[15] Federal Court of Justice (*Bundesgerichtshof*), Judgment of January 27, 1997, Case II ZR 123/94 (published in BGHZ 134, 333 [Vol. 134, page 333 et seq. of the Official Collection of Decisions in Civil Matters]).

21 Notwithstanding the extinguishment of the liability just described, there is the "liability for pre-entry charges" (*Vorbelastungshaftung*), i.e., there is an additional circumstance under which the incorporating members have to answer for the GmbH's debts: After entry in the commercial register (*Handelsregister*), the managing directors can be, by case law, obligated to conduct a balance sheet test in order to find out whether the net assets of the company have fallen under the amount of the capital subscribed, i.e., under the (nominal) capital stock amount as stated in the articles of association. If this is the case, which is likely if the company in formation already engaged in business activities, then the incorporating members are liable for the difference between the amount of the capital subscribed and the net assets as they can be inferred from the balance sheet as of the date of the GmbH's entry in the commercial register (*Handelsregister*). This liability is called "liability for pre-entry charges" (*Vorbelastungshaftung*).[16] Thus, during the period of being a company in formation, most business activities of the company are carried out at the risk of the incorporating members, rather than at the risk of the creditors.

C. Membership Interests

I. Acquisition and Transfer of Membership Interests

22 Upon incorporation of the company, every member must accept at least one membership interest in exchange for his initial contribution (*Stammeinlage*), i.e., his contribution to the capital stock. It is also possible for some or all members to accept more than one membership interest. Every membership interest must have a par value, and this par value must be denominated in whole euros. The minimum par value for a single membership interest is one euro. There is no need for every membership interest to have the same par value, but the sum of the par values of all membership interests must be equal to the capital stock.

Membership interests are transferable and inheritable. In order to transfer membership interests by contract, the contract requires notarial form, as does an agreement upon which a member's obligation to transfer a membership interest is established. In practice, the articles of association oftentimes subject the transfer of membership interests to further requirements, in particular to the approval of the company and/or of the meeting of the members (*Vinkulierung*).

23 Since the reform of the GmbH Act in 2008, membership interests may also be effectively acquired in good faith from an unentitled person (i.e., a person who has no property interest in the membership interest) under certain conditions (see § 16(3) of the GmbH Act).[17] However, it is necessary for the membership interest to actually exist, as there can be no acquisition in good faith of non-existent membership interests.

Provided that the membership interest exists, an acquisition in good faith is possible if the (unentitled) transferor is entered as the owner of the membership interest in the list of

---

[16] Federal Court of Justice (*Bundesgerichtshof*), Judgment of March 9, 1981, Case II ZR 54/80 (published in BGHZ 80, 129 [Vol. 80, page 128 et seq. of the Official Collection of Decisions in Civil Matters]); Federal Court of Justice (*Bundesgerichtshof*), Judgment of January 27, 1997, Case II ZR 123/94 (published in BGHZ 134, 333 [Vol. 134, page 333 et seq. of the Official Collection of Decisions in Civil Matters]).

[17] See further *Altgen,* The Acquisition of GmbH Shares in Good Faith, 9 German Law Journal 1141 et seq. (2008).

members recorded in the commercial register (*Handelsregister*), i.e., if the list of members is incorrect. This would be the case if, for example, the list of members had not been updated following the sale of a membership interest. The occurrence of an incorrect list of members is rather unlikely as, according to § 40(3) of the GmbH Act, the notary (*Notar*) who took part in the transfer of membership interests must sign the list instead of the managing directors, file it with the commercial register (*Handelsregister*), and deliver a copy of the changed list to the company.

By allowing the acquisition of membership interests in good faith, the law seeks to protect those who rely on the validity of public records. Failure to protect these interests would mean great uncertainty when purchasing membership interests in a GmbH, as the buyer could never be sure that the seller was the actual owner. However, the protection of buyers in good faith is limited, as the law also seeks to balance the legitimate interests of the existing members: If, at the time of the acquisition of the membership interest, the list of members has been incorrect for less than three years, it is a further precondition that the error be attributable to the entitled person. Thus, if a member is diligent in having the list of members updated without undue delay after he purchases the membership interest, but the list of members is still incorrect (e.g., because of a technical error at the commercial register (*Handelsregister*)), he is not at fault and will not lose ownership to the purported buyer. In either case, if a notice of pendency (*Widerspruch*), which serves to notify third parties of disputed ownership, is attached to the list of members, then an acquisition in good faith is impossible, because the buyer would have known of the dubious title had he checked the records.

In 2017, the rules concerning the list of members were amended. These days, the **23a** list of members needs to state not only the surname, first name, date of birth, and place of residence of the members, as well as the par values and the serial numbers of the membership interests, but also the respective percentage of participation in the capital stock represented by the respective par value of a membership interest. This amendment is due to changes in the applicable anti-money laundering laws and to the introduction of the transparency register (*Transparenzregister*). Since then, legal entities such as the GmbH have to provide details about their (ultimate) beneficial owners via the transparency register, unless this information can be retrieved electronically from entries in certain other public registers (such as the commercial register (*Handelsregister*)). In particular, certain authorities have (full) access to the content of the transparency register; since 2020, members of the public also have (limited) access.

II. Financial Rights of the Members Deriving from the Membership Interests

The most important financial right of a member is his entitlement to net income. **24** § 29 of the GmbH Act states that, in principle, members are entitled to the annual net profit (plus any profit carried forward and minus any loss carried forward). In the absence of a different criterion in the articles of association, the distribution is effected in proportion to the par value of the membership interests.

The legal entitlement to the full annual net profit notwithstanding, the articles of association typically provide for a more moderate approach to income participation. Any business that has real business opportunities for the future needs to undertake further investments that need to be financed. Retained earnings are oftentimes a cheaper source of finance than bank loans, etc., and the use of internal finance in the form of retained earnings is much less complicated (and more cost efficient) than an increase in capital. At the same time, however, members of GmbHs, particularly in family businesses, oftentimes rely on an outflow of profits as a source of their personal income.

There is one important limitation to any payout policy: In any case, the restrictions on distributions set forth in § 30 of the GmbH Act and on payments to members set forth in § 64, Sentence 3 of the GmbH Act must be observed (see below para. 39 et seq.).

D. Financial Rules Governing the GmbH – The Concept of Legal Capital

25 Contrary to several other jurisdictions, creditor protection in German company law is based on the concept of legal capital and thus on the idea of the "guarantee function" of the capital stock.[18] This function of the capital stock can be regarded as a trade-off for the privilege of the limited liability of the members (§ 13(2) of the GmbH Act). The capital stock is reserved for the satisfaction of creditors and may not be used for distributions to members. It serves as an "equity cushion". This does not mean that the initial contributions by the members are, as assets, put aside and preserved, e.g., for a financial crisis or restructuring, for insolvency proceedings or for the liquidation of the company. Rather, the initial contributions serve as working capital and can therefore decrease in value due to unfortunate or loss-generating business operations. However, they may not be used for distributions to members.

26 The concept of legal capital is based on three main features:[19] first, the raising of capital and the rendering of contributions in an economically substantive way ("effective" raising of capital and "effective" rendering of contributions); second, the restrictions concerning distributions to the members ("capital maintenance rules") and the treatment of member loans (*Gesellschafterdarlehen*); and, third, the duty of the managing directors to file for insolvency in the case of illiquidity or over-indebtedness. These features are closely related to the minimum capital stock amount requirement and to the provisions of the Commercial Code (*Handelsgesetzbuch*) pertaining to balance sheets. Obviously, restrictions on distributions are more protective of creditors, the more conservative the applicable accounting principles are.[20]

Whether a payment from the company to a member constitutes, on the one hand, a distribution, or on the other hand, a transfer in exchange for consideration, is determined from a balance sheet point of view (*bilanzielle Betrachtungsweise*). This means that a transfer of value from the company to the member is examined for whether the member transferred an adequate amount of consideration in exchange. If the member did not do so, then the balance sheet would reflect a reduction in the assets of the company, and the transfer of value would therefore qualify as a distribution.

The effective raising of capital and the effective rendering of contributions, the capital maintenance rules and the rules concerning member loans are dealt with below. The

---

[18] See further *Miola,* Legal Capital and Limited Liability Companies: the European Perspective, 2 European Company and Financial Law Review (ECFR) 413 et seq. (2005); for a critical analysis of the concept of legal capital see *Armour,* Legal Capital: An Outdated Concept?, 7 European Business Organization Law Review (EBOR) 5 et seq. (2006).

[19] For a comparison to the corporate financial system of most U.S. states see *Beurskens/Noack,* The Reform of German Private Limited Company: Is the GmbH Ready for the 21st Century?, 9 German Law Journal 1069, 1080 et seq. (2008).

[20] See also *Miola,* Legal Capital and Limited Liability Companies: the European Perspective, 2 European Company and Financial Law Review (ECFR) 413, 468 (2005).

same holds true with regard to the minimum capital stock amount requirement and some basic features of the accounting provisions of the Commercial Code (*Handelsgesetzbuch*). Although the duty to file for insolvency is best understood as being a part of the system of legal capital of an incorporated entity, the relevant statutory provisions as well as the consequences of a delayed filing for insolvency are explained in the part addressing the responsibilities of managing directors and their liability (see below para. 68 et seq.).

I. The Capital Stock of the GmbH

The capital stock (*Stammkapital*) of the GmbH is provided for in the articles of as- **27**
sociation (§ 3(1) of the GmbH Act) and registered in the commercial register (*Handelsregister*). The GmbH Act provides for a minimum capital stock (*Mindeststammkapital*). According to § 5(1) of the GmbH Act, the minimum capital stock amount is 25,000 euros (with the exception of the entrepreneurial company (limited liability)). Normally, the amount needed for the actual business purpose of the company is much higher than the minimum capital stock amount. Consequently, the minimum amount fixed by law is not intended to guarantee that every GmbH has a capital stock appropriate for its business purpose. Instead, the minimum capital stock requirement only means that no GmbH may be incorporated and entered in the commercial register (*Handelsregister*) unless the capital stock is 25,000 euros or more. Thus, the minimum capital stock requirement may be best regarded as a signal of the seriousness of the GmbH's incorporating members.

The capital stock amount is fixed in the sense that it is not affected by profits and losses. It is thus a constant figure in the balance sheet. This is due to the general rule for balance sheets in § 266 of the Commercial Code (*Handelsgesetzbuch*). According to the Commercial Code (*Handelsgesetzbuch*), the capital stock amount as provided in the articles of association is entered under "capital subscribed" ("*gezeichnetes Kapital*") in the balance sheet.

§ 266 of the Commercial Code (*Handelsgesetzbuch*) demonstrates that the capital **28**
stock does not rank among the assets of the company (on the left side of the balance sheet) but rather among liabilities (on the right side of the balance sheet).

Example: According to § 266 of the Commercial Code (*Handelsgesetzbuch*), a balance sheet (with only some of the most important items) may be structured as follows:

Assets		**Liabilities**	
A. Non-current assets		A. Equity	
I. Intangible asset items		I. Capital subscribed	300,000
II. Tangible assets		II. Capital reserve	
III. Financial assets		III. Retained earnings	
		IV. Profit carried forward/ loss carried forward	
		V. Annual net profit/ annual deficit	
B. Current assets		B. Provisions	
I. Inventory	150,000		
II. Claims and other asset items			
III. Securities			
IV. Cash on hand, …, balance with banks, checks	150,000		
C. Deferred expenses		C. Liabilities	
		I. Bond issues	
		II. Liabilities to banks	
		III. Trade payables	
		IV. Other liabilities	
D. Deferred tax assets		D. Deferred income	
E. Positive difference from the offsetting of assets and liabilities		E. Deferred tax liabilities	
Total assets	**300,000**	**Total liabilities**	**300,000**

29 Although the capital stock is fixed in the sense described above, it may be subject to change, but only through a capital increase (§ 55 of the GmbH Act) or a capital reduction (§ 58 of the GmbH Act). For such a change, the members must amend the articles of association. The resolution providing for such an amendment is to be certified by a notary (*Notar*), and the amendment of the articles of association must be registered for entry in the commercial register (*Handelsregister*). Only after the completed capital increase or capital reduction may the item "capital subscribed" in the balance sheet be amended accordingly.

Since the introduction of the concept of "authorized capital" ("*genehmigtes Kapital*") into GmbH law in 2008, a capital increase can also be effected in an easier way: For a maximum of five years after the entry of the company (or after the entry of the respective amendment of the articles of association) in the commercial register, the articles of association may authorize the managing directors to increase the capital stock up to a certain par value through the issuance of new membership interests in exchange for contributions (§ 55a of the GmbH Act). There are limits to such an authorization concerning its amount and the possibility of providing for in-kind contributions: First, the par value of the authorized capital may not exceed half of the capital stock existent at the time of the authorization. Second, the issuance of membership interests in exchange for in-kind contributions is only permissible if the authorization expressly so provides.

Additionally, the articles of association may provide for a duty of the members to make additional contributions (*Nachschusspflicht*). That means that the members may resolve to call in further payments beyond the par values of the membership interests. Additional contributions are regarded as equity but do not form part of the capital subscribed. The GmbH Act distinguishes between provisions in the articles of association that install an unlimited duty to make additional contributions and provisions that limit such a duty to a certain amount (see §§ 26–28 of the GmbH Act).

Member loans are not regarded as equity. They are treated as liabilities and, as a rule, must be separately entered as such in the balance sheet (§ 42(3) of the GmbH Act). In an insolvency proceeding, member loans are subject to special rules (see below para. 46 et seq.). **30**

II. The Effective Raising of Capital and the Effective Rendering of Contributions

Until 2008, the managing directors and the members of a GmbH had to observe extremely formalistic rules of the legal capital concept. Meanwhile, some of these rules, in particular the rules concerning so-called member loans in lieu of equity (*eigenkapitalersetzende Gesellschafterdarlehen*), have been abolished, and others have been amended and streamlined. Especially with regard to the law concerning so-called undisclosed in-kind contributions and loans to members, the GmbH Act is less formalistic today. Notwithstanding these facts, the "effective" raising of capital and the "effective" rendering of contributions (*effektive Kapitalaufbringung*) are still key elements of GmbH law and its legal capital concept (see §§ 5, 7, 19 of the GmbH Act). Here, the term "effective" means "economically substantive". That is, a contribution must be rendered so that there is an actual transfer of value to the GmbH, and that such transfer of value has not been reversed in some way, e.g., by repayments to the members. **31**

1. The General Standards

With regard to a GmbH, cash contributions and in-kind contributions are permissible. In either case, the raising of capital and thus the rendering of the contributions must be conducted in an economically substantive ("effective") way. To achieve this goal, § 19 of the GmbH Act contains some key provisions that prevent the circumvention of the rules. First, the members may not be released from their obligations to render contributions. In addition, a set-off against the company's claim to a contribution with a claim against the company is usually not permitted. Finally, members may not assert a right of retention to the object of an in-kind contribution because of claims unrelated to the object. **32**

Before the registration of the company in the commercial register (*Handelsregister*) may be effected, certain requirements regarding the rendering of contributions have to be met (see § 7(2) of the GmbH Act). These requirements differ with regard to cash contributions on the one hand and in-kind contributions on the other hand. Regarding cash contributions, at least one-fourth of the par value must be rendered with regard to each membership interest. The value of in-kind contributions is often difficult to ascertain, and in-kind contributions are often indivisible. Thus in-kind contributions must be rendered to the company completely. In total, so much must be paid in to the capital stock that the aggregate amount of the paid-in cash contributions, plus the aggregate par value of those membership interests for which in-kind contributions are to be rendered, amounts to half of the minimum capital stock.

As long as the incorporating members have not fulfilled their remaining contribution obligations, there is an unsettled debt of the members to the company. The debt **33** is payable after the members resolve to call in the remaining contribution obligations (§ 46, No. 2 of the GmbH Act) or when the company becomes insolvent. Concerning in-kind contributions, a special rule regarding their value at the time of the registration of the company for entry in the commercial register (*Handelsregister*) applies. If, at this point in time, the value of an in-kind contribution does not equal the par value of the membership interest accepted therefor, then the member must render the deficit in cash. In the case of insolvency, the insolvency receiver (*Insolvenzverwalter*) can claim payment of any missing amounts without a resolution of the members.

34 As the general provisions concerning the effective raising of capital and the effective rendering of contributions are rather strict, attempts to evade them were frequent. Case law, however, has found ways to limit the likelihood of success of these attempts and, since 2008, the GmbH Act contains special rules relating to so-called undisclosed in-kind contributions (§ 19(4) of the GmbH Act) and to so-called back and forth payments of contributions (§ 19(5) of the GmbH Act).

2. Special Rules Concerning Undisclosed In-Kind Contributions

35 The undisclosed in-kind contribution (*verdeckte Sacheinlage*) is defined in § 19(4) of the GmbH Act. "Undisclosed in-kind contribution" means a cash contribution that, from an economic perspective and based on a common understanding between the company and the member reached in connection with the acceptance of the obligation of the cash contribution, is to be assessed wholly or partially as an in-kind contribution. In other words, the purported cash contribution is merely a subterfuge enabling the member to render an in-kind contribution without having to comply with the stringent valuation requirements.

Example: A typical scenario for an undisclosed in-kind contribution is as follows: According to the articles of association, a member was obligated to render a cash contribution. With regard to his membership interest, this member paid the respective amount of money to the company. In accordance with a common understanding between the company and the member, however, the money was then used to purchase a truck from the member, i.e., the money was, in the end, re-transferred to the member as agreed upon before. Thus, from an economic point of view, the member did not make a cash contribution but rather used the truck as the object of the in-kind contribution.

36 Traditional case law followed a very strict approach for the treatment of undisclosed in-kind contributions: the contracts pertaining to the in-kind contribution and the legal acts for their performance were ineffective, and the value of items actually transferred to the company was meaningless with respect to the member's still existing contribution obligation.

Today, undisclosed in-kind contributions still do not release a member from his obligation to render a cash contribution. However, contrary to traditional case law, the contracts pertaining to the in-kind contribution and the legal acts for their performance are effective. The value of the asset (e.g., a claim, moveable or real property, or a patent) transferred to the company is deducted from the still-existing cash contribution obligation of the member. This means that the transactions between the member and the company are reviewed from an economic perspective rather than in a formalistic way: The transfer of an asset is acknowledged to the extent that the item transferred had a real value.

The member bears the burden of proving the value of the asset. In practice, however, it is frequently difficult to present such proof. Therefore, undisclosed in-kind contributions still involve enormous risks for the members. Furthermore, managing directors who are involved in the rendering of undisclosed in-kind contributions breach their duty of disclosure to the court, incurring personal liability to the company for possible damages and risking criminal conviction (see § 82 of the GmbH Act).

3. Special Rules Concerning Back and Forth Payments of Contributions

There are transactions between a member and the company that cannot be assessed **37** as an undisclosed in-kind contribution, but which nonetheless qualify as circumventions of the strict provisions concerning the rendering of contributions. Such transactions are called back and forth payments (*Hin- und Herzahlen*). § 19(5) of the GmbH Act deals with such transactions; it is subsidiary to § 19(4) of the GmbH Act, i.e., to the rules concerning undisclosed in-kind contributions. The approach of § 19(5) of the GmbH Act is less strict than the formerly existing rules developed by the Federal Court of Justice as it is possible today for the member to be released from his contribution obligation.

Transactions between members and the GmbH are classified as back and forth payments if, prior to the contribution, the member and the GmbH agreed to a payment to the member that corresponds economically to a repayment of the contribution. In such a case the objects to be rendered in exchange for the membership interests are not deemed to be rendered irrevocably at the unrestricted disposal of the managing directors in the sense of § 8(2) of the GmbH Act. § 19(5) of the GmbH Act states that, in such an instance, the member is released from his contribution obligation only if the GmbH has a claim to repayment of the payment to the member that is nominally and economically equal in value and that is due at any time, or may become due through termination by the company without notice.

Example: A member had to render 10,000 euros to the GmbH as part of a capital increase through the creation of new membership interests. The member transferred the amount to a bank account of the GmbH, but soon thereafter the GmbH paid out a "loan" (in the corresponding amount) to the member. In practice, it is a question of proof whether these transactions were undertaken pursuant to an agreement between the member and the GmbH prior to rendering the contribution. If this is the case, then the member is only released from his obligation to render the 10,000 euros if the economic value of the GmbH's claim to repayment of the loan equals 10,000 euros and if the loan is to be repaid upon the GmbH's request. Accordingly, the financial situation of the member and the terms of the loan agreement are of importance.

III. Capital Maintenance Rules

If the rules concerning the effective raising of capital and the effective rendering of **38** contributions are complied with, it is assured that the capital stock is, initially, covered by the contributions of the members. Under the legal capital concept, additional rules aim at maintaining this status: the capital maintenance rules (*Kapitalerhaltungsregeln*).

As mentioned above, capital contributions serve as the working capital of the GmbH. Thus, they may be invested, which might lead to profits. Profits (and other equity items such as capital reserves or retained earnings) may be distributed to the members to the extent that these equity items in the balance sheet exceed the capital stock. The use of the working capital may also lead to losses, and no legal provision can prevent such developments. However, to the extent that, due to losses, the assets of the company no longer cover the capital stock amount, distributions are unlawful.

GmbH law seeks to guarantee that no distributions to members result in a repayment of initially paid-in contributions. Obviously, this is a far-reaching restriction for payout policy considerations.

The heart of the capital maintenance rules can be found in §§ 30 and 31 of the GmbH Act.[21] These provisions are accompanied by § 64, Sentence 3 of the GmbH Act.

1. The Prohibition of Unlawful Distributions to Members

39 According to § 30 of the GmbH Act, the assets of the company necessary to maintain the capital stock may not be distributed to the members. This provision provides a degree of creditor protection by establishing the capital stock as the above mentioned "equity cushion" for the creditors. The capital stock serves as a barrier for payments to the members.

40 In order to comply with § 30 of the GmbH Act, the managing directors must, at least in difficult cases, make an interim balance sheet before a distribution can take place. The balance sheet test of § 30 of the GmbH Act can best be demonstrated by the following example.

Example: The *X-GmbH* is a GmbH with two members, *A* and *B*, and the sole managing director *C*. According to the articles of association, *A* has to render a cash contribution in the amount of 150,000 euros while *B* is obligated to transfer IT equipment in the total value of 150,000 euros as an in-kind contribution. Both of them have fully rendered their contributions. The opening balance sheet then looks as follows:

Assets		**Liabilities**	
A. Non-current assets		A. Equity	
I. Intangible asset items		I. Capital subscribed	300,000
II. Tangible assets		II. Capital reserve	
III. Financial assets		III. Retained earnings	
		IV. Profit carried forward/ loss carried forward	
		V. Annual net profit/ annual deficit	
B. Current assets		B. Provisions	
I. Inventory	150,000		
II. Claims and other asset items			
III. Securities			
IV. Cash on hand, …, balance with banks, checks	150,000		
C. Deferred expenses		C. Liabilities	
		I. Bond issues	
		II. Liabilities to banks	
		III. Trade payables	
		IV. Other liabilities	
D. Deferred tax assets		D. Deferred income	
E. Positive difference from the offsetting of assets and liabilities		E. Deferred tax liabilities	
Total assets	**300,000**	**Total liabilities**	**300,000**

[21] For other elements of capital maintenance rules – such as the restrictions on the acquisition of membership interests by the GmbH itself – see § 33 of the GmbH Act and *Cahn/Donald*, Comparative Company Law – Text and Cases on the Laws Governing Corporations in Germany, the UK and the USA, 292 et seq.

After a period of successful business activity, *A* and *B* adopt the resolution to distribute 100,000 euros in total (i.e., 50,000 euros to each of them). They instruct the managing director *C* to transfer the appropriate amounts from the company bank account to their personal bank accounts. At this point in time, the balance sheet of the *X-GmbH* looks as follows:

Assets		**Liabilities**	
A. Non-current assets		A. Equity	
I. Intangible asset items	40,000	I. Capital subscribed	300,000
II. Tangible assets	230,000	II. Capital reserve	50,000
III. Financial assets	90,000	III. Retained earnings	
		IV. Profit carried forward/ loss carried forward	20,000
		V. Annual net profit/ annual deficit	10,000
B. Current assets		B. Provisions	
I. Inventory	140,000		
II. Claims and other asset items	170,000		
III. Securities	40,000		
IV. Cash on hand, …, balance with banks, checks	60,000		
C. Deferred expenses		C. Liabilities	
		I. Bond issues	
		II. Liabilities to banks	210,000
		III. Trade payables	120,000
		IV. Other liabilities	60,000
D. Deferred tax assets		D. Deferred income	
E. Positive difference from the offsetting of assets and liabilities		E. Deferred tax liabilities	
Total assets	**770,000**	**Total liabilities**	**770,000**

In order to determine whether a distribution in this situation is lawful, i.e., in order to determine to what extent the assets of the company are necessary to maintain the capital stock, the managing directors and/or the members must make the following calculation: First, all assets have to be summed-up. In the example, the total of assets is 770,000 euros. Second, all liabilities (including provisions but excluding equity) have to summed-up. In the example, the total of liabilities is 390,000 euros. Third, the total of liabilities has to be deducted from the total assets. In the example, the result of this calculation is 380,000 euros. This amount is also called net assets (*Reinvermögen*). Fourth, the net assets have to be compared to the capital subscribed. To the extent the net assets exceed the capital subscribed, a distribution is lawful within the meaning of § 30 of the GmbH Act. In the example, only up to 80,000 euros (380,000 euros minus 300,000 euros) may be lawfully distributed.

Accordingly, a distribution of 100,000 euros, as it was resolved upon, would be (partially) unlawful. In such a situation, the managing director is, as an exception to the rule, not bound by the resolution of the members because he may not violate the law.

It should be noted that even a distribution of 80,000 euros might lead to liability issues. While a distribution of 80,000 euros is in accordance with § 30 of the GmbH Act, it might cause liquidity constraints, as the *X-GmbH* only has cash or a balance with banks in the amount of 60,000 euros. Thus, the managing director may face the consequence of § 64, Sentence 3 of the GmbH Act if the payments to the members must have led, in the eyes of a prudent businessman, to the illiquidity of the company. Illiquidity, however, cannot be reliably determined by an interpretation of the balance sheet. Instead, it is necessary to analyze, for example, cash flow statements (see also para. 44).

2. Consequences of Unlawful Distributions

41 The consequences of any distribution not meeting the preconditions set out in § 30 of the GmbH Act are laid down in § 31 of the GmbH Act. In case of a breach of § 30 of the GmbH Act, the company must first be reimbursed for unlawful payments by their recipients. Bona fide recipients are partly protected if the reimbursement is less than the amount required to satisfy the creditors.

Recipients in this sense are predominantly the members of the GmbH that received unlawful distributions. However, not only these recipients, but also the remaining members may be liable (§ 31(3) of the GmbH Act): If reimbursement cannot be obtained from the recipients, the other members are liable in proportion to their membership interests and to the extent required to satisfy the creditors of the GmbH (but only up to the capital stock amount). Finally, the managing directors also face liability in the case of unlawful distributions according to § 43(3) of the GmbH Act (see below para. 66).

§ 31 of the GmbH Act constitutes a claim of the GmbH against the aforementioned recipients. This claim of the GmbH cannot be pursued by a creditor of the GmbH.

3. Exceptions

42 § 30 of the GmbH Act contains two important exceptions to the definition of unlawful distributions: First, § 30 of the GmbH Act does not apply to payments that occur during the existence of a control agreement (*Beherrschungsvertrag*) or a profit transfer agreement (*Gewinnabführungsvertrag*) under the rules of the Stock Corporation Act (*Aktiengesetz*) (see below para. 91 et seq.) or that are covered by a claim to consideration or repayment against the member that is nominally and economically equal in value. The reason for this exception is that cash pooling agreements in groups of companies are permissible, regardless of the company's net assets.[22] As a result, an interim balance sheet is no longer necessary. Second, the distribution restrictions of § 30 of the GmbH Act do not apply to repayments of member loans and payments of claims arising from legal acts that are economically equivalent to member loans. The consequences of repayments of member loans are governed by rules contained in the Insolvency Code (*Insolvenzordnung*) (see below para. 46 et seq.) and also by § 64, Sentence 3 of the GmbH Act.

4. The Accompanying Solvency Test in § 64, Sentence 3 of the GmbH Act

43 The concept of §§ 30 and 31 of the GmbH Act with its balance sheet approach and its preclusion of the distribution of the capital stock demonstrates the significant difference from the alternative means of protecting creditors of companies with limited liability against distributions to members, namely the so-called solvency test based approaches.

Instead of the concept of capital maintenance, a solvency test approach is employed in some jurisdictions as a mechanism for creditor protection. Different from the concept of capital maintenance, the solvency test allows distributions to members under two conditions: First, the company remains able, despite the distributions, to

---

[22] For a comprehensive analysis see *Vetter/Schwandtner*, Cash Pooling Under the Revised German Private Limited Companies Act (GmbHG), 9 German Law Journal 1155 et seq. (2008).

pay its debts as they become due in the ordinary course of business. Second, the company's assets must exceed its liabilities. Thus, the solvency test neither depends on a mere balance sheet approach, nor recognizes the barrier function of the capital stock.[23]

Despite calls for the introduction of solvency tests into the GmbH Act and the abolishment of the existent capital maintenance rules, such solvency tests have not replaced the provisions of §§ 30 and 31 of the GmbH Act. One of the main reasons for the adherence to the traditional approach might be that a balance sheet test is simpler and perhaps more reliable than a solvency test. However, since 2008, the managing directors are not fully released from the task of checking the solvency of the GmbH. According to § 64, Sentence 3 of the GmbH Act, the managing directors are liable for payments to members to the extent that such payments must have led, in the eyes of a prudent businessman, to the illiquidity of the company. § 64, Sentence 3 of the GmbH Act is applicable to any transfer to members (including repayments of member loans), i.e., also to distributions.[24] **44**

Contrary to the considerations concerning §§ 30 and 31 of the GmbH Act, the solvency of a GmbH cannot be determined on the basis of a balance sheet analysis. The balance sheet might give an indication as to whether the company will remain solvent after a distribution to members. For example, high figures for current assets (such as securities or balance with banks) might be such an indicator. However, this potential liquidity can be offset by liabilities that become due in the nearer future. Thus, a definite answer can only be given on the basis of a cash flow statement which is concerned with the flow of cash in and out of the GmbH. Such a statement is a useful tool to determine the short-term and mid-term ability of the GmbH to satisfy claims as they become due.

As a summary, one might state that, in effect, the managing directors have to comply with both sets of rules: the capital maintenance concept, including its balance sheet test, and the solvency test. This enhances the level of creditor protection, but also raises liability concerns for managing directors when making distributions. **45**

IV. The Treatment of Member Loans

Member loans, i.e., loans given by members to the company, are common business practice and a means of financing that can be witnessed in many countries. From jurisdiction to jurisdiction, however, the classification and regulation of these loans differ. In Germany, member loans are not considered as equity, but as debt. In the case of insolvency, however, these loans are subordinate to the claims of all other creditors of the company (§ 39(1), No. 5 of the Insolvency Code (*Insolvenzordnung*)).[25] **46**

---

[23] Cf. *Rickford,* Legal Approaches to Restricting Distributions to Shareholders: Balance Sheet Tests and Solvency Tests, 7 European Business Organization Law Review (EBOR) 135 et seq. (2006); *Veil*, Capital Maintenance – The Regime of the Capital Directive versus Alternative Systems, in Legal Capital in Europe, 75 et seq. (Marcus Lutter ed., 2006).

[24] For an in-depth discussion of the problems concerning § 64, Sentence 3 of the GmbH Act see *Casper,* Liability of the Managing Director and the Shareholder in the GmbH (Private Limited Company) in Crisis, 9 German Law Journal 1125, 1126 et seq. (2008).

[25] See further *Verse,* Shareholder Loans in Corporate Insolvency – A New Approach to an Old Problem, 9 German Law Journal 1109, 1112 et seq. (2008); for an economic analysis see also *Gelter,* The Subordination of Shareholder Loans in Bankruptcy, 26 International Review of Law and Economics, 478 et seq. (2006); *Gelter/Roth,* Subordination of Shareholder Loans from a Legal and Economic Perspective, 5 Journal for Institutional Comparisons 40 (2007).

Prior to 2008, the GmbH Act contained complicated rules for member loans granted when a prudent businessman would have increased the capital stock of the company. Under such circumstances (known as a crisis of business), the member loans were regarded as given in lieu of equity, and thus treated as equity in an insolvency proceeding.[26] In addition to the applicable provisions in the GmbH Act, case law had further complicated this area of the law.

47 Today, the GmbH Act does not contain any provisions concerning member loans in lieu of equity. The respective provisions were abolished in the 2008 reform. The rules now in force are simpler and have increased the flexibility of corporate financing: The repayment of a member loan is no longer subject to the capital maintenance rule of § 30 of the GmbH Act. This means that a repayment of a member loan will not be regarded as an unlawful distribution (see above para. 42).

In the case of insolvency, however, claims to the repayment of member loans are not only subordinate to other claims. In addition, there are special rules for repayments of member loans made during the insolvency proceeding or in the year preceding the initiation of an insolvency proceeding.[27] Such transactions may be avoided by the insolvency receiver according to §§ 129 et seq. of the Insolvency Code (*Insolvenzordnung*):[28] If a member loan was repaid to the member in the year preceding the date on which the petition for the initiation of an insolvency proceeding was filed, then the insolvency receiver is entitled to bring an action against the members on behalf of the insolvent debtor. In such a case, the members have to refund the amount received to the insolvent company (§ 135(1) of the Insolvency Code (*Insolvenzordnung*)).

48 **Example:** The *A-GmbH* has three shareholders: *X*, *Y* and *Z*. *M* is the managing director. In 2018, *X* and *Y* each gave an interest-free loan to the *A-GmbH* in the amount of 50,000 euros. In mid-2019, the *A-GmbH* repaid this amount to *X*. According to a balance sheet test, the assets thereby distributed to *X* were, in the sense of § 30 of the GmbH Act, necessary for the maintenance of the capital stock of the *A-GmbH*. In January 2020, the *A-GmbH* became over-indebted, and *M* filed a petition for the initiation of an insolvency proceeding. In February 2020, the insolvency proceedings were initiated by the insolvency court.

In this case, the insolvency receiver may recover the 50,000 euros from *X*. However, *X's* duty of repayment does not arise under §§ 30 and 31 of the GmbH Act, even though the 50,000 euros were necessary for the maintenance of the capital stock of the *A-GmbH*. The reason for this is that § 30(1), Sentence 3 of the GmbH Act explicitly states that § 30 of the GmbH Act is not to be applied to the repayment of a member loan. From the perspective of the GmbH Act, the repayment of the 50,000 euros did not violate the capital maintenance rules.

Instead, *X's* obligation arises under insolvency law. As the repayment of the 50,000 euros was a legal act that satisfied the member's claim to repayment of a loan, and as this act was performed during the last year prior to the petition for initiation of the insolvency proceedings, the act is avoidable according to § 135 of the Insolvency Code (*Insolvenzordnung*) so that the insolvency receiver may avoid the act. Accordingly, *X* is obligated to repay the 50,000 euros under § 142(1) of the Insolvency Code (*Insolvenzordnung*).

---

[26] See, e.g., *Huber/Habersack,* Special Rules for Shareholder Loans: Which Consequences Would Arise for Shareholders if the System of Legal Capital Should be Abolished?, in Legal Capital in Europe, 308 (Marcus Lutter ed., 2006).

[27] See *Verse,* Shareholder Loans in Corporate Insolvency – A New Approach to an Old Problem, 9 German Law Journal 1109, 1118 et seq. (2008).

[28] §§ 129 et seq. of the Insolvency Code (*Insolvenzordnung*) empower the insolvency receiver to avoid legal acts – as far as they have been performed before the initiation of the insolvency proceeding – that are a detriment to the insolvency creditors; cf. *Nacke*, The Law of Insolvency and Security Interests, in Key Aspects of German Business Law, 127, 134 (Michael Wendler et al. eds., 2008).

Y's position is also affected by insolvency law. As he is, in addition to his position as a shareholder, a creditor of the *A-GmbH*, he has a claim for repayment of the loan. During the insolvency proceeding of a GmbH, however, claims to repayment of member loans are subordinated. This means that these claims will only be satisfied in priority after the claims of the ordinary insolvency creditors. From an economic perspective, *Y's* claim is worthless.

In addition to the above-mentioned restrictions on repayments of member loans, § 64, Sentence 3 of the GmbH Act addresses all kinds of payments to members, i.e., also payments that qualify as repayments of member loans. As mentioned above, managing directors who have repaid member loans are personally liable if the company became illiquid as a consequence of such repayments. Only payments that were, even after this point in time, consistent with the care of a prudent businessman are exempt. Accordingly, managing directors of a GmbH cannot repay member loans without facing a certain degree of risk of personal liability. Thus, they must be permanently aware of the solvency of the company whenever repaying member loans. **49**

E. Corporate Governance of the GmbH

The German stock corporation law is known for falling into the category of the so-called two-tier board system of corporate governance (also called the dual board system). Stock corporations have, first of all, a management board (*Vorstand*) that manages the stock corporation's affairs in its own responsibility and is, to a large extent, free from the influence of shareholders. In addition to the management board, there is also a supervisory board (*Aufsichtsrat*) that is primarily concerned with the functions of control and supervision.[29] **50**

For GmbHs there is, in general, no need to have a supervisory board. Thus, the GmbH Act provides only for the managing directors (*Geschäftsführer*) and the meeting of the members (*Gesellschafterversammlung*) as mandatory bodies of the GmbH. **51**

However, there are two exceptions to this rule. First, the articles of association may provide that, at the discretion of the members, a supervisory board is to be established. Second, co-determination laws may make a supervisory board mandatory. If there are more than five hundred employees, co-determination laws become applicable and demand a supervisory board for the GmbH: either due to the Act on the One-Third Participation of Employees on the Supervisory Board (*Gesetz über die Drittelbeteiligung der Arbeitnehmer im Aufsichtsrat*) (also called the One-Third Participation Act (*Drittelbeteiligungsgesetz*)) or, but only if there are more than two thousand employees, due to the Act on the Co-Determination of Employees (*Gesetz über die Mitbestimmung der Arbeitnehmer*) (also called the Co-Determination Act (*Mitbestimmungsgesetz*)). In the latter case, half of the members of the supervisory board are elected by the employees (and not by the meeting of the members) and managing directors are appointed by the so-composed supervisory board (and not by the meeting of the members).[30] Since 2015, in both these cases it is also necessary to deter-

---

[29] For further details see *Jungmann,* The Effectiveness of Corporate Governance in One-Tier and Two-Tier Board Systems, 3 European Company and Financial Law Review (ECFR) 426 et seq. (2006).

[30] For a more detailed description of the German system of co-determination see *Cahn/Donald,* Comparative Company Law – Text and Cases on the Laws Governing Corporations in Germany, the UK and the USA, 359 et seq. and *Sandrock,* The Colossus of German Supervisory Codetermination: An Institution in Crisis, 16 European Business Law Review, 83 et seq. (2005).

mine targets for the percentage of women on the supervisory board and among the managing directors.

Most GmbHs, however, have much less than five hundred or two thousand employees, respectively. Nonetheless, some of such GmbHs voluntarily opted to have a supervisory board or decided to install a (rather informal) advisory board, which oftentimes also fulfils networking functions.

I. Managing Directors

52 The GmbH is managed and represented by at least one managing director (§ 35 of the GmbH Act). The managing directors are appointed (and dismissed) at the meeting of the members (§ 46, No. 5 of the GmbH Act). There is one exception to this rule: If the Co-Determination Act (*Mitbestimmungsgesetz*) makes it mandatory to have a supervisory board, then it is the task of the supervisory board to appoint and dismiss managing directors.

If there is, due to death, dismissal or resignation of the managing director(s), no managing director in office, then the GmbH is "leadershipless". In such a case of "leadershiplessness" (*Führungslosigkeit*) the company is represented by the members – but only in the event that declarations of intent are delivered to, or documents are served on, the company. Accordingly, it is safeguarded that, at every point in time, declarations of intent can be delivered to the company and that documents can be served on the company. For all other situations that require the GmbH to be represented, it is necessary to appoint a new managing director or at least a temporary managing director (*Notgeschäftsführer*). The concept of leadershiplessness provides for one exception to the rule that the GmbH needs to be represented by managing directors: In the case of leadershiplessness, every member has the right and, even more important, potentially the duty to file for insolvency of the GmbH (see below para. 68 et seq.).

53 In general, the appointment of a managing director is revocable by the meeting of the members at any time, without prejudice to claims to compensation arising from existing contracts. Although a managing director is not an employee of the GmbH, a contract for services will typically form the basis for his relationship to the GmbH. Such a contract for services will contain remuneration rules, etc., and may also provide for a notice period for the cancellation of the contract. Thus, the revocation of the appointment as a managing director and the termination of his service contract are two separate issues.

Traditionally, German law was not very strict with regard to the necessary qualifications of managing directors. The same held true with regard to disqualification rules. As part of the 2008 reform of the GmbH Act, however, some provisions (see, e.g., § 6(2) of the GmbH Act) were enacted that resemble, to a certain extent, director disqualification rules in force in other jurisdictions.[31] Such rules disqualify a person from holding the office of a managing director if he has been convicted of intentionally committed criminal offences such as delayed filing for insolvency (*Insolvenzverschleppung*), specific insolvency criminal offences, providing false information, making false statements, etc. By August 2023 at the latest, the GmbH Act needs to be amended again in this regard in order to comply with the Directive (EU) 2019/1151 of June 20, 2019, amending Directive (EU) 2017/1132 as regards the use of digital tools and processes in company law. This directive makes it mandatory for EU Member States to have "rules on disqualification of directors".

---

[31] For a comparative analysis see *Hirte/Lanzius/Mock,* Directors' disqualification and creditor protection, in Legal Capital in Europe, 254, 261 et seq. (Marcus Lutter ed., 2006).

Under GmbH law, there is no need for a managing director also to be a member of the GmbH. § 6(3) of the GmbH Act explicitly states that members or other persons may be appointed as managing directors. Whether the managing directors are also members depends solely on the intentions of the members. Especially in family businesses run by smaller GmbHs, the managing directors are typically appointed from among the members. 54

According to § 35 of the GmbH Act, a GmbH is represented by the managing directors in and out of court. If there is more than one managing director, then all managing directors are only jointly empowered to represent the GmbH. However, the articles of association may provide that (some or all of the) managing directors have the power of sole representation (*Einzelvertretungsbefugnis*). 55

A managing director is a so-called representative belonging to a body (*organschaftlicher Vertreter*). Contrary to other persons that are authorized to represent a GmbH either by law or by contract, representatives belonging to a body fall into another category of representatives. Their power to represent the GmbH derives automatically from their holding of a position in one of the (representative) bodies of the GmbH. The power of representation of the managing directors is, with regard to third parties, unrestricted and unrestrictable: Although managing directors are obligated to the company to adhere to the limitations on the scope of their power of representation as determined by the articles of association or by the resolutions of the members, such a limitation on the power of representation has no legal effect against third parties (§ 37 of the GmbH Act). 55a

II. Supervision of the Managing Directors

The members supervise the managing directors (see § 46, No. 6 of the GmbH Act) and direct the managing directors to the extent permitted by law through resolutions, which are approved at the meetings of the members. Unlike the members of the management board of a stock corporation who are empowered to manage the stock corporation in their own discretion and under their own responsibility, the managing directors of a GmbH are under the command of the members. This means that the meeting of the members of a GmbH may pass resolutions on management matters, and that these resolutions are binding on the managing director(s), unless they are illegal. 56

Example: The meeting of the members passes a resolution according to which the managing director shall (a) stop the production of a certain product and (b) make a distribution to the members in the amount of 100,000 euros. – In general, the managing director must execute the two resolutions even if, in his professional opinion, the resolutions are not in the best interest of the company. However, if the distribution of the 100,000 euros contravened § 30 of the GmbH Act, the managing director would not be bound by the resolution.

As a consequence of the far reaching influence of the members and their superior decision-making powers, the managing director must inform the members of important management concerns that go beyond the scope of daily management activities in order to give the members the opportunity to adopt a resolution. 57

This particularity of the GmbH Act has a remarkable effect upon the governance of groups of companies. If a daughter company is in the legal form of a stock corporation, it will tend to be a "stubborn daughter", as the members of the management lead the stock corporation under their own responsibility and are – some statutory and case law exceptions notwithstanding – basically free of shareholder influence (see §§ 76, 119 of the Stock Corporation Act (*Aktiengesetz*)). In order to implement the authority to issue binding directives to a daughter company in the legal form of a stock corporation, the parent company must therefore arrange for a so-called control agreement (*Beherrschungsvertrag*) (see § 291 of the Stock Corporation Act (*Aktiengesetz*)), which necessitates the approval of the shareholder meetings of both companies. A daughter company in the legal form of a GmbH, on the contrary, will be – even without the existence of a control agreement (*Beherrschungsvertrag*) – an "obedient daughter", as the managing directors have to implement the resolutions of the members due to the (general) provisions of the GmbH Act. Accordingly, GmbHs are much more common than stock corporations as controlled undertakings in a group of companies (see below para. 91 et seq.).

58 If a supervisory board is established – either at the discretion of the members (and pursuant to the articles of association) or due to co-determination requirements – then this corporate body is also entrusted with supervisory tasks. § 52 of the GmbH Act (or the relevant provision in the applicable co-determination act, respectively) states that, unless the articles of association provide otherwise, numerous provisions of the Stock Corporation Act (*Aktiengesetz*) become applicable in such a case. Through § 111(4) of the Stock Corporation Act (*Aktiengesetz*), there will then be a list of activities of the managing directors that need the prior consent of the supervisory board.

III. Meetings of the Members

59 The statutory rights of the meeting of the members are defined in § 46 of the GmbH Act.[32] They may be amended in the articles of association. Among the typical subjects on which the meeting of the members passes resolutions are the adoption of the annual financial statements and the appropriation of the profit or loss, the calling-in of contributions and the repayment of additional contributions, amendments of the articles of association (including alterations of the capital stock amount), and, as mentioned above, the appointment and the dismissal as well as the discharge (*Entlastung*) of managing directors (also called the ratification of the acts of the managing directors).

Such resolutions are adopted in meetings of the members. A meeting is convened by the managing directors and must take place whenever it appears necessary in the interest of the company. In any case, a meeting of the members must be convened for the adoption of the annual financial statements and the resolution on the appropriation of the profit or loss.

60 There are few rules concerning meetings of the members in the GmbH Act. Resolutions are adopted by the majority of the votes cast, and each euro of a membership interest confers one vote. In addition to these provisions, there is case law concerning the validity of resolutions. If, for example, a resolution of the members is "unlawful", a minority member can bring an action for a declaration of voidness (*Nichtigkeitsklage*) or an action for rescission (*Anfechtungsklage*), i.e., actions to set aside the resolution of the meeting of the members by a court decision.

Although the action for rescission is mentioned several times in the GmbH Act, the GmbH Act itself does not contain provisions regulating the action for rescission. Instead, the courts apply §§ 241 et seq. of the Stock Corporation Act (*Aktiengesetz*) by way of analogy. As a general rule, a member is entitled to file a lawsuit on the ground that the resolution of a meeting of the members violated either a statutory provision or a provision of the articles of association, i.e., on the ground that the

---

[32] For a comprehensive list as well as for further competencies of the meeting of the members see *Müller*, The GmbH – A Guide to the German Limited Liability Company, 44 et seq.

resolution is defective. Thus, the action for rescission is an action to set aside a resolution of the members: The member's lawsuit leads to a judicial review with the aim of declaring the resolution of the members to be void. The action for rescission must be filed within a certain period of time (generally within one month) after the adoption of a resolution.

The action for a declaration of voidness is similar to the action for rescission. It is used, however, in cases where the resolution is obviously and profoundly defective, i.e., where a severe violation of the law or of the articles of association is present. In such cases, the resolution is automatically void. However, before its voidness is regarded as binding for all members as well as the managing directors, it is necessary for a court to declare the resolution void. In contrast to the action for rescission, there is no time limit to file an action for a declaration of voidness.

The outcome of an action for a declaration of voidness or an action for rescission is binding for all members and the managing directors.

IV. Participation Rights and Protection Rights of the Members

The rights of members of a GmbH are not limited to financial rights. Typically, **61** members are not treated as pure investors by the GmbH Act. Rather, they are members in the true sense of the word, and therefore enjoy participation rights and protection rights.

Above all, members have the right to participate and to vote in the meetings of the members. However, their participation rights and protection rights go even further. Every member has quite far-reaching information and inspection rights. According to § 51a of the GmbH Act, the managing directors must, upon demand, give information on the affairs of the company and grant permission to inspect the books and records without undue delay. Permission may be denied only if there is a concern that a member will misuse his rights for non-company purposes and if a "not insubstantial" disadvantage will be thereby inflicted on the company.

While this information and inspection right is a strong tool also for minority members, as it may not be restricted in the articles of association, the most powerful protection right is the above-mentioned right of any single member to file an action for rescission to declare a resolution of the meeting of the members to be void.

F. Responsibility and Liability of Managing Directors

Managing directors have numerous duties. Some of them are exclusively owed to- **62** wards the company.[33] These are the so-called fiduciary duties, i.e., the duty of care and the duty of loyalty (see below para. 64 et seq.). In case of a violation of these duties, the GmbH has a claim against its managing directors. In addition, there are some duties that rather serve public policy purposes and that are closely related to the concept of limited liability. These are the duty to file for insolvency and the duty not to make "illegal payments" (see below para. 68 et seq.). A violation of the duty to file for insolvency may also lead to claims of creditors directly against the managing

---

[33] For a general (but not GmbH law-specific) overview see *Wagner,* Officers' and Directors' Liability Under German Law — A Potemkin Village, 16 Theoretical Inquiries in Law, 69 et seq. (2015).

directors, and the breach of some of these duties might even lead to criminal conviction.[34]

63 The concept of limited liability means that generally neither the members nor the managing directors can be held personally liable for the debts of the company. This becomes apparent in § 13(2) of the GmbH Act. According to this provision, only company assets are available to satisfy the claims of the company's creditors. If the assets of the company are insufficient to pay the debts, the company is regarded as insolvent. The insolvency estate consists only of the company's assets, which may cause severe losses for the creditors. This fundamental risk faced by the GmbH's creditors is nevertheless accepted.

As mentioned above, a basic idea of German company law is that the concept of limited liability can only be justified to the extent that a reasonable degree of creditor protection can be ensured. Consequently, the law must provide means of creditor protection if insolvency proceedings are not initiated despite the occurrence of insolvency. In other words, as the absence of personal liability is the dominant privilege of the GmbH, it must be balanced by special liability in cases of its abuse. This is the justification for the duty to file for insolvency and for the severe consequences of delayed filing for insolvency which complements the general standard of conduct of managing directors, i.e., the duty of care and the duty of loyalty.

I. The Fiduciary Duties

64 Managing directors of a GmbH are jointly and severally liable to the company for the resulting damages if they breach their duties. They have the duty of care as well as the duty of loyalty. As these duties are owed towards the company, any claim for damages arising from their breach belongs to the company.

If a person acts like a managing director without being appointed managing director and is generally recognized by third parties as a managing director, then such persons – classified as being "shadow managing directors" – also owe the duty of care and the duty of loyalty towards the company. Shadow managing directors who breach their duties are also liable to the company for the arising damages.

1. The Duty of Care

65 The most fundamental duty of a managing director is the duty of care: The managing directors must exercise the care of a prudent businessman in the affairs of the company (§ 43(1) of the GmbH Act). This rule is designed to protect, above all, the interests of the company itself. As an incidental effect, however, it will serve the interests of the creditors as well.

The duty of care would expose the managing directors to an excessive risk of liability if overly strict standards of care were imposed. Therefore, the law grants a significant degree of protection to the managing directors of a GmbH, as it is acknowledged by case law that the managing directors enjoy a broad range of entrepreneurial discretion when making business decisions.[35] Unlike in the Stock Corpora-

[34] Cf. *Ladiges,* Criminal Liability of Directors of a Private Limited Company Seated in Germany, 24 Criminal Law Forum, 87, 95 et seq. (2013).

[35] Federal Court of Justice (*Bundesgerichtshof*), Judgment of November 4, 2002, Case II ZR 224/00 (published in BGHZ 152, 280 [Vol. 152, page 280 et seq. of the Official Collection of Decisions in Civil Matters]).

tion Act (*Aktiengesetz*), the so-called business judgment rule, which protects the members of the management board of a German stock corporation to an even greater extent, is not explicitly regulated in the GmbH Act. According to § 93(1) of the Stock Corporation Act (*Aktiengesetz*), the members of the management board shall not be deemed to have violated their duty of care if they had good reasons to assume that they were acting on the basis of adequate information and for the benefit of the stock corporation when making a business judgment.[36] The business judgment rule thus establishes a "safe harbor" for the members of the management board of a stock corporation.

Because the GmbH Act does not contain a similar provision and because the typical member of a GmbH has slightly different attitudes towards the readiness of the managing directors to accept risk than a shareholder in a stock corporation has towards the managing directors, it might be argued that the GmbH Act is somewhat stricter with regard to the duty of care of the managing directors. In any case, however, the managing directors of a GmbH have a broad entrepreneurial discretion when making business decisions.

In addition to the duty of care, the managing directors must observe § 30 of the **66** GmbH Act, according to which the assets of the company necessary to maintain the capital stock may not be distributed to the members. If managing directors do not comply with this provision, then the members, as the recipients, have to reimburse the company (see above para. 41), but the managing director is also obligated to pay compensation for unlawful distributions. Even if the managing directors executed a resolution of the members when making the distribution that contravened § 30 of the GmbH Act, the managing directors may be liable. § 43(3) of the GmbH Act explicitly states that the obligation of the managing directors to pay compensation for unlawful distributions is not terminated by the fact that the managing directors acted in compliance with a resolution of the members insofar as the compensation is necessary for the satisfaction of the company's creditors.

2. The Duty of Loyalty

The duty of loyalty means that managing directors are not allowed to put their per- **67** sonal interest above the interest of the GmbH. Consequently, contracts and transactions between the company and the managing directors must not be too favorable to the managing directors; they must be made "at arms' length", i.e., in a way in which the company would also have dealt with disinterested persons. Furthermore, according to the corporate opportunity doctrine, managing directors must not exploit so-called corporate opportunities, which means that they are not allowed to take advantage of opportunities for themselves that originally were opportunities of the GmbH.[37]

---

[36] For more details see *Deipenbrock,* The 'Business Judgment Rule' and the Problem of Hindsight Bias – Observations from a German Company Law Perspective, 27 European Business Law Review 197 et seq. (2016).

[37] For a more detailed description of the elements of the duty of loyalty see *Cahn/Donald,* Comparative Company Law – Text and Cases on the Laws Governing Corporations in Germany, the UK and the USA, 400 et seq.

II. The Duty to File for Insolvency and the Consequences of Delayed Filing for Insolvency

68 The most severe danger threatening managing directors with personal liability derives from § 15a of the Insolvency Code (*Insolvenzordnung*), which creates the duty to file for insolvency upon the occurrence of certain events. § 15a of the Insolvency Code (*Insolvenzordnung*) states that the managing directors must file a petition for the initiation of an insolvency proceeding if the company becomes illiquid or over-indebted. In such an instance, the filing of the petition must occur without undue delay and, in any case, no later than three weeks after the point in time in which the company became illiquid or over-indebted.[38]

The duty to file for insolvency of the GmbH becomes a duty of every single member of the GmbH in the case of "leadershiplessness" (*Führungslosigkeit*) (see above para. 52). In this regard, the law does not differentiate between majority/controlling members and members having only a small investment. Members are, however, exempted from the duty to file for insolvency if they had no knowledge of the illiquidity and the over-indebtedness or of the leadershiplessness of the GmbH.

The company law of most jurisdictions provides for liability rules of managing directors of an incorporated legal entity (*Kapitalgesellschaft*) in the vicinity of insolvency.[39] Without the duty to file for insolvency if an incorporated legal entity becomes illiquid or over-indebted, the privilege of limited liability of members/shareholders of an incorporated legal entity is hardly justifiable.[40] The reason is that in such a situation, the funds of the incorporated legal entity are by definition not sufficient for the satisfaction of the claims of the creditors. Upon the occurrence of over-indebtedness, members/shareholders of the incorporated legal entity cannot lose more than they already lost, but may profit from risky business activities. In effect, any further business activities of the incorporated legal entity are carried out solely at the risk of creditors. Thus, without any duty to file for insolvency (and corresponding sanctions in case of breach of such a duty), members/shareholders have, to the detriment of the creditors, perverse incentives with regard to the continuation of the business.[41] In some jurisdictions, such an unjustifiable continuation of the business is called "wrongful trading".[42]

German tort law and the GmbH Act provide for rather draconian sanctions if managing directors do not comply with their duty to file for insolvency. The managing directors are liable to the company for any payments made after the company's illiquidity occurred or its over-indebtedness was ascertained, and they are also liable to persons who became creditors of the company after this point in time (see below para. 73 et seq.). The only exceptions exist in cases in which payments were made in

---

[38] Cf. *Ladiges,* Criminal Liability of Directors of a Private Limited Company Seated in Germany, 24 Criminal Law Forum, 87, 96 et seq. (2013).

[39] Cf. *Kalss/Adensamer/Oelkers,* Director's Duties in the Vicinity of Insolvency – A Comparative Analysis with Reports from Germany, Austria, Belgium, Denmark, England, Finland, France, Italy, the Netherlands, Norway, Spain and Sweden, in Legal Capital in Europe, 112 et seq. (Marcus Lutter ed., 2006).

[40] Cf. *Schmidt, Karsten,* Grounds for Insolvency and Liability for Delays in Filing for Insolvency Proceedings – Necessary Supplement to Capital Protection, in Legal Capital in Europe, 144, 156 et seq. (Marcus Lutter ed., 2006).

[41] See *Schillig,* The Transition from Corporate Governance to Bankruptcy Governance – Convergence of German and US law?, 7 European Company and Financial Law Review (ECFR) 116, 118 et seq. (2010).

[42] See, e.g., Sec. 214 of the U.K. Insolvency Act 1986.

accordance with the care of a prudent businessman, or in which the managing directors neither knew nor ought to have known of the insolvency of the company.[43]

The cases concerning § 15a of the Insolvency Code (*Insolvenzordnung*) (and its **69**
predecessors contained in the GmbH Act) are countless, and the case law is complex.[44] In general, the courts are rather rigid in their judgment of when illiquidity or over-indebtedness arises. Thus, liability under § 15a of the Insolvency Code (*Insolvenzordnung*) and the accompanying provisions of the GmbH Act and the Civil Code is a serious risk for managing directors. In order to understand these immense personal risks, two fundamental considerations must be taken into account.

1. The Definition of Over-Indebtedness

It is extremely difficult to determine precisely when a commercial company such **70**
as a GmbH becomes illiquid or over-indebted. This holds especially true with regard to over-indebtedness.

In short, over-indebtedness exists if the assets of the debtor no longer cover the existing liabilities. During a crisis, but especially in the case of a start-up company, the total liabilities can easily exceed the value of the assets. However, this does not necessarily mean that the company is in a condition that justifies the initiation of insolvency proceedings. The reason is that, the figures on the balance sheet notwithstanding, the company might nevertheless be healthy and thus able to survive the crisis.

Since 2008, the law applies a "double-stage assessment". It emphasizes the criteri- **71**
on "ability of the company to survive on the market" even more. According to § 19 of the Insolvency Code (*Insolvenzordnung*), over-indebtedness exists if the assets of the debtor no longer cover the existing liabilities, unless the continuation of the business is predominantly likely according to the circumstances.

For quite a long time, statutory and case law followed a "single-stage assessment" for the determination of over-indebtedness. According to this approach, a special "insolvency balance sheet" had to be prepared in order to decide whether the company was over-indebted. This approach, however, had to answer an enigmatic question: How should the assets of the company be valued – with liquidation values or on the basis of a going concern valuation? The traditional approach was as follows: The going concern value of the company is only to be employed if, according to all circumstances, such continuation of the company is deemed highly likely.

Under the double-stage assessment applicable today, a thorough and careful prog- **72**
nosis by the managing directors as to whether the company can survive and fulfill its obligations in the near future is the predominant factor for determining whether the company is over-indebted. If this continuation prognosis (*Fortführungsprognose*) is positive, the company is not over-indebted and no insolvency proceedings need to be initiated. If it is negative, an insolvency balance sheet must be drawn up with liquidation values. On this basis, the assets will be compared to the liabilities of the company. From the perspective of the company, the advantage of the double-stage assess-

---

[43] See further *Schillig,* The Transition from Corporate Governance to Bankruptcy Governance – Convergence of German and US law?, 7 European Company and Financial Law Review (ECFR) 116, 126 et seq. (2010).

[44] On the problems associated with the consequences of delayed filing for insolvency see *Casper,* Liability of the Managing Director and the Shareholder in the GmbH (Private Limited Company) in Crisis, 9 German Law Journal 1125, 1137 et seq. (2008); see also (including a comparative perspective) *Schmidt, Karsten,* Grounds for Insolvency and Liability for Delays in Filing for Insolvency Proceedings – Necessary Supplement to Capital Protection, in Legal Capital in Europe, 144 et seq. (Marcus Lutter ed., 2006).

ment is thus the fact that in case of a positive prognosis, over-indebtedness is excluded regardless of the ratio of assets to liabilities, whereas with the single-stage approach over-indebtedness may occur even if the prospects of the company are positive.

2. The Amount of Damages Awarded in Case of Breach of the Duty to File for Insolvency

73 The breach of the duty to file for insolvency (§ 15a(1) of the Insolvency Code (*Insolvenzordnung*)) is a civil and criminal offence, as well as a violation of both German tort law and public policy (see § 823(2) of the Civil Code (*Bürgerliches Gesetzbuch*) and § 15a(4) and (5) of the Insolvency Code (*Insolvenzordnung*)). Compensation can be sought for damages primarily under German tort law.

As mentioned above, the duty to file for insolvency is a duty of the managing directors. Accordingly, the managing directors are to be held liable in a case of a breach of this duty. Quite often however, the managing directors of a GmbH resign from their position and leave the company prior to insolvency. Thus, the company is without leadership (see above). In such a case of leadershiplessness (*Führungslosigkeit*), according to § 35(1) of the GmbH Act the members replace the directors in many respects. Consequently, the members then have the duty to file for insolvency, and in such a case, the members can be held liable if they breach this duty (§§ 15(1), 15a(3) of the Insolvency Code (*Insolvenzordnung*)).

74 In the case of a breach of the duty to file for insolvency, a challenge arises, namely to quantify the amount of damages suffered by insolvency creditors as a result of a delayed filing for insolvency.

According to case law, there are two categories of creditors, and the claims of these creditors are treated differently.[45] On the one hand, there are those creditors who already were creditors of the GmbH at the time in which the company became insolvent. These creditors ("old creditors") suffer because the insolvency dividend they receive at the end of an insolvency proceeding is lower due to the delayed filing for insolvency. On the other hand, there are creditors who became creditors only due to the fact that the filing for insolvency occurred so late. These creditors ("new creditors") would not have entered into contracts or other relationships with the GmbH at all if the filing for insolvency had occurred at the proper time.

75 The damages suffered by the "old creditors" are, once the insolvency proceeding is initiated, asserted by the insolvency receiver collectively for all creditors (§ 92 of the Insolvency Code (*Insolvenzordnung*)). These damages are commonly called "(reduced) insolvency dividend damages" ("*Quotenschaden*" or "*Quotenverschlechterungsschaden*") because they amount to the difference of the hypothetical insolvency dividend (i.e., the dividend the creditors would have received if the insolvency proceeding had been initiated in due time) from the actual insolvency dividend. The managing directors have to pay enough into the insolvency estate so that all "old creditors" finally receive the hypothetical insolvency dividend.

76 The damages suffered by the "new creditors" are not asserted by the insolvency receiver collectively, and "new creditors" are not limited to a claim for only the "(re-

[45] Federal Court of Justice (*Bundesgerichtshof*), Judgment of March 30, 1998, Case II ZR 146/98 (published in BGHZ 138, 211 [Vol. 138, page 211 et seq. of the Official Collection of Decisions in Civil Matters]).

duced) insolvency dividend damages".[46] Rather, "new creditors" must bring an individual lawsuit against the managing directors on their own behalf. In such a lawsuit, however, they may recover the full damages they suffered due to entering into transactions with the already insolvent GmbH.

III. The Refund of Illegal Payments

As mentioned above, the GmbH Act states that the managing directors are obligated to compensate the company for payments that were made after the occurrence of the company's illiquidity or after the ascertainment of its over-indebtedness (§ 64, Sentence 1 of the GmbH Act). The same obligation exists for the managing directors with respect to payments to members, insofar as the payments must have led to the illiquidity of the company (§ 64, Sentence 3 of the GmbH Act). Such payments are identified as "illegal payments". **77**

With regard to § 64, Sentence 1 of the GmbH Act, courts follow a rather strict approach and award excessive damages on the basis of § 64 of the GmbH Act. Managing directors are basically liable for any transfer of assets that occurred when the company was already illiquid or over-indebted. However, payments are not characterized as "illegal" in the aforementioned sense if the reduction of the assets of a GmbH caused by payments made after the occurrence of the GmbH's illiquidity or after the ascertainment of its over-indebtedness are directly compensated in connection with such payments[47] (as, e.g., in a mere asset swap).

Similar to § 31 of the GmbH Act (see above para. 41), § 64, Sentence 1 of the GmbH Act constitutes a claim of the GmbH which cannot be pursued by a creditor of the GmbH. In case of insolvency of the GmbH, however, the claim arising according to § 64, Sentence 1 of the GmbH Act is pursued by the insolvency receiver. In practice, insolvency receivers sue the managing directors for illegal payments quite often, and such claims can exceed claims aiming at the compensation of the "(reduced) insolvency dividend damages". The addition of all these payments sometimes leads to a total liability of the managing directors that may exceed their personal funds.

G. Personal Liability of Members

In principle, members do not bear the risk of being personally liable for the debts of the GmbH. However, an efficient creditor protection system requires exceptions to this general rule. Thus, basically all jurisdictions apply the concept of "piercing the corporate veil" with many variations. In Germany, this concept itself is not recognized by the GmbH Act and it is only rarely applied by case law. However, there are a few special statutory provisions leading to personal liability of the members of a GmbH, and case law has invented liability of members in cases of a so-called "in- **78**

[46] Federal Court of Justice (*Bundesgerichtshof*), Judgment of June 6, 1994, Case II ZR 292/91 (published in BGHZ 126, 181 [Vol. 126, page 181 et seq. of the Official Collection of Decisions in Civil Matters]).

[47] Federal Court of Justice (*Bundesgerichtshof*), Judgment of November 18, 2014, Case II ZR 231/13 (published in BGHZ 203, 218 [Vol. 203, page 218 et seq. of the Official Collection of Decisions in Civil Matters]).

fringement endangering the survival of the company by extraction of indispensable financial resources" (see below).

I. Statutory Provisions

79 The members (and the managing directors) are jointly and severally liable to the company for damages suffered because of false information given during the incorporation of the company (§ 9a of the GmbH Act). A member (or managing director) is released from these obligations only if he neither knew, nor, with the exercise of the care of a prudent businessman, ought to have known the facts upon which liability arose (§ 9a of the GmbH Act). The same rule applies when a capital increase is registered for entry in the commercial register (*Handelsregister*) (§ 57(4) of the GmbH Act).

In addition to that, members may be obligated to refund illegal payments (see above para. 77). Furthermore, in the case of "leadershiplessness" (*Führungslosigkeit*), members can be held liable (under tort law provisions) for breaching their then-existing duty to file for insolvency (see above para. 68).

II. Infringement Endangering the Survival of the Company by Extraction of Indispensable Financial Resources

80 In addition to the statutorily defined liabilities of members in the aforementioned context, there has been an extensive (academic) discussion about piercing the corporate veil under German law. In the past, the following circumstances were regarded as possible exceptions to the limited liability concept: (i) commingling of assets/failure to segregate funds of separate legal entities, (ii) the use of the company as a mere façade, for example to commit fraud or other wrong, and (iii) gross undercapitalization.

The courts, however, were rather reluctant to follow such arguments. Indeed, it is true to state that the traditional legal system in Germany does not accept exceptions to the rule of the limited liability of members. Nonetheless, a kind of "piercing of the corporate veil" doctrine was established under the case law of the Federal Court of Justice (*Bundesgerichtshof*) in the years 2001 to 2009.[48] In some landmark rulings, the Federal Court of Justice (*Bundesgerichtshof*) applied different concepts for the liability of members. Finally, it held that members are liable for damages and losses caused by an "infringement endangering the survival of the company by extraction of indispensable financial resources" (*existenzgefährdender Eingriff*).

81 Originally, the line of arguments of the Federal Court of Justice (*Bundesgerichtshof*) was as follows: The privilege of limited personal liability (§ 13(2) of the GmbH Act) was granted under the condition that members treat the capital stock as an estate reserved for the satisfaction of the company's creditors. If members intervene in the management of the company in a way that does not respect the minimum conditions for the company's survival, or at least for paying off the debts of the company, then the members (partially) lose their privilege of limited liability. Therefore, in an insolvency proceeding, members have to replenish the company's assets wrongfully spent. If no insol-

---

[48] Federal Court of Justice (*Bundesgerichtshof*), Judgment of September 17, 2001, Case II ZR 178/99 (published in BGHZ 149, 10 [Vol. 149, page 10 et seq. of the Official Collection of Decisions in Civil Matters]) ("Bremer Vulkan"); Federal Court of Justice (*Bundesgerichtshof*), Judgment of June 24, 2002, Case II ZR 300/00 (published in BGHZ 151, 181 [Vol. 151, page 181 et seq. of the Official Collection of Decisions in Civil Matters]) ("KBV").

vency proceeding can be initiated (e.g., due to a lack of funds), the company's creditors can assert their claims directly against the members.

Meanwhile, however, the Federal Court of Justice (*Bundesgerichtshof*) has changed the construction of the member's liability for an infringement endangering the survival of the company by extraction of indispensable financial resources.[49] While maintaining the designation "*existenzgefährdender Eingriff*", the court now technically refrains from piercing the corporate veil. This construction bars the company's creditors from asserting their claims directly against the members under all circumstances. Instead, the company has a claim to compensation against its members under the preconditions of § 826 of the Civil Code (*Bürgerliches Gesetzbuch*). As a tort law provision, § 826 of the Civil Code (*Bürgerliches Gesetzbuch*) grants a claim to compensation if the tortfeasor acts against public policy.[50] According to the meanwhile well-established case law, an infringement endangering the survival of the company by extraction of indispensable financial resources conflicts with public policy and thus constitutes a tort claim of the company against the member. This construction avoids the need to grant the creditors a direct claim against the members if no insolvency proceeding is initiated. Because the company always has an independent claim to compensation, it at least theoretically never lacks funds.

In addition, the Federal Court of Justice (*Bundesgerichtshof*) has explicitly stated **82** that even a gross undercapitalization does not per se lead to the application of the doctrine of the infringement endangering the survival of the company by extraction of indispensable financial resources.[51] Consequently, the current status of the case law can be regarded as further proof of the reluctance of German courts to accept the concept of piercing the corporate veil.

However, members are not free from all concerns of personal liability. The personal liability under § 826 of the Civil Code (*Bürgerliches Gesetzbuch*) for an infringement endangering the survival of the company by extraction of indispensable financial resources in relation to the company is still unrestricted. For example, the Federal Court of Justice (*Bundesgerichtshof*) has also held that this liability under § 826 of the Civil Code (*Bürgerliches Gesetzbuch*) can even arise when the infringement takes place during the liquidation proceedings.[52] In addition, there might be an infringement endangering the survival of the company by extraction of indispensable financial resources when the merger of a legal entity that is virtually insolvent is de-facto used to circumvent the liquidation of this legal entity under the provisions of the Insolven-

---

[49] Federal Court of Justice (*Bundesgerichtshof*), Judgment of July 16, 2007, Case II ZR 3/04 (published in BGHZ 173, 246 [Vol. 173, page 246 et seq. of the Official Collection of Decisions in Civil Matters]) ("Trihotel"); for further details see *Casper,* Liability of the Managing Director and the Shareholder in the GmbH (Private Limited Company) in Crisis, 9 German Law Journal 1125, 1132 et seq. (2008).

[50] Federal Court of Justice (*Bundesgerichtshof*), Judgment of July 16, 2007, Case II ZR 3/04 (published in BGHZ 173, 246 [Vol. 173, page 246 et seq. of the Official Collection of Decisions in Civil Matters]) ("Trihotel").

[51] Federal Court of Justice (*Bundesgerichtshof*), Judgment of April 28, 2008, Case II ZR 264/06 (published in BGHZ 176, 204 [Vol. 176, page 204 et seq. of the Official Collection of Decisions in Civil Matters]) ("Gamma").

[52] Federal Court of Justice (*Bundesgerichtshof*), Judgment of February 9, 2009, Case II ZR 292/07 (published in BGHZ 179, 344 [Vol. 179, page 344 et seq. of the Official Collection of Decisions in Civil Matters]) ("Sanitary").

cy Code (*Insolvenzordnung*) and thereby causes the insolvency of the target entity in the merger transaction.[53]

H. Structural Alterations and the Termination of the GmbH

I. Amendment of the Articles of Association and Changes in the Capital Stock

83 An amendment of the articles of association may only be effected through a resolution of the members. § 53(2) of the GmbH Act requires a three-fourths majority for any such amendment. An exception exists with regard to a voluntary increase of the payments that the members are obligated to make. Such a change of the articles of association may only be resolved upon with the consent of all affected members. For all amendments, the resolution of the members must be certified by a notary (*Notar*) and must be registered for entry in the commercial register (*Handelsregister*).

§§ 55 et seq. of the GmbH Act concern the capital increase and the capital reduction. With regard to a capital increase, the law provides means for protecting minority members, while basically all provisions concerning a capital reduction seek to protect the creditors of the GmbH. The capital stock amount cannot be reduced below the statutory minimum of 25,000 euros.

II. The Termination of the Legal Entity

84 The termination of a GmbH requires three consecutive steps: First, the company needs to be dissolved; second, the company must enter liquidation; and, third, the company must be deregistered from the commercial register (*Handelsregister*) by the court of registry (*Registergericht*).

The dissolution of a GmbH occurs, inter alia, through the expiration of the time provided in the articles of association, through a resolution of the members (with a majority of three-fourths of the votes cast) or through the initiation of an insolvency proceeding. The dissolution must be registered for entry in the commercial register (*Handelsregister*) (§ 65 of the GmbH Act). After the dissolution, the company continues to exist, but it can only conduct the business necessary to achieve its liquidation. Through a unanimous resolution of the members, it remains possible at this stage of the termination to resume the former business and exit the termination process.

Subsequent to the dissolution, the company will be liquidated. The process is normally carried out by the managing directors (as liquidators) according to the provisions of §§ 65 et seq. of the GmbH Act. The company ultimately ceases to exist as a legal entity after its deregistration in the commercial register (*Handelsregister*), but not before all the company's assets have been distributed (§ 69 of the GmbH Act). This distribution, however, may not be performed before the debts of the company have been paid off or provided with security, or during the year following the dissolution.

---

[53] Federal Court of Justice (*Bundesgerichtshof*), Judgment of November 6, 2018, Case II ZR 199/17 (published in BGHZ 220, 179 [Vol. 220, page 179 et seq. of the Official Collection of Decisions in Civil Matters]).

A different process is followed if an insolvency proceeding is initiated. If the company is insolvent according to the provisions of the Insolvency Code (*Insolvenzordnung*), an application to initiate insolvency proceedings can be filed with the court by any creditor. The managing directors can also file for insolvency (and have to do so in case of illiquidity or over-indebtedness; see above para. 68 et seq.). The order of the insolvency court to initiate insolvency proceedings initiates the dissolution of the company. Instead of liquidation by the managing directors, the insolvency receiver and the insolvency court will control the process from thereon. **85**

Insolvency proceedings are governed by the Insolvency Code (*Insolvenzordnung*). In Germany, there are neither distinctive acts of Parliament for personal bankruptcy and corporate insolvency nor for liquidation and reorganization procedures. In general, an insolvency proceeding serves to satisfy the creditors of the GmbH collectively by disposing of the assets of the GmbH and distributing the proceeds to its creditors. This will typically lead to a dissolution and liquidation of the insolvent GmbH. Part of the disposition of the assets may entail the sale of the business (or parts thereof) as a whole. In such a case, the business will continue to exist, but it will be held by another legal entity.

An alternative aim of an insolvency proceeding is making a different arrangement in a so-called insolvency plan (*Insolvenzplan*), which is a special insolvency procedure for the reorganization of an insolvent estate, particularly aiming at the survival of the business.[54] This allows the continuation of the existence of the insolvent GmbH. Once the insolvency plan is accepted by the creditors, the insolvency proceedings will follow the provisions of the insolvency plan.

In 2012, the Act on the Further Facilitation of Corporate Reorganization (*Gesetz zur weiteren Erleichterung der Sanierung von Unternehmen*, commonly simply referred to with its abbreviation "*ESUG*") came into force and amended the Insolvency Code (*Insolvenzordnung*). This act extended the possibilities of insolvent GmbHs to administer and direct the insolvency estate themselves under the supervision of a trustee (*Sachwalter*) (rather than under the command of an insolvency receiver (*Insolvenzverwalter*)) in a self-administration procedure (*Eigenverwaltung*), especially in cases in which the reorganization of the insolvent GmbH is not obviously futile. In addition, it became possible to affect the position of the members of the GmbH in the insolvency plan. Particularly, it can now be provided in the insolvency plan to convert claims of creditors into membership interests (debt-to-equity swap). **85a**

III. Mergers and Acquisitions

The acquisition of a GmbH involves either the acquisition of the membership interests or the purchase of the assets of the company. In the former case (often called a "share deal"), the structure of the GmbH is not per se affected, because the existing members are simply replaced by new members. **86**

The situation is slightly different in the latter case (often called an "asset deal"), as all assets are transferred to the purchasing party. Although the company itself becomes, in this regard, an empty shell, in general all rights and obligations of the company remain with the company. However, employment contracts will be taken over "by the new business" by virtue of § 613a of the Civil Code (*Bürgerliches Ge-*

[54] Cf. *Nacke*, The Law of Insolvency and Security Interests, in Key Aspects of German Business Law, 127, 136 (Michael Wendler et al. eds., 2008).

setzbuch). Certain limitations notwithstanding, this rule has to be applied in cases of corporate insolvency and corporate reorganization as well. According to this provision, it is not possible to sell a business without its employees.

87 In the case of a merger, one entity becomes the universal successor (*Gesamtrechtsnachfolger*) of one or several other legal entities. Mergers (as well as de-mergers (*Spaltung*) and also mere changes of the legal form of an entity (*Formwechsel*)) are governed by the Transformation Act (*Umwandlungsgesetz*).[55] When a GmbH is merged into another legal entity, the members of the GmbH receive either membership interests (or shares) in the surviving company and/or another consideration.

I. The GmbH in Groups of Companies

I. Sources and Terminology of the Law of Groups of Companies

88 It is a worldwide observable phenomenon that legal entities are affiliated with other legal entities. This can be the result of the acquisition of other entities or by the intent of a legal entity to segment its activities. In general, in such a group of companies, each legal entity has its own assets and liabilities as well as its own management and employees. The key questions of the law of groups of companies (*Konzernrecht*) are, however: To what extent are the entities belonging to the group separate and independent legal entities? And to what extent are there interdependencies that mingle things together? Answering these questions is difficult as the legal form does not match with the economic functions of the group of companies. In addition, the answers to these questions depend on the perspective chosen; they diverge in company law, in tax law, in insolvency law, etc.

89 It may be regarded as a German particularity that there are statutory provisions governing the law of groups of companies. However, the relevant rules are part of the Stock Corporation Act (*Aktiengesetz*), and the GmbH Act does not contain provisions that parallel §§ 15 et seq. and §§ 291 et seq. of the Stock Corporation Act (*Aktiengesetz*). The law pertaining to GmbHs in a group of companies is – as in most jurisdictions – rather based on case law. To a good extent, however, provisions of the Stock Corporation Act (*Aktiengesetz*) are applied by way of analogy.

In addition, some provisions of the Commercial Code (*Handelsgesetzbuch*) – especially those pertaining to balance sheets – and provisions in the numerous taxation acts play an important role in the law of groups of companies. In this context, typically female versions of expressions describing the degree of kinship are used. One talks about "*Muttergesellschaft*" (typically translated to "parent company" in a gender-neutral way) and "*Tochtergesellschaft*", i.e. about a "daughter company" (rather than "subsidiaries"). In addition, German law refers to the term "undertaking" (*Unternehmen*) in the context of the law of groups of companies. Following this terminology, legal entities in a group of companies are "affiliated undertakings" (*verbundene Unternehmen*).

---

[55] For details see *Rosengarten/Burmeister/Klein*, Mergers and Acquisitions in Germany (2nd ed., 2016); for an overview see *Müller*, The GmbH – A Guide to the German Limited Liability Company, 123 et seq.

II. The Exercise of Control – Controlled and Controlling Undertakings

90 The exercise of control of one undertaking over another is one of the core topics of the law of groups of companies. § 17 of the Stock Corporation Act (*Aktiengesetz*) defines controlled undertakings (*abhängige Unternehmen*) as well as controlling undertakings (*herrschende Unternehmen*). According to this provision (which is also relevant for GmbHs), controlled undertakings are independent legal entities over which another legal entity can, indirectly or directly, exercise a controlling influence. If the majority of the membership interests of a GmbH are held by another undertaking, then such a GmbH is assumed to be controlled by the other undertaking.[56]

German law of groups of companies recognizes two ways of how control over another undertaking is exercised. Both forms of control are dealt with in the Stock Corporation Act (*Aktiengesetz*), and both can also be exercised by and/or over GmbHs. The law distinguishes between situations in which control in the aforementioned sense derives from a mere de-facto control situation (*faktischer Konzern*) and situations in which there is an affiliation agreement (*Unternehmensvertrag*) establishing control.

91 In the latter of the aforementioned cases, a contractual group of companies (*Vertragskonzern*) has been established, typically based on a control agreement (*Beherrschungsvertrag*) – and sometimes supplemented by a profit transfer agreement (*Gewinnabführungsvertrag*) – pursuant to § 291 of the Stock Corporation Act (*Aktiengesetz*).

An affiliation agreement (*Unternehmensvertrag*) is more than a mere contract between two legal entities, as it effectually resembles an amendment of the articles of association.[57] Therefore, an affiliation agreement (*Unternehmensvertrag*) must be in writing and requires the approval of the meeting of the members (with a three-quarter majority). An affiliation agreement (*Unternehmensvertrag*) only becomes effective upon registration in the commercial register (*Handelsregister*).

As directives of a parent company (being the sole or at least majority shareholder of the daughter company) are – unlike in stock corporation law – binding upon the managing directors of a GmbH (see above para. 57), one might wonder why control agreements are also widely recognized in GmbH groups of companies.

In addition to the benefits relating to tax law issues (see below para. 96), the key advantage is that the role of the management of both, of the parent company and of the daughter company, will be clearly defined in the affiliation agreement (*Unternehmensvertrag*). Accordingly, the legitimacy of the influence of a parent company cannot be called into question, and any remaining uncertainty is eliminated.

92 This has to be contrasted with mere de-facto-control situations. The exercise of de-facto-control is not unlawful per se. However, exercising influence in such a way undermines or even contradicts the idea of distinct legal entities with a separate management in groups of companies. The conflict of interest inherent to such situations is dealt with in two provisions of the Stock Corporation Act (*Aktiengesetz*).

---

[56] For a more detailed description of the various degrees of affiliation, see *Scheuch,* Konzernrecht: An Overview of the German Regulation of Corporate Groups and Resulting Liability Issues, 13 European Company Law 191, 192 (2016).

[57] Federal Court of Justice (*Bundesgerichtshof*), Judgment of October 24, 1988, Case II ZR 311/87 (published in BGHZ 105, 311 [Vol. 105, page 311 et seq. of the Official Collection of Decisions in Civil Matters]).

According to § 311 of the Stock Corporation Act (*Aktiengesetz*), in the absence of a control agreement (*Beherrschungsvertrag*), the controlling undertaking may not use its influence to cause a controlled undertaking to carry out a detrimental legal transaction or to take or fail to take measures to its detriment, unless the detriment is compensated. In case the controlling undertaking exercises undue influence, the controlled undertaking and its shareholders/members are entitled to sue the controlling undertaking for damages according to § 317 of the Stock Corporation Act (*Aktiengesetz*). Keeping all accumulated tax advantages for the controlling undertaking and not sharing them with the controlled undertaking can be seen as an example for exercising undue influence.[58]

III. Protection of Outside Members

93 If one legal entity is in a position to be able to exercise control over another entity, the interests of minority shareholders are potentially infringed, as the controlling undertaking might put its own interests over the interests of the controlled undertaking. The exercise of control can exploit the business activities of the controlled undertaking to the detriment of its shareholders/members.

This is most evident in situations in which a control agreement (*Beherrschungsvertrag*) is supplemented by a profit transfer agreement (*Gewinnabführungsvertrag*). This leads to a pooling of the profits and losses of both entities. Accordingly, the net income of one of the entities may be excluded from being available for distribution to the shareholders/members due to the losses of the other entity.

94 As a majority of three-quarters in the meeting of the members is sufficient to approve an affiliation agreement (*Unternehmensvertrag*) of a GmbH (see above para. 91), some of the members might be out-voted. For this reason, the protection of outside members (*außenstehende Gesellschafter*) is a further central topic addressed by the law of groups of companies. According to §§ 304 and 305 of the Stock Corporation Act (*Aktiengesetz*), a profit transfer agreement (*Gewinnabführungsvertrag*) shall provide adequate compensation for outside members by means of recurring payments in proportion to their holding in the capital stock. Furthermore, an affiliation agreement (*Unternehmensvertrag*) shall include the obligation of the other party of such an agreement to purchase, upon demand, the membership interests of any outside member for an adequate consideration. Such consideration may consist of the shares/membership interests of the controlling undertaking or of cash payments.

IV. Protection of Creditors

95 The concept of creditor protection is widely observable throughout German company law. The same holds true with regard to the law of groups of companies, which puts a clear focus on the protection of creditors. The creditors of the daughter company are protected by § 302 of the Stock Corporation Act (*Aktiengesetz*), which constitutes the obligation of the parent company to compensate each annual deficit of the daughter company arising during the term of the affiliation agreement (*Unternehmensvertrag*), insofar as this is not compensated with amounts taken from other

---

[58] Federal Court of Justice (*Bundesgerichtshof*), Judgment of March 1, 1999, Case II ZR 312/97 (published in BGHZ 141, 79 [Vol. 141, page 79 et seq. of the Official Collection of Decisions in Civil Matters]).

retained earnings that were allocated to them during the term of the affiliation agreement (*Unternehmensvertrag*). In addition, § 303 of the Stock Corporation Act (*Aktiengesetz*) grants a special protection in the case of the termination of an affiliation agreement (*Unternehmensvertrag*). These provisions are applied to GmbHs as members of groups of companies by way of analogy.[59]

V. Impact of Corporate Tax Law

Law and practice of groups of companies have to be seen in the context of tax law. **96** The pooling of profits and losses especially under the existence of an affiliation agreement (*Unternehmensvertrag*) (see above para. 91 et seq.) is also advantageous with regard to corporate tax (*Körperschaftsteuer*). The relevant tax law provisions allow a consolidated reporting of profits and losses so that profits of one entity can be offset by the losses of another entity (and vice-versa). This means that both entities are regarded as one fiscal unit for corporate tax purposes (*Organschaft*).

Example: If the annual profit of the parent company equals the annual deficit of the daughter company, and there was no profit transfer agreement (*Gewinnabführungsvertrag*), the parent company would have to pay corporate tax on its annual profit, while the daughter company simply does not owe corporate tax to the tax authorities. With a profit transfer agreement (*Gewinnabführungsvertrag*) in place, however, both entities are regarded as one fiscal unit so that neither the parent company nor the daughter company has to pay corporate tax as the consolidated net income of the group of companies is zero.

A fiscal unit scheme of a group of companies may also be effective with regard to value added tax (*Umsatzsteuer*), trade tax (*Gewerbesteuer*), etc. For these reasons, an affiliation agreement (*Unternehmensvertrag*) between the members of a group of companies is rather common in Germany.

VI. Groups of Companies in Insolvency Proceedings

If one entity in a group of companies becomes insolvent, this has far-reaching legal **97** and de facto implications for the other members of the group of companies. In light of the still increasing economic importance of groups of companies, the Insolvency Code (*Insolvenzordnung*) was amended in 2018 by the Act on the Facilitation of the Handling of the Insolvency of Groups of Companies (*Gesetz zur Erleichterung der Bewältigung von Konzerninsolvenzen*).

Since then, the Insolvency Code (*Insolvenzordnung*) contains mechanisms for the cooperation of the insolvency receivers (*Insolvenzverwalter*) as well as of the relevant courts and creditor committees of several insolvency proceedings in cases where two or more of the insolvent legal entities belong to the same group of companies. In particular, there can be a competent coordinating court that appoints a coordinator of the proceedings. Thus, German insolvency law provides for special rules concerning insolvent groups of companies.

---

[59] Cf. *Scheuch,* Konzernrecht: An Overview of the German Regulation of Corporate Groups and Resulting Liability Issues, 13 European Company Law 191, 197 (2016).

Chapter 2. Bilingual Versions of the Statutory Provisions Concerning Companies with Limited Liability

A. Act pertaining to Companies with Limited Liability

Abschnitt 1 Errichtung der Gesellschaft

§ 1 Zweck; Gründerzahl

Gesellschaften mit beschränkter Haftung können nach Maßgabe der Bestimmungen dieses Gesetzes zu jedem gesetzlich zulässigen Zweck durch eine oder mehrere Personen errichtet werden.

§ 2 Form des Gesellschaftsvertrags

(1) Der Gesellschaftsvertrag bedarf notarieller Form. Er ist von sämtlichen Gesellschaftern zu unterzeichnen.

(1a) Die Gesellschaft kann in einem vereinfachten Verfahren gegründet werden, wenn sie höchstens drei Gesellschafter und einen Geschäftsführer hat. Für die Gründung im vereinfachten Verfahren ist das in der Anlage bestimmte Musterprotokoll zu verwenden. Darüber hinaus dürfen keine vom Gesetz abweichenden Bestimmungen getroffen werden. Das Musterprotokoll gilt zugleich als Gesellschafterliste. Im Übrigen finden auf das Musterprotokoll die Vorschriften dieses Gesetzes über den Gesellschaftsvertrag entsprechende Anwendung.

(2) Die Unterzeichnung durch Bevollmächtigte ist nur auf Grund einer notariell errichteten oder beglaubigten Vollmacht zulässig.

§ 3 Inhalt des Gesellschaftsvertrags

(1) Der Gesellschaftsvertrag muß enthalten:

Chapter 1 Founding of the Company

§ 1 Purpose; Number of Incorporators

Companies with limited liability may be founded, in compliance with the provisions of this Act, for any statutorily permissible purpose by one or more persons.

§ 2 Form of the Articles of Association

(1) The articles of association require notarial form. They are to be signed by all members.

(1a) The company may be incorporated through a simplified procedure if it has no more than three members and one managing director. For the incorporation through the simplified procedure, the model protocol provided in the appendix is to be used. Beyond that, no provisions may be made that deviate from the Act. The model protocol is also regarded as the list of members. Apart from that, the provisions of this Act concerning the articles of association apply accordingly to the model protocol.

(2) Signature through an agent is only permissible based on a power of attorney constituted or authenticated by a notary (*Notar*).

§ 3 Contents of the Articles of Association

(1) The articles of association must contain:

1. die Firma und den Sitz der Gesellschaft,

2. den Gegenstand des Unternehmens,

3. den Betrag des Stammkapitals,

4. die Zahl und die Nennbeträge der Geschäftsanteile, die jeder Gesellschafter gegen Einlage auf das Stammkapital (Stammeinlage) übernimmt.

(2) Soll das Unternehmen auf eine gewisse Zeit beschränkt sein oder sollen den Gesellschaftern außer der Leistung von Kapitaleinlagen noch andere Verpflichtungen gegenüber der Gesellschaft auferlegt werden, so bedürfen auch diese Bestimmungen der Aufnahme in den Gesellschaftsvertrag.

1. the company name and the registered office of the company,

2. the purpose of the business,

3. the capital stock amount,

4. the number and the par values of the membership interests that each member accepts in exchange for his contribution to the capital stock (initial contribution).

(2) If the business will be limited to a certain term, or if additional obligations in relation to the company, other than the rendering of capital contributions, will be imposed on the members, then these provisions also require inclusion in the articles of association.

§ 4 Firma

Die Firma der Gesellschaft muß, auch wenn sie nach § 22 des Handelsgesetzbuchs oder nach anderen gesetzlichen Vorschriften fortgeführt wird, die Bezeichnung „Gesellschaft mit beschränkter Haftung“ oder eine allgemein verständliche Abkürzung dieser Bezeichnung enthalten. Verfolgt die Gesellschaft ausschließlich und unmittelbar steuerbegünstigte Zwecke nach den §§ 51 bis 68 der Abgabenordnung kann die Abkürzung „gGmbH“ lauten.

§ 4 Company Name

The company name must contain the designation “Gesellschaft mit beschränkter Haftung”, or a generally understood abbreviation of this designation, even if it continues to be used according to § 22 of the Commercial Code (*Handelsgesetzbuch*) or according to other statutory provisions. If the company exclusively and directly pursues tax-privileged purposes in accordance with §§ 51 through 68 of the Fiscal Code (*Abgabenordnung*), the abbreviation may be “gGmbH”.

§ 4a Sitz der Gesellschaft

Sitz der Gesellschaft ist der Ort im Inland, den der Gesellschaftsvertrag bestimmt.

§ 4a Registered Office of the Company

The registered office of the company is the place in Germany provided in the articles of association.

§ 5 Stammkapital; Geschäftsanteil

(1) Das Stammkapital der Gesellschaft muß mindestens fünfundzwanzigtausend Euro betragen.

(2) Der Nennbetrag jedes Geschäftsanteils muss auf volle Euro lauten. Ein Gesellschafter kann bei Errichtung der Gesellschaft mehrere Geschäftsanteile übernehmen.

§ 5 Capital Stock; Membership Interest

(1) The capital stock of the company must amount to at least twenty-five thousand euros.

(2) The par value of each membership interest must be denominated in whole euros. A member may accept multiple membership interests upon founding of the company.

(3) Die Höhe der Nennbeträge der einzelnen Geschäftsanteile kann verschieden bestimmt werden. Die Summe der Nennbeträge aller Geschäftsanteile muss mit dem Stammkapital übereinstimmen.

(4) Sollen Sacheinlagen geleistet werden, so müssen der Gegenstand der Sacheinlage und der Nennbetrag des Geschäftsanteils, auf den sich die Sacheinlage bezieht, im Gesellschaftsvertrag festgesetzt werden. Die Gesellschafter haben in einem Sachgründungsbericht die für die Angemessenheit der Leistungen für Sacheinlagen wesentlichen Umstände darzulegen und beim Übergang eines Unternehmens auf die Gesellschaft die Jahresergebnisse der beiden letzten Geschäftsjahre anzugeben.

(3) Different par values may be provided for the individual membership interests. The sum of the par values of all membership interests must be equal to the capital stock.

(4) If in-kind contributions will be rendered, then the object of the in-kind contribution, and the par value of the membership interest to which the in-kind contribution relates, must be determined in the articles of association. The members must present any facts that are material to the adequacy of any rendering of in-kind contributions in a report on the incorporation using in-kind contributions and, upon the transfer of a business to the company, state the annual profits or losses of the preceding two fiscal years.

§ 5a Unternehmergesellschaft

(1) Eine Gesellschaft, die mit einem Stammkapital gegründet wird, das den Betrag des Mindeststammkapitals nach § 5 Abs. 1 unterschreitet, muss in der Firma abweichend von § 4 die Bezeichnung „Unternehmergesellschaft (haftungsbeschränkt)" oder „UG (haftungsbeschränkt)" führen.

(2) Abweichend von § 7 Abs. 2 darf die Anmeldung erst erfolgen, wenn das Stammkapital in voller Höhe eingezahlt ist. Sacheinlagen sind ausgeschlossen.

(3) In der Bilanz des nach den §§ 242, 264 des Handelsgesetzbuchs aufzustellenden Jahresabschlusses ist eine gesetzliche Rücklage zu bilden, in die ein Viertel des um einen Verlustvortrag aus dem Vorjahr geminderten Jahresüberschusses einzustellen ist. Die Rücklage darf nur verwandt werden

1. für Zwecke des § 57c;

2. zum Ausgleich eines Jahresfehlbetrags, soweit er nicht durch einen Gewinnvortrag aus dem Vorjahr gedeckt ist;

§ 5a Entrepreneurial Company

(1) A company that is incorporated with a capital stock below the minimum capital stock amount according to § 5(1) must include the designation "Unternehmergesellschaft (haftungsbeschränkt)" or "UG (haftungsbeschränkt)" in the company name, notwithstanding § 4.

(2) Notwithstanding § 7(2), the registration may be first effected when the capital stock has been fully paid in. In-kind contributions are prohibited.

(3) In the balance sheet of the annual financial statements to be drawn up according to §§ 242 and 264 of the Commercial Code (*Handelsgesetzbuch*), a statutory reserve is to be provided for in which one-fourth of the annual net profit less any loss carried forward from the previous year is to be allocated. The reserve may only be used

1. for § 57c purposes;

2. to compensate for an annual deficit, insofar as it is not covered by a profit carried forward from the previous year;

3. zum Ausgleich eines Verlustvortrags aus dem Vorjahr, soweit er nicht durch einen Jahresüberschuss gedeckt ist.

3. to compensate for a loss carried forward from the previous year, insofar as it is not covered by an annual net profit.

(4) Abweichend von § 49 Abs. 3 muss die Versammlung der Gesellschafter bei drohender Zahlungsunfähigkeit unverzüglich einberufen werden.

(4) Notwithstanding § 49(3), the meeting of the members must be called without undue delay in the event of imminent illiquidity.

(5) Erhöht die Gesellschaft ihr Stammkapital so, dass es den Betrag des Mindeststammkapitals nach § 5 Abs. 1 erreicht oder übersteigt, finden die Absätze 1 bis 4 keine Anwendung mehr; die Firma nach Absatz 1 darf beibehalten werden.

(5) If the company raises its capital stock such that the minimum capital stock amount according to § 5(1) is met or surpassed, then Subsections 1 to 4 no longer apply; the company name according to Subsection 1 may be retained.

§ 6 Geschäftsführer

§ 6 Managing Director

(1) Die Gesellschaft muß einen oder mehrere Geschäftsführer haben.

(1) The company must have one or more managing directors.

(2) Geschäftsführer kann nur eine natürliche, unbeschränkt geschäftsfähige Person sein. Geschäftsführer kann nicht sein, wer

1. als Betreuter bei der Besorgung seiner Vermögensangelegenheiten ganz oder teilweise einem Einwilligungsvorbehalt (§ 1903 des Bürgerlichen Gesetzbuchs) unterliegt,

2. aufgrund eines gerichtlichen Urteils oder einer vollziehbaren Entscheidung einer Verwaltungsbehörde einen Beruf, einen Berufszweig, ein Gewerbe oder einen Gewerbezweig nicht ausüben darf, sofern der Unternehmensgegenstand ganz oder teilweise mit dem Gegenstand des Verbots übereinstimmt,

3. wegen einer oder mehrerer vorsätzlich begangener Straftaten

(2) Only a natural person of full legal capacity may be a managing director. A managing director may not be someone who

1. is wholly or partially subject to an obligation to obtain consent as a person whose financial matters are supervised (§ 1903 of the Civil Code (*Bürgerliches Gesetzbuch*)),

2. may not practice a profession, a branch of a profession, a trade, or a branch of a trade based on a court judgment or an executable decision of an administrative agency, if the business purpose coincides wholly or partially with the subject-matter of the prohibition,

3. has been convicted because of one or more intentionally committed criminal offenses

a) des Unterlassens der Stellung des Antrags auf Eröffnung des Insolvenzverfahrens (Insolvenzverschleppung),

a) of failing to file a petition for the initiation of an insolvency proceeding (delayed filing for insolvency),

b) nach den §§ 283 bis 283d des Strafgesetzbuchs (Insolvenzstraftaten),

b) according to §§ 283 to 283d of the Criminal Code (*Strafgesetzbuch*) (insolvency criminal offenses),

c) der falschen Angaben nach § 82 dieses Gesetzes oder § 399 des Aktiengesetzes,

d) der unrichtigen Darstellung nach § 400 des Aktiengesetzes, § 331 des Handelsgesetzbuchs, § 313 des Umwandlungsgesetzes oder § 17 des Publizitätsgesetzes oder

e) nach den §§ 263 bis 264a oder den §§ 265b bis 266a des Strafgesetzbuchs zu einer Freiheitsstrafe von mindestens einem Jahr

verurteilt worden ist; dieser Ausschluss gilt für die Dauer von fünf Jahren seit der Rechtskraft des Urteils, wobei die Zeit nicht eingerechnet wird, in welcher der Täter auf behördliche Anordnung in einer Anstalt verwahrt worden ist.

Satz 2 Nr. 3 gilt entsprechend bei einer Verurteilung im Ausland wegen einer Tat, die mit den in Satz 2 Nr. 3 genannten Taten vergleichbar ist.

(3) Zu Geschäftsführern können Gesellschafter oder andere Personen bestellt werden. Die Bestellung erfolgt entweder im Gesellschaftsvertrag oder nach Maßgabe der Bestimmungen des dritten Abschnitts.

(4) Ist im Gesellschaftsvertrag bestimmt, daß sämtliche Gesellschafter zur Geschäftsführung berechtigt sein sollen, so gelten nur die der Gesellschaft bei Festsetzung dieser Bestimmung angehörenden Personen als die bestellten Geschäftsführer.

(5) Gesellschafter, die vorsätzlich oder grob fahrlässig einer Person, die nicht Geschäftsführer sein kann, die Führung der Geschäfte überlassen, haften der Gesellschaft solidarisch für den Schaden, der dadurch entsteht, dass diese Person die ihr gegenüber der Gesellschaft bestehenden Obliegenheiten verletzt.

c) of false disclosure according to § 82 of this Act or § 399 of the Stock Corporation Act (*Aktiengesetz*),

d) of false statements according to § 400 of the Stock Corporation Act (*Aktiengesetz*), § 331 of the Commercial Code (*Handelsgesetzbuch*), § 313 of the Transformation Act (*Umwandlungsgesetz*), or § 17 of the Public Disclosure Act (*Publizitätsgesetz*), or

e) according to §§ 263 to 264a or to §§ 265b to 266a of the Criminal Code (*Strafgesetzbuch*) and sentenced to a term of imprisonment of at least one year;

this disqualification applies for the duration of five years from the moment in which the judgment becomes res judicata, while the time during which the offender has been institutionalized pursuant to an administrative ruling will not be counted.

Sentence 2, No. 3 applies accordingly to a foreign conviction because of an act that is comparable to the acts named in Sentence 2, No. 3.

(3) Members or other persons may be appointed as managing directors. The appointment is effected either in the articles of association or in compliance with the provisions of the Third Chapter.

(4) If the articles of association provide that all members will be entitled to participate in the management, then only the persons who are members of the company upon the determination of this provision are regarded as the appointed managing directors.

(5) Members who intentionally or through gross negligence relinquish the management of the business to a person who may not be a managing director are jointly and severally liable to the company for the damage that arises when this person breaches his duties to the company.

§ 7 Anmeldung der Gesellschaft

(1) Die Gesellschaft ist bei dem Gericht, in dessen Bezirk sie ihren Sitz hat, zur Eintragung in das Handelsregister anzumelden.

(2) Die Anmeldung darf erst erfolgen, wenn auf jeden Geschäftsanteil, soweit nicht Sacheinlagen vereinbart sind, ein Viertel des Nennbetrags eingezahlt ist. Insgesamt muß auf das Stammkapital mindestens soviel eingezahlt sein, daß der Gesamtbetrag der eingezahlten Geldeinlagen zuzüglich des Gesamtnennbetrags der Geschäftsanteile, für die Sacheinlagen zu leisten sind, die Hälfte des Mindeststammkapitals gemäß § 5 Abs. 1 erreicht.

(3) Die Sacheinlagen sind vor der Anmeldung der Gesellschaft zur Eintragung in das Handelsregister so an die Gesellschaft zu bewirken, daß sie endgültig zur freien Verfügung der Geschäftsführer stehen.

§ 7 Registration of the Company

(1) The company is to be registered for entry in the commercial register (*Handelsregister*) at the court of the district in which it has its registered office.

(2) The registration may first be effected when, for each membership interest, insofar as no in-kind contributions are agreed upon, one-fourth of the par value has been paid in. In total, so much must be paid in to the capital stock that the aggregate amount of the paid-in cash contributions, plus the aggregate par value of the membership interests for which in-kind contributions are to be rendered, amounts to half of the minimum capital stock according to § 5(1).

(3) The in-kind contributions are to be rendered to the company before the registration of the company for entry in the commercial register (*Handelsregister*) such that they are irrevocably at the unrestricted disposal of the managing directors.

§ 8 Inhalt der Anmeldung

(1) Der Anmeldung müssen beigefügt sein:

1. der Gesellschaftsvertrag und im Fall des § 2 Abs. 2 die Vollmachten der Vertreter, welche den Gesellschaftsvertrag unterzeichnet haben, oder eine beglaubigte Abschrift dieser Urkunden,

2. die Legitimation der Geschäftsführer, sofern dieselben nicht im Gesellschaftsvertrag bestellt sind,

3. eine von den Anmeldenden unterschriebene Liste der Gesellschafter nach den Vorgaben des § 40,

4. im Fall des § 5 Abs. 4 die Verträge, die den Festsetzungen zugrunde liegen oder zu ihrer Ausführung geschlossen worden sind, und der Sachgründungsbericht,

§ 8 Contents of the Registration

(1) The following must be appended to the registration:

1. the articles of association and, in the case of § 2(2), the powers of attorney of the representatives who have signed the articles of association, or an authenticated copy of these documents,

2. the legitimating documents of the managing directors, if the managing directors are not appointed in the articles of association,

3. a list of the members signed by the registrants in accordance with the requirements of § 40,

4. in the case of § 5(4), the contracts that are the basis of the determinations or that have been entered into for their performance, and the report on the incorporation using in-kind contributions,

5. wenn Sacheinlagen vereinbart sind, Unterlagen darüber, daß der Wert der Sacheinlagen den Nennbetrag der dafür übernommenen Geschäftsanteile erreicht.

6. (weggefallen)

(2) In der Anmeldung ist die Versicherung abzugeben, daß die in § 7 Abs. 2 und 3 bezeichneten Leistungen auf die Geschäftsanteile bewirkt sind und daß der Gegenstand der Leistungen sich endgültig in der freien Verfügung der Geschäftsführer befindet. Das Gericht kann bei erheblichen Zweifeln an der Richtigkeit der Versicherung Nachweise (unter anderem Einzahlungsbelege) verlangen.

(3) In der Anmeldung haben die Geschäftsführer zu versichern, daß keine Umstände vorliegen, die ihrer Bestellung nach § 6 Abs. 2 Satz 2 Nr. 2 und 3 sowie Satz 3 entgegenstehen, und daß sie über ihre unbeschränkte Auskunftspflicht gegenüber dem Gericht belehrt worden sind. Die Belehrung nach § 53 Abs. 2 des Bundeszentralregistergesetzes kann schriftlich vorgenommen werden; sie kann auch durch einen Notar oder einen im Ausland bestellten Notar, durch einen Vertreter eines vergleichbaren rechtsberatenden Berufs oder einen Konsularbeamten erfolgen.

(4) In der Anmeldung sind ferner anzugeben:

1. eine inländische Geschäftsanschrift,

2. Art und Umfang der Vertretungsbefugnis der Geschäftsführer.

(5) Für die Einreichung von Unterlagen nach diesem Gesetz gilt § 12 Abs. 2 des Handelsgesetzbuchs entsprechend.

5. if in-kind contributions are agreed upon, documentation that the value of the in-kind contributions amounts to the par value of the membership interests accepted therefor.

6. (repealed)

(2) In the registration, the representation is to be given that the renderings designated in § 7(2) and (3) for the membership interests have been made and that the object rendered is irrevocably at the unrestricted disposal of the managing directors. The court may, upon substantial doubt as to the correctness of the representation, demand evidence (inter alia payment receipts).

(3) In the registration, the managing directors must assert that no circumstances exist that conflict with their appointment according to § 6(2), Sentence 2, No. 2 and 3, as well as Sentence 3, and that they have been instructed on their unlimited duty of disclosure to the court. The instruction according to § 53(2) of the Federal Central Register Act (*Bundeszentralregistergesetz*) may be performed in writing; it may also be effected by a notary (*Notar*) or a notary (*Notar*) who has been authorized in a foreign country, by a representative of a comparable legal advisory profession, or by a consular officer.

(4) Furthermore, the following are to be stated in the registration:

1. a domestic business address,

2. the type and extent of the power of representation of the managing directors.

(5) For the filing of documentation according to this Act, § 12(2) of the Commercial Code (*Handelsgesetzbuch*) applies accordingly.

§ 9 Überbewertung der Sacheinlagen

(1) Erreicht der Wert einer Sacheinlage im Zeitpunkt der Anmeldung der Gesellschaft zur Eintragung in das Handelsregister nicht den Nennbetrag des dafür übernommenen Geschäftsanteils, hat der Gesellschafter in Höhe des Fehlbetrags eine Einlage in Geld zu leisten. Sonstige Ansprüche bleiben unberührt.

(2) Der Anspruch der Gesellschaft nach Absatz 1 Satz 1 verjährt in zehn Jahren seit der Eintragung der Gesellschaft in das Handelsregister.

§ 9 Overvaluation of the In-Kind Contributions

(1) If the value of an in-kind contribution at the time of the registration of the company for entry in the commercial register (*Handelsregister*) does not equal the par value of the membership interest accepted therefor, then the member must render a cash contribution in the amount of the deficit. Other claims remain unaffected.

(2) The claim of the company according to Subsection 1, Sentence 1 becomes time-barred ten years from the entry of the company in the commercial register (*Handelsregister*).

§ 9a Ersatzansprüche der Gesellschaft

(1) Werden zum Zweck der Errichtung der Gesellschaft falsche Angaben gemacht, so haben die Gesellschafter und Geschäftsführer der Gesellschaft als Gesamtschuldner fehlende Einzahlungen zu leisten, eine Vergütung, die nicht unter den Gründungsaufwand aufgenommen ist, zu ersetzen und für den sonst entstehenden Schaden Ersatz zu leisten.

(2) Wird die Gesellschaft von Gesellschaftern durch Einlagen oder Gründungsaufwand vorsätzlich oder aus grober Fahrlässigkeit geschädigt, so sind ihr alle Gesellschafter als Gesamtschuldner zum Ersatz verpflichtet.

(3) Von diesen Verpflichtungen ist ein Gesellschafter oder ein Geschäftsführer befreit, wenn er die die Ersatzpflicht begründenden Tatsachen weder kannte noch bei Anwendung der Sorgfalt eines ordentlichen Geschäftsmannes kennen mußte.

(4) Neben den Gesellschaftern sind in gleicher Weise Personen verantwortlich, für deren Rechnung die Gesellschafter

§ 9a Claims to Compensation of the Company

(1) If false information was given for the purpose of founding the company, then the members and managing directors, as joint and several debtors, must render missing payments to the company, compensate the company for remuneration that is not absorbed by the incorporation expenses, and pay compensation to the company for any other arising damages.

(2) If the company is damaged by members through contributions or incorporation expenses intentionally or through gross negligence, then all members, as joint and several debtors, are obligated to pay compensation.

(3) A member or a managing director is released from these obligations if he neither knew, nor, with the exercise of the care of a prudent businessman, ought to have known the facts establishing the duty to pay compensation.

(4) In addition to the members, the persons on whose behalf the members have accepted membership interests are

Geschäftsanteile übernommen haben. Sie können sich auf ihre eigene Unkenntnis nicht wegen solcher Umstände berufen, die ein für ihre Rechnung handelnder Gesellschafter kannte oder bei Anwendung der Sorgfalt eines ordentlichen Geschäftsmannes kennen mußte.

responsible in the same manner. They may not invoke their own lack of knowledge concerning such circumstances that a member acting on their behalf knew or, with the exercise of the care of a prudent businessman, ought to have known.

§ 9b Verzicht auf Ersatzansprüche

(1) Ein Verzicht der Gesellschaft auf Ersatzansprüche nach § 9a oder ein Vergleich der Gesellschaft über diese Ansprüche ist unwirksam, soweit der Ersatz zur Befriedigung der Gläubiger der Gesellschaft erforderlich ist. Dies gilt nicht, wenn der Ersatzpflichtige zahlungsunfähig ist und sich zur Abwendung des Insolvenzverfahrens mit seinen Gläubigern vergleicht oder wenn die Ersatzpflicht in einem Insolvenzplan geregelt wird.

(2) Ersatzansprüche der Gesellschaft nach § 9a verjähren in fünf Jahren. Die Verjährung beginnt mit der Eintragung der Gesellschaft in das Handelsregister oder, wenn die zum Ersatz verpflichtende Handlung später begangen worden ist, mit der Vornahme der Handlung.

§ 9b Waiver of Claims to Compensation

(1) A waiver of the company of claims to compensation according to § 9a or a settlement of the company concerning these claims is ineffective insofar as the compensation is necessary for the satisfaction of the creditors of the company. This does not apply if the party obligated to pay compensation is illiquid and settles with his creditors for the avoidance of an insolvency proceeding, or if the duty to pay compensation is governed in an insolvency plan.

(2) The claims to compensation of the company according to § 9a become time-barred after five years. The statute of limitations begins to run with the entry of the company in the commercial register (*Handelsregister*) or, if the act giving rise to the obligation to pay compensation has been committed later, with the performance of the act.

§ 9c Ablehnung der Eintragung

(1) Ist die Gesellschaft nicht ordnungsgemäß errichtet und angemeldet, so hat das Gericht die Eintragung abzulehnen. Dies gilt auch, wenn Sacheinlagen nicht unwesentlich überbewertet worden sind.

(2) Wegen einer mangelhaften, fehlenden oder nichtigen Bestimmung des Gesellschaftsvertrages darf das Gericht die Eintragung nach Absatz 1 nur ablehnen, soweit diese Bestimmung, ihr Fehlen oder ihre Nichtigkeit

§ 9c Refusal of Entry

(1) If the company is not properly founded and registered, then the court must refuse entry. This also applies if in-kind contributions have been not immaterially overvalued.

(2) The court may refuse the entry because of a defective, lacking, or void provision of the articles of association according to Subsection 1 only insofar as this provision, its lack or its voidness

1. Tatsachen oder Rechtsverhältnisse betrifft, die nach § 3 Abs. 1 oder auf Grund anderer zwingender gesetzlicher Vorschriften in dem Gesellschaftsvertrag bestimmt sein müssen oder die in das Handelsregister einzutragen oder von dem Gericht bekanntzumachen sind,

2. Vorschriften verletzt, die ausschließlich oder überwiegend zum Schutze der Gläubiger der Gesellschaft oder sonst im öffentlichen Interesse gegeben sind, oder

3. die Nichtigkeit des Gesellschaftsvertrages zur Folge hat.

1. pertains to facts or legal relationships that, according to § 3(1) or based on other mandatory statutory provisions, must be provided in the articles of association, are to be entered into the commercial register (*Handelsregister*), or are to be published by the court,

2. violates provisions that are exclusively or predominantly for the protection of the creditors of the company or are otherwise in the public interest, or

3. results in the voidness of the articles of association.

§ 10 Inhalt der Eintragung

(1) Bei der Eintragung in das Handelsregister sind die Firma und der Sitz der Gesellschaft, eine inländische Geschäftsanschrift, der Gegenstand des Unternehmens, die Höhe des Stammkapitals, der Tag des Abschlusses des Gesellschaftsvertrags und die Personen der Geschäftsführer anzugeben. Ferner ist einzutragen, welche Vertretungsbefugnis die Geschäftsführer haben.

(2) Enthält der Gesellschaftsvertrag Bestimmungen über die Zeitdauer der Gesellschaft oder über das genehmigte Kapital, so sind auch diese Bestimmungen einzutragen. Wenn eine Person, die für Willenserklärungen und Zustellungen an die Gesellschaft empfangsberechtigt ist, mit einer inländischen Anschrift zur Eintragung in das Handelsregister angemeldet wird, sind auch diese Angaben einzutragen; Dritten gegenüber gilt die Empfangsberechtigung als fortbestehend, bis sie im Handelsregister gelöscht und die Löschung bekannt gemacht worden ist, es sei denn, dass die fehlende Empfangsberechtigung dem Dritten bekannt war.

(3) (weggefallen)

§ 10 Contents of the Entry

(1) The company name and registered office of the company, a domestic business address, the purpose of the business, the capital stock amount, the day of conclusion of the articles of association, and the persons to be managing directors are to be stated in the entry in the commercial register (*Handelsregister*). Furthermore, which power of representation the managing directors have is to be entered.

(2) If the articles of association contain provisions about the duration of the company or about the authorized capital, then these provisions are also to be entered. If a person who is authorized to take delivery of declarations of intent and service of process on the company is registered with a domestic address for entry in the commercial register (*Handelsregister*), then this information is also to be entered; in relation to third parties, the authorization to take delivery is considered to continue until it has been deregistered from the commercial register (*Handelsregister*) and the deregistration has been published, unless the lacking authorization to take delivery was known to the third party.

(3) (repealed)

§ 11 Rechtszustand vor der Eintragung

(1) Vor der Eintragung in das Handelsregister des Sitzes der Gesellschaft besteht die Gesellschaft mit beschränkter Haftung als solche nicht.

(2) Ist vor der Eintragung im Namen der Gesellschaft gehandelt worden, so haften die Handelnden persönlich und solidarisch.

§ 11 Legal Status before Entry

(1) Before entry in the commercial register (*Handelsregister*) for the registered office of the company, the company with limited liability as such does not exist.

(2) If acts have been taken in the name of the company before entry, then the acting persons are personally and jointly and severally liable.

§ 12 Bekanntmachungen der Gesellschaft

Bestimmt das Gesetz oder der Gesellschaftsvertrag, dass von der Gesellschaft etwas bekannt zu machen ist, so erfolgt die Bekanntmachung im Bundesanzeiger (Gesellschaftsblatt). Daneben kann der Gesellschaftsvertrag andere öffentliche Blätter oder elektronische Informationsmedien als Gesellschaftsblätter bezeichnen.

§ 12 Publications of the Company

If the Act or the articles of association provide that something is to be published by the company, then the publication is effected in the Federal Gazette (*Bundesanzeiger*) (company bulletin). In addition, the articles of association may designate other public newspapers or electronic information media as company bulletins.

Abschnitt 2 Rechtsverhältnisse der Gesellschaft und der Gesellschafter

Chapter 2 Legal Relationships of the Company and the Members

§ 13 Juristische Person; Handelsgesellschaft

(1) Die Gesellschaft mit beschränkter Haftung als solche hat selbständig ihre Rechte und Pflichten; sie kann Eigentum und andere dingliche Rechte an Grundstücken erwerben, vor Gericht klagen und verklagt werden.

(2) Für die Verbindlichkeiten der Gesellschaft haftet den Gläubigern derselben nur das Gesellschaftsvermögen.

(3) Die Gesellschaft gilt als Handelsgesellschaft im Sinne des Handelsgesetzbuchs.

§ 13 Legal Person; Commercial Company

(1) The company with limited liability as such has its rights and duties independently; it may acquire property and other in rem rights to real property, and sue and be sued in court.

(2) Only the company assets are subject to the creditors of the company for the company's liabilities.

(3) The company is regarded as a commercial company within the meaning of the Commercial Code (*Handelsgesetzbuch*).

§ 14 Einlagepflicht

Auf jeden Geschäftsanteil ist eine Einlage zu leisten. Die Höhe der zu leistenden Einlage richtet sich nach dem bei der Errichtung der Gesellschaft im Gesellschaftsvertrag festgesetzten Nennbetrag des Geschäftsanteils. Im Fall der Kapitalerhöhung bestimmt sich die Höhe der zu leistenden Einlage nach dem in der Übernahmeerklärung festgesetzten Nennbetrag des Geschäftsanteils.

§ 14 Duty of Contribution

A contribution is to be rendered for each membership interest. The amount of the contribution to be rendered is determined by the par value of the membership interest determined in the articles of association upon the founding of the company. In the event of a capital increase, the amount of the contribution to be rendered is determined according to the par value of the membership interest determined in the declaration of acceptance.

§ 15 Übertragung von Geschäftsanteilen

(1) Die Geschäftsanteile sind veräußerlich und vererblich.

(2) Erwirbt ein Gesellschafter zu seinem ursprünglichen Geschäftsanteil weitere Geschäftsanteile, so behalten dieselben ihre Selbständigkeit.

(3) Zur Abtretung von Geschäftsanteilen durch Gesellschafter bedarf es eines in notarieller Form geschlossenen Vertrags.

(4) Der notariellen Form bedarf auch eine Vereinbarung, durch welche die Verpflichtung eines Gesellschafters zur Abtretung eines Geschäftsanteils begründet wird. Eine ohne diese Form getroffene Vereinbarung wird jedoch durch den nach Maßgabe des vorigen Absatzes geschlossenen Abtretungsvertrag gültig.

(5) Durch den Gesellschaftsvertrag kann die Abtretung der Geschäftsanteile an weitere Voraussetzungen geknüpft, insbesondere von der Genehmigung der Gesellschaft abhängig gemacht werden.

§ 15 Transfer of Membership Interests

(1) The membership interests are transferable and inheritable.

(2) If a member acquires membership interests in addition to his original membership interest, then the membership interests maintain their independence.

(3) A contract entered into in notarial form is required for the transfer of membership interests by members.

(4) An agreement upon which an obligation of a member to transfer a membership interest is established also requires notarial form. An agreement reached without this form, however, becomes valid through a transfer contract entered into according to the requirements of the previous Subsection.

(5) Through the articles of association, the transfer of the membership interests may be made dependent on further requirements, in particular on the approval of the company.

§ 16 Rechtsstellung bei Wechsel der Gesellschafter oder Veränderung des Umfangs ihrer Beteiligung; Erwerb vom Nichtberechtigten

(1) Im Verhältnis zur Gesellschaft gilt im Fall einer Veränderung in den Perso-

§ 16 Legal Status upon Replacement of the Members or Change in the Extent of Their Participation; Acquisition from an Unentitled Person

(1) In the event of a change in the persons who are members or in the extent of

nen der Gesellschafter oder des Umfangs ihrer Beteiligung als Inhaber eines Geschäftsanteils nur, wer als solcher in der im Handelsregister aufgenommenen Gesellschafterliste (§ 40) eingetragen ist. Eine vom Erwerber in Bezug auf das Gesellschaftsverhältnis vorgenommene Rechtshandlung gilt als von Anfang an wirksam, wenn die Liste unverzüglich nach Vornahme der Rechtshandlung in das Handelsregister aufgenommen wird.

their participation, someone is only considered to be an owner of a membership interest in relation to the company if he is entered in the list of members (§ 40) recorded in the commercial register (*Handelsregister*). A legal act performed by the acquirer with regard to the relationship to the company is considered effective ab initio if the list is recorded in the commercial register (*Handelsregister*) without undue delay after the performance of the legal act.

(2) Für Einlageverpflichtungen, die in dem Zeitpunkt rückständig sind, ab dem der Erwerber gemäß Absatz 1 Satz 1 im Verhältnis zur Gesellschaft als Inhaber des Geschäftsanteils gilt, haftet der Erwerber neben dem Veräußerer.

(2) The acquirer, in addition to the transferor, is liable for contribution obligations that are in arrears at the time from which the acquirer is considered to be owner of the membership interest in relation to the company according to Subsection 1, Sentence 1.

(3) Der Erwerber kann einen Geschäftsanteil oder ein Recht daran durch Rechtsgeschäft wirksam vom Nichtberechtigten erwerben, wenn der Veräußerer als Inhaber des Geschäftsanteils in der im Handelsregister aufgenommenen Gesellschafterliste eingetragen ist. Dies gilt nicht, wenn die Liste zum Zeitpunkt des Erwerbs hinsichtlich des Geschäftsanteils weniger als drei Jahre unrichtig und die Unrichtigkeit dem Berechtigten nicht zuzurechnen ist. Ein gutgläubiger Erwerb ist ferner nicht möglich, wenn dem Erwerber die mangelnde Berechtigung bekannt oder infolge grober Fahrlässigkeit unbekannt ist oder der Liste ein Widerspruch zugeordnet ist. Die Zuordnung eines Widerspruchs erfolgt aufgrund einer einstweiligen Verfügung oder aufgrund einer Bewilligung desjenigen, gegen dessen Berechtigung sich der Widerspruch richtet. Eine Gefährdung des Rechts des Widersprechenden muss nicht glaubhaft gemacht werden.

(3) The acquirer may effectively acquire a membership interest or a right therein from an unentitled person through a legal transaction if the transferor is entered as the owner of the membership interest in the list of members recorded in the commercial register (*Handelsregister*). This does not apply if the list has been incorrect with regard to the membership interest for less than three years at the time of the acquisition, and the incorrectness is not attributable to the entitled person. Furthermore, an acquisition in good faith is not possible if the lacking entitlement was known or, as a result of gross negligence, unknown to the acquirer, or if a notice of pendency is attached to the list. The attachment of a notice of pendency is effected based on an interim injunction or based on the consent of the person against whose entitlement the objection is directed. A threat to the right of the objecting party need not be credibly shown.

§ 17 (weggefallen)

§ 17 (repealed)

§ 18 Mitberechtigung am Geschäftsanteil

(1) Steht ein Geschäftsanteil mehreren Mitberechtigten ungeteilt zu, so können sie die Rechte aus demselben nur gemeinschaftlich ausüben.

(2) Für die auf den Geschäftsanteil zu bewirkenden Leistungen haften sie der Gesellschaft solidarisch.

(3) Rechtshandlungen, welche die Gesellschaft gegenüber dem Inhaber des Anteils vorzunehmen hat, sind, sofern nicht ein gemeinsamer Vertreter der Mitberechtigten vorhanden ist, wirksam, wenn sie auch nur gegenüber einem Mitberechtigten vorgenommen werden. Gegenüber mehreren Erben eines Gesellschafters findet diese Bestimmung nur in bezug auf Rechtshandlungen Anwendung, welche nach Ablauf eines Monats seit dem Anfall der Erbschaft vorgenommen werden.

§ 18 Co-entitlement to the Membership Interest

(1) If a membership interest belongs to multiple co-entitled persons undividedly, then they may only exercise the rights deriving from the membership interest jointly.

(2) They are jointly and severally liable to the company for the contributions to be made for the membership interest.

(3) Unless there is a joint representative of the co-entitled persons, legal acts that the company must perform in relation to the owner of the interest are effective even if they are only taken in relation to one co-entitled person. In relation to multiple heirs of a member, this provision applies only with respect to legal acts that are taken after the expiration of one month after the accrual of the inheritance.

§ 19 Leistung der Einlagen

(1) Die Einzahlungen auf die Geschäftsanteile sind nach dem Verhältnis der Geldeinlagen zu leisten.

(2) Von der Verpflichtung zur Leistung der Einlagen können die Gesellschafter nicht befreit werden. Gegen den Anspruch der Gesellschaft ist die Aufrechnung nur zulässig mit einer Forderung aus der Überlassung von Vermögensgegenständen, deren Anrechnung auf die Einlageverpflichtung nach § 5 Abs. 4 Satz 1 vereinbart worden ist. An dem Gegenstand einer Sacheinlage kann wegen Forderungen, welche sich nicht auf den Gegenstand beziehen, kein Zurückbehaltungsrecht geltend gemacht werden.

(3) Durch eine Kapitalherabsetzung können die Gesellschafter von der Verpflichtung zur Leistung von Einlagen höchstens in Höhe des Betrags befreit werden, um den das Stammkapital herabgesetzt worden ist.

§ 19 Rendering of the Contributions

(1) The payments for the membership interests are to be rendered according to the proportion of the cash contributions.

(2) The members may not be released from the obligation to render the contributions. A set-off against the claim of the company is only permissible with a claim arising from the transfer of assets, the deduction of which from the contribution obligation has been agreed to according to § 5(4), Sentence 1. No right of retention may be asserted with regard to the object of an in-kind contribution because of claims that do not relate to the item.

(3) Through a capital reduction, the members may be released from the obligation to render contributions only up to the amount of the value by which the capital stock has been reduced.

(4) Ist eine Geldeinlage eines Gesellschafters bei wirtschaftlicher Betrachtung und aufgrund einer im Zusammenhang mit der Übernahme der Geldeinlage getroffenen Abrede vollständig oder teilweise als Sacheinlage zu bewerten (verdeckte Sacheinlage), so befreit dies den Gesellschafter nicht von seiner Einlageverpflichtung. Jedoch sind die Verträge über die Sacheinlage und die Rechtshandlungen zu ihrer Ausführung nicht unwirksam. Auf die fortbestehende Geldeinlagepflicht des Gesellschafters wird der Wert des Vermögensgegenstandes im Zeitpunkt der Anmeldung der Gesellschaft zur Eintragung in das Handelsregister oder im Zeitpunkt seiner Überlassung an die Gesellschaft, falls diese später erfolgt, angerechnet. Die Anrechnung erfolgt nicht vor Eintragung der Gesellschaft in das Handelsregister. Die Beweislast für die Werthaltigkeit des Vermögensgegenstandes trägt der Gesellschafter.

(4) If, from an economic perspective and based on a common understanding reached in connection with the acceptance of the obligation of the cash contribution, a cash contribution of a member is to be assessed wholly or partially as an in-kind contribution (undisclosed in-kind contribution), then the member is not released from his contribution obligation. However, the contracts pertaining to the in-kind contribution and the legal acts for their performance are not ineffective. The value of the asset at the time of the registration of the company for entry in the commercial register (*Handelsregister*) or at the time of its transfer to the company, if this occurs later, is deducted from the still-existing cash contribution duty of the member. The deduction is not effected before entry of the company in the commercial register (*Handelsregister*). The member bears the burden of proving the value of the asset.

(5) Ist vor der Einlage eine Leistung an den Gesellschafter vereinbart worden, die wirtschaftlich einer Rückzahlung der Einlage entspricht und die nicht als verdeckte Sacheinlage im Sinne von Absatz 4 zu beurteilen ist, so befreit dies den Gesellschafter von seiner Einlageverpflichtung nur dann, wenn die Leistung durch einen vollwertigen Rückgewähranspruch gedeckt ist, der jederzeit fällig ist oder durch fristlose Kündigung durch die Gesellschaft fällig werden kann. Eine solche Leistung oder die Vereinbarung einer solchen Leistung ist in der Anmeldung nach § 8 anzugeben.

(5) If, before the contribution, a payment to the member was agreed to that corresponds economically to a repayment of the contribution, and that is not to be assessed as an undisclosed in-kind contribution within the meaning of Subsection 4, then the member is released from his contribution obligation only if the payment is covered by a claim to repayment that is nominally and economically equal in value and that is due at any time, or may become due through termination without notice by the company. Such a payment or an agreement for such a payment is to be stated in the registration according to § 8.

(6) Der Anspruch der Gesellschaft auf Leistung der Einlagen verjährt in zehn Jahren von seiner Entstehung an. Wird das Insolvenzverfahren über das Vermögen der Gesellschaft eröffnet, so tritt die Verjährung nicht vor Ablauf von sechs Monaten ab dem Zeitpunkt der Eröffnung ein.

(6) The claim of the company to rendering of contributions becomes time-barred ten years after its accrual. If an insolvency proceeding is initiated concerning the assets of the company, then the claim does not become time-barred until the expiration of six months from the time of the initiation of the insolvency proceeding.

§ 20 Verzugszinsen

Ein Gesellschafter, welcher den auf die Stammeinlage eingeforderten Betrag nicht zur rechten Zeit einzahlt, ist zur Entrichtung von Verzugszinsen von Rechts wegen verpflichtet.

§ 20 Default Interest

A member who does not pay in the amount called in for the initial contribution at the correct time is obligated as a matter of law to pay default interest.

§ 21 Kaduzierung

(1) Im Fall verzögerter Einzahlung kann an den säumigen Gesellschafter eine erneute Aufforderung zur Zahlung binnen einer zu bestimmenden Nachfrist unter Androhung seines Ausschlusses mit dem Geschäftsanteil, auf welchen die Zahlung zu erfolgen hat, erlassen werden. Die Aufforderung erfolgt mittels eingeschriebenen Briefes. Die Nachfrist muß mindestens einen Monat betragen.

(2) Nach fruchtlosem Ablauf der Frist ist der säumige Gesellschafter seines Geschäftsanteils und der geleisteten Teilzahlungen zugunsten der Gesellschaft verlustig zu erklären. Die Erklärung erfolgt mittels eingeschriebenen Briefes.

(3) Wegen des Ausfalls, welchen die Gesellschaft an dem rückständigen Betrag oder den später auf den Geschäftsanteil eingeforderten Beträgen der Stammeinlage erleidet, bleibt ihr der ausgeschlossene Gesellschafter verhaftet.

§ 21 Forfeiture

(1) In the case of a delayed payment, a renewed request for payment within a to-be-determined extension period may be issued to the defaulting member under threat of his forfeiture of the membership interest for which the payment is to be made. The request is effected by means of a registered letter. The extension of time must amount to at least one month.

(2) After an unsuccessful expiration of the period, the defaulting member is to be declared in forfeiture of his membership interest and of the partial payments rendered in favor of the company. The declaration is effected by means of a registered letter.

(3) The forfeiting member remains liable to the company for the deficiency that the company incurs in the amount in arrears, or in the amounts of the initial contribution that are later called in for the membership interest.

§ 22 Haftung der Rechtsvorgänger

(1) Für eine von dem ausgeschlossenen Gesellschafter nicht erfüllte Einlageverpflichtung haftet der Gesellschaft auch der letzte und jeder frühere Rechtsvorgänger des Ausgeschlossenen, der im Verhältnis zu ihr als Inhaber des Geschäftsanteils gilt.

(2) Ein früherer Rechtsvorgänger haftet nur, soweit die Zahlung von dessen Rechtsnachfolger nicht zu erlangen ist; dies ist bis zum Beweis des Gegenteils

§ 22 Liability of Predecessors in Interest

(1) The preceding and each earlier predecessor in interest to the forfeiting member, who is considered to be owner of the membership interest in relation to the company, is also liable to the company for a contribution obligation not fulfilled by the forfeiting member.

(2) An earlier predecessor in interest is only liable insofar as the payment cannot be obtained from his successor in interest; this is to be presumed until the con-

anzunehmen, wenn der letztere die Zahlung nicht bis zum Ablauf eines Monats geleistet hat, nachdem an ihn die Zahlungsaufforderung und an den Rechtsvorgänger die Benachrichtigung von derselben erfolgt ist.

(3) Die Haftung des Rechtsvorgängers ist auf die innerhalb der Frist von fünf Jahren auf die Einlageverpflichtung eingeforderten Leistungen beschränkt. Die Frist beginnt mit dem Tag, ab welchem der Rechtsnachfolger im Verhältnis zur Gesellschaft als Inhaber des Geschäftsanteils gilt.

(4) Der Rechtsvorgänger erwirbt gegen Zahlung des rückständigen Betrags den Geschäftsanteil des ausgeschlossenen Gesellschafters.

§ 23 Versteigerung des Geschäftsanteils

Ist die Zahlung des rückständigen Betrags von Rechtsvorgängern nicht zu erlangen, so kann die Gesellschaft den Geschäftsanteil im Wege öffentlicher Versteigerung verkaufen lassen. Eine andere Art des Verkaufs ist nur mit Zustimmung des ausgeschlossenen Gesellschafters zulässig.

§ 24 Aufbringung von Fehlbeträgen

Soweit eine Stammeinlage weder von den Zahlungspflichtigen eingezogen, noch durch Verkauf des Geschäftsanteils gedeckt werden kann, haben die übrigen Gesellschafter den Fehlbetrag nach Verhältnis ihrer Geschäftsanteile aufzubringen. Beiträge, welche von einzelnen Gesellschaftern nicht zu erlangen sind, werden nach dem bezeichneten Verhältnis auf die übrigen verteilt.

§ 25 Zwingende Vorschriften

Von den in den §§ 21 bis 24 bezeichneten Rechtsfolgen können die Gesellschafter nicht befreit werden.

trary is proven if the successor in interest has not rendered payment before the expiration of one month after the request for payment has been effected to him, and notice of the same has been effected to the predecessors in interest.

(3) The liability of the predecessor in interest is limited to the renderings called in for the contribution obligation within the period of five years. The period begins on the day on which the successor in interest is considered to be the owner of the membership interest in relation to the company.

(4) The predecessor in interest acquires the membership interest of the forfeiting member against payment of the amount in arrears.

§ 23 Auction of the Membership Interest

If the payment of the amount in arrears cannot be obtained from the predecessors in interest, then the company may sell the membership interest by way of a public auction. Another type of sale is only permissible with the consent of the forfeiting member.

§ 24 Raising of Deficiencies

Insofar as an initial contribution may neither be collected from the parties obligated to pay, nor be covered through the sale of the membership interest, the remaining members must raise the deficit in proportion to their membership interests. Portions that cannot be acquired from individual members are apportioned among the others according to the aforementioned proportion.

§ 25 Mandatory Provisions

The members may not be released from the legal consequences designated in §§ 21 to 24.

§ 26 Nachschusspflicht

(1) Im Gesellschaftsvertrag kann bestimmt werden, daß die Gesellschafter über die Nennbeträge der Geschäftsanteile hinaus die Einforderung von weiteren Einzahlungen (Nachschüssen) beschließen können.

(2) Die Einzahlung der Nachschüsse hat nach Verhältnis der Geschäftsanteile zu erfolgen.

(3) Die Nachschußpflicht kann im Gesellschaftsvertrag auf einen bestimmten, nach Verhältnis der Geschäftsanteile festzusetzenden Betrag beschränkt werden.

§ 26 Duty to Make Additional Contributions

(1) The articles of association may provide that the members may resolve to call in further payments (additional contributions) beyond the par values of the membership interests.

(2) The payment of additional contributions must be made in proportion to the membership interests.

(3) The duty to make additional contributions may be limited in the articles of association to a certain amount to be determined in proportion to the membership interests.

§ 27 Unbeschränkte Nachschusspflicht

(1) Ist die Nachschußpflicht nicht auf einen bestimmten Betrag beschränkt, so hat jeder Gesellschafter, falls er die Stammeinlage vollständig eingezahlt hat, das Recht, sich von der Zahlung des auf den Geschäftsanteil eingeforderten Nachschusses dadurch zu befreien, daß er innerhalb eines Monats nach der Aufforderung zur Einzahlung den Geschäftsanteil der Gesellschaft zur Befriedigung aus demselben zur Verfügung stellt. Ebenso kann die Gesellschaft, wenn der Gesellschafter binnen der angegebenen Frist weder von der bezeichneten Befugnis Gebrauch macht, noch die Einzahlung leistet, demselben mittels eingeschriebenen Briefes erklären, daß sie den Geschäftsanteil als zur Verfügung gestellt betrachte.

(2) Die Gesellschaft hat den Geschäftsanteil innerhalb eines Monats nach der Erklärung des Gesellschafters oder der Gesellschaft im Wege öffentlicher Versteigerung verkaufen zu lassen. Eine andere Art des Verkaufs ist nur mit Zustimmung des Gesellschafters zulässig. Ein nach Deckung der Verkaufskosten und des rückständigen Nachschusses

§ 27 Unlimited Duty to Make Additional Contributions

(1) If the duty to make additional contributions is not limited to a certain amount, then each member has the right, if he has fully paid in the initial contribution, to release himself from the payment of the additional contribution called in for the membership interest if he, within one month after the request for the payment, places the membership interest at the disposal of the company for satisfaction from the membership interest. In the same way, the company may, if the member within the stated period neither makes use of the aforementioned power nor renders payment, declare to the member by means of a registered letter that it regards the membership interest as being placed at its disposal.

(2) The company is obligated to sell the membership interest by means of a public auction within one month after the declaration of the member or of the company. Another type of sale is only permissible with the consent of the member. A surplus remaining after covering the costs of sale and the additional contribution in arrears belongs to the member.

verbleibender Überschuß gebührt dem Gesellschafter.

(3) Ist die Befriedigung der Gesellschaft durch den Verkauf nicht zu erlangen, so fällt der Geschäftsanteil der Gesellschaft zu. Dieselbe ist befugt, den Anteil für eigene Rechnung zu veräußern.

(4) Im Gesellschaftsvertrag kann die Anwendung der vorstehenden Bestimmungen auf den Fall beschränkt werden, daß die auf den Geschäftsanteil eingeforderten Nachschüsse einen bestimmten Betrag überschreiten.

(3) If the satisfaction of the company through sale is not to be achieved, then the membership interest devolves to the company. The company is entitled to transfer the membership interest for its own account.

(4) In the articles of association, the application of the foregoing provisions may be limited to the case in which the additional contributions called in for the membership interest exceed a certain amount.

§ 28 Beschränkte Nachschusspflicht

(1) Ist die Nachschußpflicht auf einen bestimmten Betrag beschränkt, so finden, wenn im Gesellschaftsvertrag nicht ein anderes festgesetzt ist, im Fall verzögerter Einzahlung von Nachschüssen die auf die Einzahlung der Stammeinlagen bezüglichen Vorschriften der §§ 21 bis 23 entsprechende Anwendung. Das gleiche gilt im Fall des § 27 Abs. 4 auch bei unbeschränkter Nachschußpflicht, soweit die Nachschüsse den im Gesellschaftsvertrag festgesetzten Betrag nicht überschreiten.

(2) Im Gesellschaftsvertrag kann bestimmt werden, daß die Einforderung von Nachschüssen, auf deren Zahlung die Vorschriften der §§ 21 bis 23 Anwendung finden, schon vor vollständiger Einforderung der Stammeinlagen zulässig ist.

§ 28 Limited Duty to Make Additional Contributions

(1) If the duty to make additional contributions is limited to a certain amount, then the provisions of §§ 21 to 23 relating to the payment of initial contributions apply accordingly in the case of a delayed payment of additional contributions, if the articles of association do not determine otherwise. The same also applies in the case of § 27(4) to an unlimited duty to make additional contributions, insofar as the additional contributions do not exceed the amount determined in the articles of association.

(2) The articles of association may provide that the calling-in of additional contributions, to the payment of which the provisions of §§ 21 to 23 apply, is permissible even before a complete calling-in of the initial contributions.

§ 29 Ergebnisverwendung

(1) Die Gesellschafter haben Anspruch auf den Jahresüberschuß zuzüglich eines Gewinnvortrags und abzüglich eines Verlustvortrags, soweit der sich ergebende Betrag nicht nach Gesetz oder Gesellschaftsvertrag, durch Beschluß nach Absatz 2 oder als zusätzlicher Aufwand

§ 29 Appropriation of Profit or Loss

(1) The members have a claim to the annual net profit plus a profit carried forward and minus a loss carried forward, insofar as the resulting amount is not barred from distribution to the members according to statute or the articles of association, by resolution according to

auf Grund des Beschlusses über die Verwendung des Ergebnisses von der Verteilung unter die Gesellschafter ausgeschlossen ist. Wird die Bilanz unter Berücksichtigung der teilweisen Ergebnisverwendung aufgestellt oder werden Rücklagen aufgelöst, so haben die Gesellschafter abweichend von Satz 1 Anspruch auf den Bilanzgewinn.

(2) Im Beschluß über die Verwendung des Ergebnisses können die Gesellschafter, wenn der Gesellschaftsvertrag nichts anderes bestimmt, Beträge in Gewinnrücklagen einstellen oder als Gewinn vortragen.

(3) Die Verteilung erfolgt nach Verhältnis der Geschäftsanteile. Im Gesellschaftsvertrag kann ein anderer Maßstab der Verteilung festgesetzt werden.

(4) Unbeschadet der Absätze 1 und 2 und abweichender Gewinnverteilungsabreden nach Absatz 3 Satz 2 können die Geschäftsführer mit Zustimmung des Aufsichtsrats oder der Gesellschafter den Eigenkapitalanteil von Wertaufholungen bei Vermögensgegenständen des Anlage- und Umlaufvermögens in andere Gewinnrücklagen einstellen. Der Betrag dieser Rücklagen ist in der Bilanz gesondert auszuweisen; er kann auch im Anhang angegeben werden.

Subsection 2, or as an additional expenditure based on the resolution on the appropriation of the profit or loss. If the balance sheet is drawn up taking into account the partial appropriation of the profit or loss, or if the reserves are released, then the members have a claim to the unappropriated profit, notwithstanding Sentence 1.

(2) In the resolution on the appropriation of the profit or loss, the members may allocate amounts to retained earnings or carry them forward as profit if the articles of association do not provide otherwise.

(3) The distribution is effected in proportion to the membership interests. Another criterion of distribution may be determined in the articles of association.

(4) Regardless of Subsections 1 and 2 and regardless of contrary profit distribution agreements according to Subsection 3, Sentence 2, the managing directors may, with the consent of the supervisory board or of the members, allocate the equity portion of reversals of impairments of items of non-current and current assets to other retained earnings. The amount of these reserves is to be separately entered in the balance sheet; it may also be stated in the notes.

§ 30 Kapitalerhaltung

(1) Das zur Erhaltung des Stammkapitals erforderliche Vermögen der Gesellschaft darf an die Gesellschafter nicht ausgezahlt werden. Satz 1 gilt nicht bei Leistungen, die bei Bestehen eines Beherrschungs- oder Gewinnabführungsvertrags (§ 291 des Aktiengesetzes) erfolgen oder durch einen vollwertigen Gegenleistungs- oder Rückgewähranspruch gegen den Gesellschafter gedeckt sind. Satz 1 ist zudem nicht anzuwenden auf die Rückgewähr eines Gesellschafterdarlehens und Leistungen auf Forderungen aus Rechtshandlungen, die einem

§ 30 Maintenance of Capital

(1) The assets of the company necessary for the maintenance of the capital stock may not be distributed to the members. Sentence 1 does not apply to payments that occur during the existence of a control agreement or a profit transfer agreement (§ 291 of the Stock Corporation Act (*Aktiengesetz*)) or that are covered by a claim to consideration or to repayment against the member that is nominally and economically equal in value. Moreover, Sentence 1 is not to be applied to the repayment of a member loan and payments of claims arising from

Gesellschafterdarlehen wirtschaftlich entsprechen.

(2) Eingezahlte Nachschüsse können, soweit sie nicht zur Deckung eines Verlustes am Stammkapital erforderlich sind, an die Gesellschafter zurückgezahlt werden. Die Zurückzahlung darf nicht vor Ablauf von drei Monaten erfolgen, nachdem der Rückzahlungsbeschluß nach § 12 bekanntgemacht ist. Im Fall des § 28 Abs. 2 ist die Zurückzahlung von Nachschüssen vor der Volleinzahlung des Stammkapitals unzulässig. Zurückgezahlte Nachschüsse gelten als nicht eingezogen.

legal acts that are economically equivalent to a member loan.

(2) Paid-in additional contributions may be repaid to the members, insofar as they are not necessary for covering a loss of the capital stock. The repayment may not be effected before the expiration of three months after the repayment resolution is published according to § 12. In the case of § 28(2), the repayment of additional contributions is impermissible before the complete payment of the capital stock. Repaid additional contributions are considered not to have been called in.

§ 31 Erstattung verbotener Rückzahlungen

(1) Zahlungen, welche den Vorschriften des § 30 zuwider geleistet sind, müssen der Gesellschaft erstattet werden.

(2) War der Empfänger in gutem Glauben, so kann die Erstattung nur insoweit verlangt werden, als sie zur Befriedigung der Gesellschaftsgläubiger erforderlich ist.

(3) Ist die Erstattung von dem Empfänger nicht zu erlangen, so haften für den zu erstattenden Betrag, soweit er zur Befriedigung der Gesellschaftsgläubiger erforderlich ist, die übrigen Gesellschafter nach Verhältnis ihrer Geschäftsanteile. Beiträge, welche von einzelnen Gesellschaftern nicht zu erlangen sind, werden nach dem bezeichneten Verhältnis auf die übrigen verteilt.

(4) Zahlungen, welche auf Grund der vorstehenden Bestimmungen zu leisten sind, können den Verpflichteten nicht erlassen werden.

(5) Die Ansprüche der Gesellschaft verjähren in den Fällen des Absatzes 1 in zehn Jahren sowie in den Fällen des Absatzes 3 in fünf Jahren. Die Verjährung beginnt mit dem Ablauf des Tages, an welchem die Zahlung, deren Erstattung beansprucht

§ 31 Reimbursement of Prohibited Repayments

(1) Payments that are made contrary to the provisions of § 30 must be reimbursed to the company.

(2) If the recipient was in good faith, then the reimbursement may only be demanded insofar as it is necessary for the satisfaction of the company's creditors.

(3) If the reimbursement cannot be obtained from the recipient, then the other members are liable, in proportion to their membership interests, for the amount to be reimbursed, insofar as it is necessary for the satisfaction of the company's creditors. Portions that cannot be acquired from individual members are apportioned among the others according to the aforementioned proportion.

(4) The obligated parties may not be exempted from payments that are to be made based on the foregoing provisions.

(5) The claims of the company become time-barred after ten years in the cases of Subsection 1 and after five years in the cases of Subsection 3. The statute of limitations begins to run upon the expiration of the day on which the payment for

wird, geleistet ist. In den Fällen des Absatzes 1 findet § 19 Abs. 6 Satz 2 entsprechende Anwendung.

(6) Für die in den Fällen des Absatzes 3 geleistete Erstattung einer Zahlung sind den Gesellschaftern die Geschäftsführer, welchen in betreff der geleisteten Zahlung ein Verschulden zur Last fällt, solidarisch zum Ersatz verpflichtet. Die Bestimmungen in § 43 Abs. 1 und 4 finden entsprechende Anwendung.

which reimbursement is demanded is made. In the cases of Subsection 1, § 19(6), Sentence 2 applies accordingly.

(6) For the paid reimbursement of a payment in the cases of Subsection 3, the managing directors who are at fault with regard to the payment made are jointly and severally liable to the members for compensation. The provisions in § 43(1) and (4) apply accordingly.

§ 32 Rückzahlung von Gewinn

Liegt die in § 31 Abs. 1 bezeichnete Voraussetzung nicht vor, so sind die Gesellschafter in keinem Fall verpflichtet, Beträge, welche sie in gutem Glauben als Gewinnanteile bezogen haben, zurückzuzahlen.

§ 32 Repayment of Profits

If the precondition designated in § 31(1) is not met, then the members are in no case obligated to repay amounts that they received, in good faith, as shares of profit.

§ 32a (weggefallen)

§ 32a (repealed)

§ 32b (weggefallen)

§ 32b (repealed)

§ 33 Erwerb eigener Geschäftsanteile

(1) Die Gesellschaft kann eigene Geschäftsanteile, auf welche die Einlagen noch nicht vollständig geleistet sind, nicht erwerben oder als Pfand nehmen.

(2) Eigene Geschäftsanteile, auf welche die Einlage vollständig geleistet ist, darf sie nur erwerben, sofern sie im Zeitpunkt des Erwerbs eine Rücklage in Höhe der Aufwendungen für den Erwerb bilden könnte, ohne das Stammkapital oder eine nach dem Gesellschaftsvertrag zu bildende Rücklage zu mindern, die nicht zur Zahlung an die Gesellschafter verwandt werden darf. Als Pfand nehmen darf sie solche Geschäftsanteile nur, soweit der Gesamtbetrag der durch Inpfandnahme eigener Geschäftsanteile gesicherten Forderungen oder, wenn der Wert der als Pfand genommenen Geschäftsanteile niedriger ist, dieser Betrag nicht höher ist als das über das Stamm-

§ 33 The Company's Acquisition of Its Own Membership Interests

(1) The company may not acquire or take as a pledge its own membership interests for which the contributions have not been fully rendered.

(2) The company may only acquire its own membership interests for which the contribution has been fully rendered if it could, at the time of the acquisition, accumulate a reserve in the amount of the expenditures for the acquisition, without decreasing the capital stock or a reserve to be accumulated according to the articles of association that may not be used for payments to the members. The company may only take such membership interests as a pledge, insofar as the total amount of the claims secured through taking its own membership interests as a pledge or, if the value of the membership interests taken as a pledge is lower, this amount, is not greater than the

kapital hinaus vorhandene Vermögen. Ein Verstoß gegen die Sätze 1 und 2 macht den Erwerb oder die Inpfandnahme der Geschäftsanteile nicht unwirksam; jedoch ist das schuldrechtliche Geschäft über einen verbotswidrigen Erwerb oder eine verbotswidrige Inpfandnahme nichtig.

assets existing beyond the capital stock. A violation of Sentences 1 and 2 does not make the acquisition or the taking as a pledge ineffective; however, the contract forming the basis of a prohibited acquisition or for the prohibited taking as a pledge is void.

(3) Der Erwerb eigener Geschäftsanteile ist ferner zulässig zur Abfindung von Gesellschaftern nach § 29 Abs. 1, § 122i Abs. 1 Satz 2, § 125 Satz 1 in Verbindung mit § 29 Abs. 1 und § 207 Abs. 1 des Umwandlungsgesetzes, sofern der Erwerb binnen sechs Monaten nach dem Wirksamwerden der Umwandlung oder nach der Rechtskraft der gerichtlichen Entscheidung erfolgt und die Gesellschaft im Zeitpunkt des Erwerbs eine Rücklage in Höhe der Aufwendungen für den Erwerb bilden könnte, ohne das Stammkapital oder eine nach dem Gesellschaftsvertrag zu bildende Rücklage zu mindern, die nicht zur Zahlung an die Gesellschafter verwandt werden darf.

(3) Furthermore, the company's acquisition of its own membership interests is permissible for the compensation of members according to § 29(1), § 122i(1), Sentence 2, § 125, Sentence 1 in connection with § 29(1), and § 207(1) of the Transformation Act (*Umwandlungsgesetz*), if the acquisition occurs within six months after the transformation takes effect or after the court decision becomes res judicata, and if the company, at the point in time of the acquisition, could accumulate a reserve in the amount of the expenditures for the acquisition, without decreasing the capital stock or a reserve to be accumulated according to the articles of association that may not be used for payments to the members.

§ 34 Einziehung von Geschäftsanteilen

(1) Die Einziehung (Amortisation) von Geschäftsanteilen darf nur erfolgen, soweit sie im Gesellschaftsvertrag zugelassen ist.

(2) Ohne die Zustimmung des Anteilsberechtigten findet die Einziehung nur statt, wenn die Voraussetzungen derselben vor dem Zeitpunkt, in welchem der Berechtigte den Geschäftsanteil erworben hat, im Gesellschaftsvertrag festgesetzt waren.

(3) Die Bestimmung in § 30 Abs. 1 bleibt unberührt.

§ 34 Redemption of Membership Interests

(1) The redemption (amortization) of membership interests may only occur insofar as it is permitted in the articles of association.

(2) In the absence of the consent of the person entitled to a membership interest, the redemption may only take place if the requirements of the redemption were determined in the articles of association before the time at which the entitled person acquired the membership interest.

(3) The provision in § 30(1) remains unaffected.

Abschnitt 3 Vertretung und Geschäftsführung

§ 35 Vertretung der Gesellschaft

(1) Die Gesellschaft wird durch die Geschäftsführer gerichtlich und außergerichtlich vertreten. Hat eine Gesellschaft keinen Geschäftsführer (Führungslosigkeit), wird die Gesellschaft für den Fall, dass ihr gegenüber Willenserklärungen abgegeben oder Schriftstücke zugestellt werden, durch die Gesellschafter vertreten.

(2) Sind mehrere Geschäftsführer bestellt, sind sie alle nur gemeinschaftlich zur Vertretung der Gesellschaft befugt, es sei denn, dass der Gesellschaftsvertrag etwas anderes bestimmt. Ist der Gesellschaft gegenüber eine Willenserklärung abzugeben, genügt die Abgabe gegenüber einem Vertreter der Gesellschaft nach Absatz 1. An die Vertreter der Gesellschaft nach Absatz 1 können unter der im Handelsregister eingetragenen Geschäftsanschrift Willenserklärungen abgegeben und Schriftstücke für die Gesellschaft zugestellt werden. Unabhängig hiervon können die Abgabe und die Zustellung auch unter der eingetragenen Anschrift der empfangsberechtigten Person nach § 10 Abs. 2 Satz 2 erfolgen.

(3) Befinden sich alle Geschäftsanteile der Gesellschaft in der Hand eines Gesellschafters oder daneben in der Hand der Gesellschaft und ist er zugleich deren alleiniger Geschäftsführer, so ist auf seine Rechtsgeschäfte mit der Gesellschaft § 181 des Bürgerlichen Gesetzbuchs anzuwenden. Rechtsgeschäfte zwischen ihm und der von ihm vertretenen Gesellschaft sind, auch wenn er nicht alleiniger Geschäftsführer ist, unverzüglich nach ihrer Vornahme in eine Niederschrift aufzunehmen.

Chapter 3 Representation and Management

§ 35 Representation of the Company

(1) The company is represented by the managing directors in and out of court. If the company has no managing director (leadershiplessness), then the company is represented by the members in the event that declarations of intent are delivered to, or documents are served on, the company.

(2) If multiple managing directors are appointed, then they all are only jointly empowered to represent the company, unless the articles of association provide otherwise. If a declaration of intent is to be delivered to the company, then delivery to one representative of the company according to Subsection 1 is sufficient. Declarations of intent may be delivered to, and documents for the company may be served on, the representatives of the company according to Subsection 1 at the business address entered in the commercial register (*Handelsregister*). Independent hereof, delivery and service may also occur at the address of the person authorized to take delivery entered according to § 10(2), Sentence 2.

(3) If all membership interests of the company are in the possession of one member or, in addition thereto, in the possession of the company, and if he is simultaneously the sole managing director, then § 181 of the Civil Code (*Bürgerliches Gesetzbuch*) is to be applied to his legal transactions with the company. Legal transactions between him and the company represented by him are to be recorded in the minutes without undue delay after their performance, even if he is not the sole managing director.

§ 35a Angaben auf Geschäftsbriefen

(1) Auf allen Geschäftsbriefen gleichviel welcher Form, die an einen bestimmten Empfänger gerichtet werden, müssen die Rechtsform und der Sitz der Gesellschaft, das Registergericht des Sitzes der Gesellschaft und die Nummer, unter der die Gesellschaft in das Handelsregister eingetragen ist, sowie alle Geschäftsführer und, sofern die Gesellschaft einen Aufsichtsrat gebildet und dieser einen Vorsitzenden hat, der Vorsitzende des Aufsichtsrats mit dem Familiennamen und mindestens einem ausgeschriebenen Vornamen angegeben werden. Werden Angaben über das Kapital der Gesellschaft gemacht, so müssen in jedem Fall das Stammkapital sowie, wenn nicht alle in Geld zu leistenden Einlagen eingezahlt sind, der Gesamtbetrag der ausstehenden Einlagen angegeben werden.

(2) Der Angaben nach Absatz 1 Satz 1 bedarf es nicht bei Mitteilungen oder Berichten, die im Rahmen einer bestehenden Geschäftsverbindung ergehen und für die üblicherweise Vordrucke verwendet werden, in denen lediglich die im Einzelfall erforderlichen besonderen Angaben eingefügt zu werden brauchen.

(3) Bestellscheine gelten als Geschäftsbriefe im Sinne des Absatzes 1. Absatz 2 ist auf sie nicht anzuwenden.

(4) Auf allen Geschäftsbriefen und Bestellscheinen, die von einer Zweigniederlassung einer Gesellschaft mit beschränkter Haftung mit Sitz im Ausland verwendet werden, müssen das Register, bei dem die Zweigniederlassung geführt wird, und die Nummer des Registereintrags angegeben werden; im übrigen gelten die Vorschriften der Absätze 1 bis 3 für die Angaben bezüglich der Haupt- und der Zweigniederlassung, soweit nicht das ausländische Recht Abweichungen nötig macht. Befindet sich die ausländische Gesellschaft in Liquidation,

§ 35a Information in Business Letters

(1) In all business letters, regardless of form, that are addressed to a certain recipient, the legal form and the registered office of the company, the court of registry for the registered office of the company, and the number under which the company is entered in the commercial register (*Handelsregister*), as well as all managing directors and, insofar as the company establishes a supervisory board and this has a chairman, the chairman of the supervisory board, with surname and at least one full first name, must be stated. If information about the capital of the company is given, then in each case the capital stock and, if not all contributions to be rendered in cash have been paid in, the total amount of outstanding contributions, must be stated.

(2) The information according to Subsection 1, Sentence 1 is not required for notifications or reports that are issued within an existing business relationship and for which preprinted forms are usually used in which only the special information that is necessary in the particular case needs to be inserted.

(3) Order forms are considered to be business letters within the meaning of Subsection 1. Subsection 2 is not to be applied to them.

(4) In all business letters and order forms that are used by a branch office of a company with limited liability with a registered office abroad, the register in which the branch office is recorded and the registration number must be stated; apart from that, the provisions of Subsections 1 to 3 apply to the information relating to the central office and the branch office, insofar as the foreign law does not make deviations necessary. If the foreign company is in liquidation, then this fact and all liquidators are also to be stated.

so sind auch diese Tatsache sowie alle Liquidatoren anzugeben.

§ 36 Zielgrößen und Fristen zur gleichberechtigten Teilhabe von Frauen und Männern

Die Geschäftsführer einer Gesellschaft, die der Mitbestimmung unterliegt, legen für den Frauenanteil in den beiden Führungsebenen unterhalb der Geschäftsführer Zielgrößen fest. Liegt der Frauenanteil bei Festlegung der Zielgrößen unter 30 Prozent, so dürfen die Zielgrößen den jeweils erreichten Anteil nicht mehr unterschreiten. Gleichzeitig sind Fristen zur Erreichung der Zielgrößen festzulegen. Die Fristen dürfen jeweils nicht länger als fünf Jahre sein.

§ 36 Targets and Periods for the Equal Participation of Women and Men

The managing directors of a company that is subject to co-determination must determine targets for the percentage of women in the two management levels below the managing directors. If the percentage of women is, upon determining the targets, under 30 percent, then the targets may no longer be lower than the respective percentage achieved. Periods for the achievement of the targets are to be determined at the same time. The respective periods may not be longer than five years.

§ 37 Beschränkungen der Vertretungsbefugnis

(1) Die Geschäftsführer sind der Gesellschaft gegenüber verpflichtet, die Beschränkungen einzuhalten, welche für den Umfang ihrer Befugnis, die Gesellschaft zu vertreten, durch den Gesellschaftsvertrag oder, soweit dieser nicht ein anderes bestimmt, durch die Beschlüsse der Gesellschafter festgesetzt sind.

(2) Gegen dritte Personen hat eine Beschränkung der Befugnis der Geschäftsführer, die Gesellschaft zu vertreten, keine rechtliche Wirkung. Dies gilt insbesondere für den Fall, daß die Vertretung sich nur auf gewisse Geschäfte oder Arten von Geschäften erstrecken oder nur unter gewissen Umständen oder für eine gewisse Zeit oder an einzelnen Orten stattfinden soll, oder daß die Zustimmung der Gesellschafter oder eines Organs der Gesellschaft für einzelne Geschäfte erfordert ist.

§ 37 Limitations on the Power of Representation

(1) The managing directors are obligated to the company to abide by the limitations on the scope of their power to represent the company that are determined by the articles of association or, insofar as these do not provide otherwise, by the resolutions of the members.

(2) A limitation on the power of the managing directors to represent the company has no legal effect against third parties. This applies, in particular, to the case in which the representation only covers certain transactions or types of transactions, or only exists under certain circumstances or for a certain time or in particular places, or in which the consent of the members or a body of the company is necessary for single transactions.

§ 38 Widerruf der Bestellung

(1) Die Bestellung der Geschäftsführer ist zu jeder Zeit widerruflich, unbescha-

§ 38 Revocation of the Appointment

(1) The appointment of the managing directors is revocable at any time, with-

det der Entschädigungsansprüche aus bestehenden Verträgen.

(2) Im Gesellschaftsvertrag kann die Zulässigkeit des Widerrufs auf den Fall beschränkt werden, daß wichtige Gründe denselben notwendig machen. Als solche Gründe sind insbesondere grobe Pflichtverletzung oder Unfähigkeit zur ordnungsmäßigen Geschäftsführung anzusehen.

§ 39 Anmeldung der Geschäftsführer

(1) Jede Änderung in den Personen der Geschäftsführer sowie die Beendigung der Vertretungsbefugnis eines Geschäftsführers ist zur Eintragung in das Handelsregister anzumelden.

(2) Der Anmeldung sind die Urkunden über die Bestellung der Geschäftsführer oder über die Beendigung der Vertretungsbefugnis in Urschrift oder öffentlich beglaubigter Abschrift beizufügen.

(3) Die neuen Geschäftsführer haben in der Anmeldung zu versichern, daß keine Umstände vorliegen, die ihrer Bestellung nach § 6 Abs. 2 Satz 2 Nr. 2 und 3 sowie Satz 3 entgegenstehen und daß sie über ihre unbeschränkte Auskunftspflicht gegenüber dem Gericht belehrt worden sind. § 8 Abs. 3 Satz 2 ist anzuwenden.

(4) (weggefallen)

§ 40 Liste der Gesellschafter, Verordnungsermächtigung

(1) Die Geschäftsführer haben unverzüglich nach Wirksamwerden jeder Veränderung in den Personen der Gesellschafter oder des Umfangs ihrer Beteiligung eine von ihnen unterschriebene Liste der Gesellschafter zum Handelsregister einzureichen, aus welcher Name, Vorname, Geburtsdatum und Wohnort

out prejudice to claims to compensation arising from existing contracts.

(2) In the articles of association, the permissibility of revocation may be limited to cases in which important reasons make the revocation necessary. In particular, gross breach of duty or incompetence regarding proper management are to be regarded as such reasons.

§ 39 Registration of the Managing Directors

(1) Every change in the persons who are managing directors as well as the termination of the power of representation of a managing director is to be registered for entry in the commercial register (*Handelsregister*).

(2) The documents for the appointment of the managing directors or for the termination of the power of representation are to be appended to the registration in original or as a publicly authenticated copy.

(3) The new managing directors must assert in the registration that no circumstances exist that conflict with their appointment according to § 6(2), Sentence 2, No. 2 and 3, as well as Sentence 3, and that they have been instructed on their unlimited duty of disclosure to the court. § 8(3), Sentence 2 is to be applied.

(4) (repealed)

§ 40 List of the Members, Authorization to Issue Regulations

(1) The managing directors must file a list of the members signed by the managing directors with the commercial register (*Handelsregister*) without undue delay after the entry into force of every change in the persons who are members or in the extent of their participation, in which the surname, first name, date of

derselben sowie die Nennbeträge und die laufenden Nummern der von einem jeden derselben übernommenen Geschäftsanteile sowie die durch den jeweiligen Nennbetrag eines Geschäftsanteils vermittelte jeweilige prozentuale Beteiligung am Stammkapital zu entnehmen sind. Ist ein Gesellschafter selbst eine Gesellschaft, so sind bei eingetragenen Gesellschaften in die Liste deren Firma, Satzungssitz, zuständiges Register und Registernummer aufzunehmen, bei nicht eingetragenen Gesellschaften deren jeweilige Gesellschafter unter einer zusammenfassenden Bezeichnung mit Name, Vorname, Geburtsdatum und Wohnort. Hält ein Gesellschafter mehr als einen Geschäftsanteil, ist in der Liste der Gesellschafter zudem der Gesamtumfang der Beteiligung am Stammkapital als Prozentsatz gesondert anzugeben. Die Änderung der Liste durch die Geschäftsführer erfolgt auf Mitteilung und Nachweis.

(2) Hat ein Notar an Veränderungen nach Absatz 1 Satz 1 mitgewirkt, hat er unverzüglich nach deren Wirksamwerden ohne Rücksicht auf etwaige später eintretende Unwirksamkeitsgründe die Liste anstelle der Geschäftsführer zu unterschreiben, zum Handelsregister einzureichen und eine Abschrift der geänderten Liste an die Gesellschaft zu übermitteln. Die Liste muss mit der Bescheinigung des Notars versehen sein, dass die geänderten Eintragungen den Veränderungen entsprechen, an denen er mitgewirkt hat, und die übrigen Eintragungen mit dem Inhalt der zuletzt im Handelsregister aufgenommenen Liste übereinstimmen.

(3) Geschäftsführer, welche die ihnen nach Absatz 1 obliegende Pflicht verletzen, haften denjenigen, deren Beteiligung sich geändert hat, und den Gläubigern der Gesellschaft für den daraus entstandenen Schaden als Gesamtschuldner.

birth, and place of residence of the members, as well as the par values and the serial numbers of the membership interests accepted by each of the members, and the respective percentage of participation in the capital stock represented by the respective par value of a membership interest, appear. If a member is itself a company, then, in the case of registered companies, the company name, registered office provided in the articles of association, competent register and register number and, in the case of unregistered companies, the respective members under a summarized description with surname, first name, date of birth and place of residence, are to be recorded. If a member holds more than one membership interest, then, in addition, the total amount of participation in the capital stock is to be stated separately in the list of the members as a percentage. The change of the list by the managing directors is effected upon notification and evidence.

(2) If a notary (*Notar*) took part in changes according to Subsection 1, Sentence 1, then he must, without undue delay after their entry into force, without consideration of possible later-occurring reasons for ineffectiveness, sign the list instead of the managing directors, file it with the commercial register (*Handelsregister*), and deliver a copy of the changed list to the company. The list must be provided with the attestation of the notary (*Notar*) that the changed entries correspond to the changes in which he took part, and that the other entries are consistent with the content of the list last recorded in the commercial register (*Handelsregister*).

(3) Managing directors that breach the duty imposed on them according to Subsection 1 are liable as joint and several debtors to those whose participation changed and to the creditors of the company for the damages arising therefrom.

(4) Das Bundesministerium der Justiz und für Verbraucherschutz wird ermächtigt, durch Rechtsverordnung mit Zustimmung des Bundesrates nähere Bestimmungen über die Ausgestaltung der Gesellschafterliste zu treffen.

(4) The Federal Ministry of Justice and Consumer Protection (*Bundesministerium der Justiz und für Verbraucherschutz*) is authorized to enact more detailed provisions on the form of the list of members by regulation with the consent of the Federal Council (*Bundesrat*).

(5) Die Landesregierungen werden ermächtigt, durch Rechtsverordnung zu bestimmen, dass bestimmte in der Liste der Gesellschafter enthaltene Angaben in strukturierter maschinenlesbarer Form an das Handelsregister zu übermitteln sind, soweit nicht durch das Bundesministerium der Justiz und für Verbraucherschutz nach § 387 Absatz 2 des Gesetzes über das Verfahren in Familiensachen und in den Angelegenheiten der freiwilligen Gerichtsbarkeit entsprechende Vorschriften erlassen werden. Die Landesregierungen können die Ermächtigung durch Rechtsverordnung auf die Landesjustizverwaltungen übertragen.

(5) The state governments are authorized to determine by regulation that certain information contained in the list of members is to be transmitted to the commercial register (*Handelsregister*) in a structured, machine-readable form, unless such provisions are issued by the Federal Ministry of Justice and Consumer Protection (*Bundesministerium der Justiz und für Verbraucherschutz*) pursuant to Section 387(2) of the Act on Proceedings in Family Matters and in Matters of Non-contentious Jurisdiction (*Gesetz über das Verfahren in Familiensachen und in den Angelegenheiten der freiwilligen Gerichtsbarkeit*). The state governments can delegate the authorization by regulation to the state administrative agencies for justice.

§ 41 Buchführung

Die Geschäftsführer sind verpflichtet, für die ordnungsmäßige Buchführung der Gesellschaft zu sorgen.

§ 41 Accounting

The managing directors are obligated to provide for the proper accounting of the company.

§ 42 Bilanz

(1) In der Bilanz des nach den §§ 242, 264 des Handelsgesetzbuchs aufzustellenden Jahresabschlusses ist das Stammkapital als gezeichnetes Kapital auszuweisen.

(2) Das Recht der Gesellschaft zur Einziehung von Nachschüssen der Gesellschafter ist in der Bilanz insoweit zu aktivieren, als die Einziehung bereits beschlossen ist und den Gesellschaftern ein Recht, durch Verweisung auf den Geschäftsanteil sich von der Zahlung der Nachschüsse zu befreien, nicht zusteht.

§ 42 Balance Sheet

(1) In the balance sheet of the annual financial statements to be drawn up according to §§ 242 and 264 of the Commercial Code (*Handelsgesetzbuch*), the capital stock is to be entered as capital subscribed.

(2) The right of the company to call in additional contributions from the members is to be entered on the assets side in the balance sheet insofar as they have already been called in and the members do not have a right to release themselves from the payment of the additional contributions through referencing the mem-

Der nachzuschießende Betrag ist auf der Aktivseite unter den Forderungen gesondert unter der Bezeichnung „Eingeforderte Nachschüsse“ auszuweisen, soweit mit der Zahlung gerechnet werden kann. Ein dem Aktivposten entsprechender Betrag ist auf der Passivseite in dem Posten „Kapitalrücklage“ gesondert auszuweisen.

(3) Ausleihungen, Forderungen und Verbindlichkeiten gegenüber Gesellschaftern sind in der Regel als solche jeweils gesondert auszuweisen oder im Anhang anzugeben; werden sie unter anderen Posten ausgewiesen, so muß diese Eigenschaft vermerkt werden.

§ 42a Vorlage des Jahresabschlusses und des Lageberichts

(1) Die Geschäftsführer haben den Jahresabschluß und den Lagebericht unverzüglich nach der Aufstellung den Gesellschaftern zum Zwecke der Feststellung des Jahresabschlusses vorzulegen. Ist der Jahresabschluß durch einen Abschlußprüfer zu prüfen, so haben die Geschäftsführer ihn zusammen mit dem Lagebericht und dem Prüfungsbericht des Abschlußprüfers unverzüglich nach Eingang des Prüfungsberichts vorzulegen. Hat die Gesellschaft einen Aufsichtsrat, so ist dessen Bericht über das Ergebnis seiner Prüfung ebenfalls unverzüglich vorzulegen.

(2) Die Gesellschafter haben spätestens bis zum Ablauf der ersten acht Monate oder, wenn es sich um eine kleine Gesellschaft handelt (§ 267 Abs. 1 des Handelsgesetzbuchs), bis zum Ablauf der ersten elf Monate des Geschäftsjahrs über die Feststellung des Jahresabschlusses und über die Ergebnisverwendung zu beschließen. Der Gesellschaftsvertrag kann die Frist nicht verlängern. Auf den

bership interests. The amount to be paid as an additional contribution is to be entered on the assets side under receivables, separately under the designation “Called-in Additional Contributions” (“*Eingeforderte Nachschüsse*”), insofar as payment can be anticipated. An amount corresponding to the asset item is to be separately entered on the liabilities side under the item “Capital Reserve” (“*Kapitalrücklage*”).

(3) As a rule, lending, claims, and liabilities in relation to members are each to be separately entered as such or stated in the notes; if they are entered under other items, then this attribute must be noted.

§ 42a Submission of the Annual Financial Statements and Management Report

(1) The managing directors must submit the annual financial statements and the management report to the members without undue delay after drawing them up for purposes of adoption of the annual financial statements. If the annual financial statements are to be audited by an auditor, then the managing directors must submit them together with the management report and the audit report of the auditor without undue delay after receipt of the audit report. If the company has a supervisory board, then its report on the results of its audit is likewise to be submitted.

(2) The members must resolve upon the adoption of the annual financial statements and on the appropriation of profit or loss no later than the expiration of the first eight months or, in the case of a small company (§ 267(1) of the Commercial Code (*Handelsgesetzbuch*)), no later than the expiration of the first eleven months, of the fiscal year. The articles of association may not extend the period.

Jahresabschluß sind bei der Feststellung die für seine Aufstellung geltenden Vorschriften anzuwenden.

For the adoption, the provisions applicable to their drawing up are to be applied to the annual financial statements.

(3) Hat ein Abschlußprüfer den Jahresabschluß geprüft, so hat er auf Verlangen eines Gesellschafters an den Verhandlungen über die Feststellung des Jahresabschlusses teilzunehmen.

(3) If an auditor audited the annual financial statements, then he must participate in the discussions on the adoption of the annual financial statements upon demand of a member.

(4) Ist die Gesellschaft zur Aufstellung eines Konzernabschlusses und eines Konzernlageberichts verpflichtet, so sind die Absätze 1 bis 3 entsprechend anzuwenden. Das Gleiche gilt hinsichtlich eines Einzelabschlusses nach § 325 Abs. 2a des Handelsgesetzbuchs, wenn die Gesellschafter die Offenlegung eines solchen beschlossen haben.

(4) If the company is obligated to draw up consolidated financial statements and a consolidated management report, then Subsections 1 through 3 are to be applied accordingly. The same applies with respect to individual financial statements according to § 325(2a) of the Commercial Code (*Handelsgesetzbuch*) if the members have resolved upon the publication thereof.

§ 43 Haftung der Geschäftsführer

§ 43 Liability of the Managing Directors

(1) Die Geschäftsführer haben in den Angelegenheiten der Gesellschaft die Sorgfalt eines ordentlichen Geschäftsmannes anzuwenden.

(1) The managing directors must exercise the care of a prudent businessman in the affairs of the company.

(2) Geschäftsführer, welche ihre Obliegenheiten verletzen, haften der Gesellschaft solidarisch für den entstandenen Schaden.

(2) Managing directors who breach their duties are jointly and severally liable to the company for the arising damages.

(3) Insbesondere sind sie zum Ersatz verpflichtet, wenn den Bestimmungen des § 30 zuwider Zahlungen aus dem zur Erhaltung des Stammkapitals erforderlichen Vermögen der Gesellschaft gemacht oder den Bestimmungen des § 33 zuwider eigene Geschäftsanteile der Gesellschaft erworben worden sind. Auf den Ersatzanspruch finden die Bestimmungen in § 9b Abs. 1 entsprechende Anwendung. Soweit der Ersatz zur Befriedigung der Gläubiger der Gesellschaft erforderlich ist, wird die Verpflichtung der Geschäftsführer dadurch nicht aufgehoben, daß dieselben in Befolgung eines Beschlusses der Gesellschafter gehandelt haben.

(3) In particular, they are obligated to pay compensation if, contrary to the provisions of § 30, payments have been made out of the assets of the company that were necessary for the maintenance of the capital stock, or if, contrary to the provisions of § 33, the company has acquired its own membership interests. The provisions in § 9b(1) apply accordingly to the claim to compensation. Insofar as the compensation is necessary for the satisfaction of the creditors of the company, the obligation of the managing directors is not terminated by the fact that the managing directors acted in compliance with a resolution of the members.

(4) Die Ansprüche auf Grund der vorstehenden Bestimmungen verjähren in fünf Jahren.

(4) The claims based on the foregoing provisions become time-barred after five years.

§ 43a Kreditgewährung aus Gesellschaftsvermögen

Den Geschäftsführern, anderen gesetzlichen Vertretern, Prokuristen oder zum gesamten Geschäftsbetrieb ermächtigten Handlungsbevollmächtigten darf Kredit nicht aus dem zur Erhaltung des Stammkapitals erforderlichen Vermögen der Gesellschaft gewährt werden. Ein entgegen Satz 1 gewährter Kredit ist ohne Rücksicht auf entgegenstehende Vereinbarungen sofort zurückzugewähren.

§ 43a Granting of Credit out of Company Assets

Credit may not be granted out of the assets of the company that are necessary for the maintenance of the capital stock to the managing directors, other statutory representatives, Prokurists, or authorized signatories who are empowered for all business operations. Credit that is granted contrary to Sentence 1 is to be immediately repaid regardless of conflicting agreements.

§ 44 Stellvertreter von Geschäftsführern

Die für die Geschäftsführer gegebenen Vorschriften gelten auch für Stellvertreter von Geschäftsführern.

§ 44 Deputies of Managing Directors

The provisions provided for managing directors also apply to deputies of managing directors.

§ 45 Rechte der Gesellschafter

(1) Die Rechte, welche den Gesellschaftern in den Angelegenheiten der Gesellschaft, insbesondere in bezug auf die Führung der Geschäfte zustehen, sowie die Ausübung derselben bestimmen sich, soweit nicht gesetzliche Vorschriften entgegenstehen, nach dem Gesellschaftsvertrag.

(2) In Ermangelung besonderer Bestimmungen des Gesellschaftsvertrags finden die Vorschriften der §§ 46 bis 51 Anwendung.

§ 45 Rights of the Members

(1) The rights enjoyed by the members in the affairs of the company, in particular in relation to the management of the business operations, as well as the exercise of those rights, are determined according to the articles of association, insofar as no statutory provisions conflict.

(2) In the absence of specific provisions in the articles of association, the provisions of §§ 46 to 51 apply.

§ 46 Aufgabenkreis der Gesellschafter

Der Bestimmung der Gesellschafter unterliegen:

1. die Feststellung des Jahresabschlusses und die Verwendung des Ergebnisses;

§ 46 Areas of Responsibility of the Members

The following are subject to the determination of the members:

1. the adoption of the annual financial statements and the appropriation of the profit or loss;

1a. die Entscheidung über die Offenlegung eines Einzelabschlusses nach internationalen Rechnungslegungsstandards (§ 325 Abs. 2a des Handelsgesetzbuchs) und über die Billigung des von den Geschäftsführern aufgestellten Abschlusses;

1b. die Billigung eines von den Geschäftsführern aufgestellten Konzernabschlusses;

2. die Einforderung der Einlagen;

3. die Rückzahlung von Nachschüssen;

4. die Teilung, die Zusammenlegung sowie die Einziehung von Geschäftsanteilen;

5. die Bestellung und die Abberufung von Geschäftsführern sowie die Entlastung derselben;

6. die Maßregeln zur Prüfung und Überwachung der Geschäftsführung;

7. die Bestellung von Prokuristen und von Handlungsbevollmächtigten zum gesamten Geschäftsbetrieb;

8. die Geltendmachung von Ersatzansprüchen, welche der Gesellschaft aus der Gründung oder Geschäftsführung gegen Geschäftsführer oder Gesellschafter zustehen, sowie die Vertretung der Gesellschaft in Prozessen, welche sie gegen die Geschäftsführer zu führen hat.

§ 47 Abstimmung

(1) Die von den Gesellschaftern in den Angelegenheiten der Gesellschaft zu treffenden Bestimmungen erfolgen durch Beschlußfassung nach der Mehrheit der abgegebenen Stimmen.

(2) Jeder Euro eines Geschäftsanteils gewährt eine Stimme.

(3) Vollmachten bedürfen zu ihrer Gültigkeit der Textform.

1a. the decision on the publication of the individual financial statements according to international accounting standards (§ 325(2a) of the Commercial Code (*Handelsgesetzbuch*)) and on the approval of the financial statements drawn up by the managing directors;

1b. the approval of consolidated financial statements drawn up by the managing directors;

2. the calling-in of contributions;

3. the repayment of additional contributions;

4. the division, the consolidation, as well as the redemption of membership interests;

5. the appointment and the dismissal, as well as the discharge of managing directors;

6. the measures for the audit and monitoring of the management;

7. the appointment of Prokurists and of authorized signatories for all business operations;

8. the enforcement of claims to compensation that belong to the company arising from the incorporation or management against managing directors or members, as well as the representation of the company in proceedings that it must conduct against the managing directors.

§ 47 Voting

(1) The determinations to be made by the members in the affairs of the company are effected through the adoption of a resolution by the majority of the votes cast.

(2) Each euro of a membership interest confers one vote.

(3) Proxies are required to be in textual form to be valid.

(4) Ein Gesellschafter, welcher durch die Beschlußfassung entlastet oder von einer Verbindlichkeit befreit werden soll, hat hierbei kein Stimmrecht und darf ein solches auch nicht für andere ausüben. Dasselbe gilt von einer Beschlußfassung, welche die Vornahme eines Rechtsgeschäfts oder die Einleitung oder Erledigung eines Rechtsstreits gegenüber einem Gesellschafter betrifft.

(4) A member that will be discharged or released from a liability through the adoption of a resolution has no right to vote thereon and also may not exercise that of another. The same applies to the adoption of a resolution that pertains to the performance of a legal transaction or the initiation or settlement of a legal dispute in relation to a member.

§ 48 Gesellschafterversammlung

(1) Die Beschlüsse der Gesellschafter werden in Versammlungen gefaßt.

(2) Der Abhaltung einer Versammlung bedarf es nicht, wenn sämtliche Gesellschafter in Textform mit der zu treffenden Bestimmung oder mit der schriftlichen Abgabe der Stimmen sich einverstanden erklären.

(3) Befinden sich alle Geschäftsanteile der Gesellschaft in der Hand eines Gesellschafters oder daneben in der Hand der Gesellschaft, so hat er unverzüglich nach der Beschlußfassung eine Niederschrift aufzunehmen und zu unterschreiben.

§ 48 Meeting of the Members

(1) The resolutions of the members are adopted in meetings.

(2) The holding of a meeting is not required if all members declare themselves, in textual form, to be in agreement with the resolution to be adopted or with the written casting of votes.

(3) If all membership interests of the company are in the possession of one member or, in addition thereto, in the possession of the company, then he must record and sign minutes after the adoption of the resolution without undue delay.

§ 49 Einberufung der Versammlung

(1) Die Versammlung der Gesellschafter wird durch die Geschäftsführer berufen.

(2) Sie ist außer den ausdrücklich bestimmten Fällen zu berufen, wenn es im Interesse der Gesellschaft erforderlich erscheint.

(3) Insbesondere muß die Versammlung unverzüglich berufen werden, wenn aus der Jahresbilanz oder aus einer im Laufe des Geschäftsjahres aufgestellten Bilanz sich ergibt, daß die Hälfte des Stammkapitals verloren ist.

§ 49 Convening of the Meeting

(1) The meeting of the members is convened by the managing directors.

(2) Aside from the cases expressly provided for, the meeting is to be convened if it appears necessary in the interest of the company.

(3) In particular, the meeting must be convened without undue delay if it appears in the annual balance sheet, or in a balance sheet drawn up during the course of the fiscal year, that half of the capital stock has been lost.

§ 50 Minderheitsrechte

(1) Gesellschafter, deren Geschäftsanteile zusammen mindestens dem zehnten

§ 50 Minority Rights

(1) Members whose membership interests correspond, in the aggregate, to at

Teil des Stammkapitals entsprechen, sind berechtigt, unter Angabe des Zwecks und der Gründe die Berufung der Versammlung zu verlangen.

(2) In gleicher Weise haben die Gesellschafter das Recht zu verlangen, daß Gegenstände zur Beschlußfassung der Versammlung angekündigt werden.

(3) Wird dem Verlangen nicht entsprochen oder sind Personen, an welche dasselbe zu richten wäre, nicht vorhanden, so können die in Absatz 1 bezeichneten Gesellschafter unter Mitteilung des Sachverhältnisses die Berufung oder Ankündigung selbst bewirken. Die Versammlung beschließt, ob die entstandenen Kosten von der Gesellschaft zu tragen sind.

least one-tenth of the capital stock are entitled to demand the convening of a meeting upon specification of the purpose and reasons.

(2) Under the same conditions, the members have the right to demand that items be announced for the adoption of a resolution of the meeting.

(3) If the demand is not complied with or if persons to whom the demand was to be directed are not on hand, then the members designated in Subsection 1 may, upon notification of the subject-matter, effectuate the convening or the announcement themselves. The meeting resolves whether the arising costs are to be borne by the company.

§ 51 Form der Einberufung

(1) Die Berufung der Versammlung erfolgt durch Einladung der Gesellschafter mittels eingeschriebener Briefe. Sie ist mit einer Frist von mindestens einer Woche zu bewirken.

(2) Der Zweck der Versammlung soll jederzeit bei der Berufung angekündigt werden.

(3) Ist die Versammlung nicht ordnungsmäßig berufen, so können Beschlüsse nur gefaßt werden, wenn sämtliche Gesellschafter anwesend sind.

(4) Das gleiche gilt in bezug auf Beschlüsse über Gegenstände, welche nicht wenigstens drei Tage vor der Versammlung in der für die Berufung vorgeschriebenen Weise angekündigt worden sind.

§ 51 Form of the Convening

(1) The convening of the meeting is effected through invitation of the members by means of registered letters. It is to be effectuated at least one week in advance.

(2) The purpose of the meeting shall be announced each time upon the convening.

(3) If the meeting is not properly convened, then resolutions may only be adopted if all members are present.

(4) The same applies regarding resolutions on items that have not been announced in the manner prescribed for the convening at least three days before the meeting.

§ 51a Auskunfts- und Einsichtsrecht

(1) Die Geschäftsführer haben jedem Gesellschafter auf Verlangen unverzüglich Auskunft über die Angelegenheiten der Gesellschaft zu geben und die Einsicht der Bücher und Schriften zu gestatten.

§ 51a Right to Information and Right to Inspection

(1) To each member upon demand, the managing directors must give information on the affairs of the company and permission to inspect the books and records without undue delay.

(2) Die Geschäftsführer dürfen die Auskunft und die Einsicht verweigern, wenn zu besorgen ist, daß der Gesellschafter sie zu gesellschaftsfremden Zwecken verwenden und dadurch der Gesellschaft oder einem verbundenen Unternehmen einen nicht unerheblichen Nachteil zufügen wird. Die Verweigerung bedarf eines Beschlusses der Gesellschafter.

(2) The managing directors may deny information and inspection if there is a concern that the member will use it for non-company purposes and a not insubstantial disadvantage will be thereby inflicted on the company or an affiliated undertaking. The denial requires a resolution of the members.

(3) Von diesen Vorschriften kann im Gesellschaftsvertrag nicht abgewichen werden.

(3) The articles of association may not deviate from these provisions.

§ 51b Gerichtliche Entscheidung über das Auskunfts- und Einsichtsrecht

§ 51b Court Decision on the Right to Information and the Right to Inspection

Für die gerichtliche Entscheidung über das Auskunfts- und Einsichtsrecht findet § 132 Abs. 1, 3 und 4 des Aktiengesetzes entsprechende Anwendung. Antragsberechtigt ist jeder Gesellschafter, dem die verlangte Auskunft nicht gegeben oder die verlangte Einsicht nicht gestattet worden ist.

§ 132(1), (3) and (4) of the Stock Corporation Act (*Aktiengesetz*) applies accordingly to the court decision on the right to information and the right to inspection. Each member to whom the demanded information or the demanded permission to inspect has not been given is entitled to file a petition.

§ 52 Aufsichtsrat

§ 52 Supervisory Board

(1) Ist nach dem Gesellschaftsvertrag ein Aufsichtsrat zu bestellen, so sind § 90 Abs. 3, 4, 5 Satz 1 und 2, § 95 Satz 1, § 100 Abs. 1 und 2 Nr. 2 und Abs. 5, § 101 Abs. 1 Satz 1, § 103 Abs. 1 Satz 1 und 2, §§ 105, 107 Absatz 3 Satz 2 und 3 und Absatz 4, §§ 110 bis 114, 116 des Aktiengesetzes in Verbindung mit § 93 Abs. 1 und 2 Satz 1 und 2 des Aktiengesetzes, § 124 Abs. 3 Satz 2, §§ 170, 171, 394 und 395 des Aktiengesetzes entsprechend anzuwenden, soweit nicht im Gesellschaftsvertrag ein anderes bestimmt ist.

(1) If a supervisory board is to be appointed according to the articles of association, then § 90(3), (4), (5), Sentence 1 and 2, § 95, Sentence 1, § 100(1) and (2), No. 2 and (5), § 101(1), Sentence 1, § 103(1), Sentence 1 and 2, §§ 105, 107(3), Sentence 2 and 3, and (4), §§ 110 to 114, 116 of the Stock Corporation Act (*Aktiengesetz*) in connection with § 93(1) and (2), Sentence 1 and 2 of the Stock Corporation Act (*Aktiengesetz*), § 124(3), Sentence 2, §§ 170, 171, 394 and 395 of the Stock Corporation Act (*Aktiengesetz*) are to be applied accordingly, unless otherwise provided for in the articles of association.

(2) Ist nach dem Drittelbeteiligungsgesetz ein Aufsichtsrat zu bestellen, so legt die Gesellschafterversammlung für den Frauenanteil im Aufsichtsrat und unter

(2) If a supervisory board is to be appointed pursuant to the One-Third Participation Act (*Drittelbeteiligungsgesetz*), the meeting of the members determines

den Geschäftsführern Zielgrößen fest, es sei denn, sie hat dem Aufsichtsrat diese Aufgabe übertragen. Ist nach dem Mitbestimmungsgesetz, dem Montan-Mitbestimmungsgesetz oder dem Mitbestimmungsergänzungsgesetz ein Aufsichtsrat zu bestellen, so legt der Aufsichtsrat für den Frauenanteil im Aufsichtsrat und unter den Geschäftsführern Zielgrößen fest. Liegt der Frauenanteil bei Festlegung der Zielgrößen unter 30 Prozent, so dürfen die Zielgrößen den jeweils erreichten Anteil nicht mehr unterschreiten. Gleichzeitig sind Fristen zur Erreichung der Zielgrößen festzulegen. Die Fristen dürfen jeweils nicht länger als fünf Jahre sein.

targets for the percentage of women on the supervisory board and among the managing directors, unless it has delegated this task to the supervisory board. If a supervisory board is to be appointed in accordance with the Co-Determination Act (*Mitbestimmungsgesetz*), the Coal and Steel Co-Determination Act (*Montan-Mitbestimmungsgesetz*) or the Co-Determination Supplementary Act (*Mitbestimmungsergänzungsgesetz*), then the supervisory board determines targets for the percentage of women on the supervisory board and among the managing directors. If the percentage of women is, upon determining the targets, under 30 percent, then the targets may no longer be lower than the respective percentage achieved. Periods for the achievement of the targets are to be determined at the same time. The respective periods may not be longer than five years.

(3) Werden die Mitglieder des Aufsichtsrats vor der Eintragung der Gesellschaft in das Handelsregister bestellt, gilt § 37 Abs. 4 Nr. 3 und 3a des Aktiengesetzes entsprechend. Die Geschäftsführer haben bei jeder Änderung in den Personen der Aufsichtsratsmitglieder unverzüglich eine Liste der Mitglieder des Aufsichtsrats, aus welcher Name, Vorname, ausgeübter Beruf und Wohnort der Mitglieder ersichtlich ist, zum Handelsregister einzureichen; das Gericht hat nach § 10 des Handelsgesetzbuchs einen Hinweis darauf bekannt zu machen, dass die Liste zum Handelsregister eingereicht worden ist.

(3) If the members of the supervisory board are appointed prior to the entry of the company in the commercial register (*Handelsregister*), § 37(4), No. 3 and 3a of the Stock Corporation Act (*Aktiengesetz*) shall apply accordingly. The managing directors must, without undue delay, file a list of the members of the supervisory board, on which the surname, first name, practiced profession and place of residence of the members appear, with the commercial register (*Handelsregister*) upon each change in the persons who are supervisory board members; the court has to publish an indication according to § 10 of the Commercial Code (*Handelsgesetzbuch*) that the list has been filed with the commercial register (*Handelsregister*).

(4) Schadensersatzansprüche gegen die Mitglieder des Aufsichtsrats wegen Verletzung ihrer Obliegenheiten verjähren in fünf Jahren.

(4) Claims to compensation for damages against the members of the supervisory board because of a breach of their duties become time-barred after five years.

Abschnitt 4 Abänderungen des Gesellschaftsvertrags

§ 53 Form der Satzungsänderung

(1) Eine Abänderung des Gesellschaftsvertrags kann nur durch Beschluß der Gesellschafter erfolgen.

(2) Der Beschluß muß notariell beurkundet werden, derselbe bedarf einer Mehrheit von drei Vierteilen der abgegebenen Stimmen. Der Gesellschaftsvertrag kann noch andere Erfordernisse aufstellen.

(3) Eine Vermehrung der den Gesellschaftern nach dem Gesellschaftsvertrag obliegenden Leistungen kann nur mit Zustimmung sämtlicher beteiligter Gesellschafter beschlossen werden.

§ 54 Anmeldung und Eintragung der Satzungsänderung

(1) Die Abänderung des Gesellschaftsvertrags ist zur Eintragung in das Handelsregister anzumelden. Der Anmeldung ist der vollständige Wortlaut des Gesellschaftsvertrags beizufügen; er muß mit der Bescheinigung eines Notars versehen sein, daß die geänderten Bestimmungen des Gesellschaftsvertrags mit dem Beschluß über die Änderung des Gesellschaftsvertrags und die unveränderten Bestimmungen mit dem zuletzt zum Handelsregister eingereichten vollständigen Wortlaut des Gesellschaftsvertrags übereinstimmen.

(2) Bei der Eintragung genügt, sofern nicht die Abänderung die in § 10 bezeichneten Angaben betrifft, die Bezugnahme auf die bei dem Gericht eingereichten Dokumente über die Abänderung.

Chapter 4 Amendments of the Articles of Association

§ 53 Form of the Amendment of the Articles of Association

(1) An amendment of the articles of association may only be effected through a resolution of the members.

(2) The resolution must be certified by a notary (*Notar*), and requires a majority of three-fourths of the votes cast. The articles of association may additionally impose other requirements.

(3) An increase of the contributions that the members are obligated to render according to the articles of association may only be resolved upon with the consent of all affected members.

§ 54 Registration and Entry of the Amendment of the Articles of Association

(1) The amendment of the articles of association is to be registered for entry in the commercial register (*Handelsregister*). The complete wording of the articles of association is to be appended to the registration; it must be provided with the attestation of a notary (*Notar*) that the amended provisions of the articles of association are consistent with the resolution on the change of the articles of association, and that the unchanged provisions are consistent with the complete wording of the articles of association as last filed with the commercial register (*Handelsregister*).

(2) A reference to the documents on the amendment filed with the court is sufficient for the entry, unless the amendment pertains to the information designated in § 10.

(3) Die Abänderung hat keine rechtliche Wirkung, bevor sie in das Handelsregister des Sitzes der Gesellschaft eingetragen ist.

§ 55 Erhöhung des Stammkapitals

(1) Wird eine Erhöhung des Stammkapitals beschlossen, so bedarf es zur Übernahme jedes Geschäftsanteils an dem erhöhten Kapital einer notariell aufgenommenen oder beglaubigten Erklärung des Übernehmers.

(2) Zur Übernahme eines Geschäftsanteils können von der Gesellschaft die bisherigen Gesellschafter oder andere Personen, welche durch die Übernahme ihren Beitritt zu der Gesellschaft erklären, zugelassen werden. Im letzteren Fall sind außer dem Nennbetrag des Geschäftsanteils auch sonstige Leistungen, zu welchen der Beitretende nach dem Gesellschaftsvertrag verpflichtet sein soll, in der in Absatz 1 bezeichneten Urkunde ersichtlich zu machen.

(3) Wird von einem der Gesellschaft bereits angehörenden Gesellschafter ein Geschäftsanteil an dem erhöhten Kapital übernommen, so erwirbt derselbe einen weiteren Geschäftsanteil.

(4) Die Bestimmungen in § 5 Abs. 2 und 3 über die Nennbeträge der Geschäftsanteile sowie die Bestimmungen in § 19 Abs. 6 über die Verjährung des Anspruchs der Gesellschaft auf Leistung der Einlagen sind auch hinsichtlich der an dem erhöhten Kapital übernommenen Geschäftsanteile anzuwenden.

§ 55a Genehmigtes Kapital

(1) Der Gesellschaftsvertrag kann die Geschäftsführer für höchstens fünf Jahre nach Eintragung der Gesellschaft ermächtigen, das Stammkapital bis zu einem bestimmten Nennbetrag (genehmigtes Kapital) durch Ausgabe neuer Geschäftsanteile gegen Einlagen zu er-

(3) The amendment has no legal effect before it is entered in the commercial register (*Handelsregister*) for the registered office of the company.

§ 55 Increase of the Capital Stock

(1) If an increase of the capital stock is resolved upon, then the acceptance of each membership interest for the increased capital requires a declaration of the accepting party recorded or authenticated by a notary (*Notar*).

(2) The preexisting members, or other persons that declare their joining of the company through the acceptance, may be permitted to accept a membership interest. In the latter case, other payments for which the joining person will be obligated according to the articles of association, in addition to the par value of the membership interest, are to appear in the certificate designated in Subsection 1.

(3) If a membership interest for the increased capital is accepted by a person who is already a member of the company, then he acquires an additional membership interest.

(4) The provisions in § 5(2) and (3) on the par values of the membership interests, as well as the provisions in § 19(6) on the statute of limitations for the claim of the company to rendering of contributions, are also to be applied with respect to the membership interests accepted for the increased capital.

§ 55a Authorized Capital

(1) The articles of association may, for a maximum of five years after the entry of the company, authorize the managing directors to increase the capital stock up to a certain par value (authorized capital) through issuance of new membership interests in exchange for contributions.

höhen. Der Nennbetrag des genehmigten Kapitals darf die Hälfte des Stammkapitals, das zur Zeit der Ermächtigung vorhanden ist, nicht übersteigen.

The par value of the authorized capital may not exceed half of the capital stock existing at the time of the authorization.

(2) Die Ermächtigung kann auch durch Abänderung des Gesellschaftsvertrags für höchstens fünf Jahre nach deren Eintragung erteilt werden.

(2) The authorization may also be given through an amendment of the articles of association for a maximum of five years after the amendment's entry.

(3) Gegen Sacheinlagen (§ 56) dürfen Geschäftsanteile nur ausgegeben werden, wenn die Ermächtigung es vorsieht.

(3) Membership interests may only be issued in exchange for in-kind contributions (§ 56) if the authorization so provides.

§ 56 Kapitalerhöhung mit Sacheinlagen

§ 56 Capital Increase with In-kind Contributions

(1) Sollen Sacheinlagen geleistet werden, so müssen ihr Gegenstand und der Nennbetrag des Geschäftsanteils, auf den sich die Sacheinlage bezieht, im Beschluß über die Erhöhung des Stammkapitals festgesetzt werden. Die Festsetzung ist in die in § 55 Abs. 1 bezeichnete Erklärung des Übernehmers aufzunehmen.

(1) If in-kind contributions will be rendered, then their object and the par value of the membership interest to which the in-kind contribution relates must be determined in the resolution on the increase of the capital stock. The determination is to be recorded in the declaration of the accepting party designated in § 55(1).

(2) Die §§ 9 und 19 Abs. 2 Satz 2 und Abs. 4 finden entsprechende Anwendung.

(2) §§ 9 and 19(2), Sentence 2 and (4) apply accordingly.

§ 56a Leistungen auf das neue Stammkapital

§ 56a Rendering of Contributions to the New Capital Stock

Für die Leistungen der Einlagen auf das neue Stammkapital finden § 7 Abs. 2 Satz 1 und Abs. 3 sowie § 19 Abs. 5 entsprechende Anwendung.

§ 7(2), Sentence 1 and (3) as well as § 19(5) apply accordingly to rendering of contributions to the new capital stock.

§ 57 Anmeldung der Erhöhung

§ 57 Registration of the Increase

(1) Die beschlossene Erhöhung des Stammkapitals ist zur Eintragung in das Handelsregister anzumelden, nachdem das erhöhte Kapital durch Übernahme von Geschäftsanteilen gedeckt ist.

(1) The resolved-upon increase of the capital stock is to be registered for entry in the commercial register (*Handelsregister*) after the increased capital is covered through acceptance of membership interests.

(2) In der Anmeldung ist die Versicherung abzugeben, daß die Einlagen auf das neue Stammkapital nach § 7 Abs. 2 Satz 1 und Abs. 3 bewirkt sind und daß

(2) In the registration, the assertion is to be given that the contributions to the new capital stock have been rendered according to § 7(2), Sentence 1 and (3),

der Gegenstand der Leistungen sich endgültig in der freien Verfügung der Geschäftsführer befindet. § 8 Abs. 2 Satz 2 gilt entsprechend.

and that the object rendered is irrevocably at the unrestricted disposal of the managing directors. § 8(2), Sentence 2 applies accordingly.

(3) Der Anmeldung sind beizufügen:

(3) The following are to be appended to the registration:

1. die in § 55 Abs. 1 bezeichneten Erklärungen oder eine beglaubigte Abschrift derselben;

1. the declarations designated in § 55(1) or an authenticated copy thereof;

2. eine von den Anmeldenden unterschriebene Liste der Personen, welche die neuen Geschäftsanteile übernommen haben; aus der Liste müssen die Nennbeträge der von jedem übernommenen Geschäftsanteile ersichtlich sein;

2. a list of the persons who have accepted the new membership interests signed by the registrants; the par values of the membership interests accepted by each person must appear on the list;

3. bei einer Kapitalerhöhung mit Sacheinlagen die Verträge, die den Festsetzungen nach § 56 zugrunde liegen oder zu ihrer Ausführung geschlossen worden sind.

3. upon a capital increase with in-kind contributions, the contracts that are the basis of the determinations according to § 56 or that have been entered into for their performance.

(4) Für die Verantwortlichkeit der Geschäftsführer, welche die Kapitalerhöhung zur Eintragung in das Handelsregister angemeldet haben, finden § 9a Abs. 1 und 3, § 9b entsprechende Anwendung.

(4) § 9a(1) and (3) and § 9b apply accordingly to the responsibility of the managing directors that have registered the capital increase for entry in the commercial register (*Handelsregister*).

§ 57a Ablehnung der Eintragung

Für die Ablehnung der Eintragung durch das Gericht findet § 9c Abs. 1 entsprechende Anwendung.

§ 57a Refusal of Entry

§ 9c(1) applies accordingly to the refusal of entry by the court.

§ 57b (weggefallen)

§ 57b (repealed)

§ 57c Kapitalerhöhung aus Gesellschaftsmitteln

(1) Das Stammkapital kann durch Umwandlung von Rücklagen in Stammkapital erhöht werden (Kapitalerhöhung aus Gesellschaftsmitteln).

(2) Die Erhöhung des Stammkapitals kann erst beschlossen werden, nachdem der Jahresabschluß für das letzte vor der Beschlußfassung über die Kapitalerhöhung abgelaufene Geschäftsjahr (letzter Jahresabschluß) festgestellt und über die

§ 57c Capital Increase from Company Funds

(1) The capital stock may be increased through a conversion of reserves to capital stock (capital increase from company funds).

(2) The increase of the capital stock may be first resolved upon after the annual financial statements for the preceding fiscal year elapsing before the adoption of the resolution on the capital increase (preceding annual financial statements) has

Ergebnisverwendung Beschluß gefaßt worden ist.

been adopted, and the resolution on the appropriation of profit and loss has been adopted.

(3) Dem Beschluß über die Erhöhung des Stammkapitals ist eine Bilanz zugrunde zu legen.

(3) A balance sheet is to be relied on for the resolution on the increase of the capital stock.

(4) Neben den §§ 53 und 54 über die Abänderung des Gesellschaftsvertrags gelten die §§ 57d bis 57o.

(4) §§ 57d to 57o apply in addition to §§ 53 and 54 on the amendment of the articles of association.

§ 57d Ausweisung von Kapital- und Gewinnrücklagen

§ 57d Entry of Capital Reserves and Retained Earnings

(1) Die Kapital- und Gewinnrücklagen, die in Stammkapital umgewandelt werden sollen, müssen in der letzten Jahresbilanz und, wenn dem Beschluß eine andere Bilanz zugrunde gelegt wird, auch in dieser Bilanz unter „Kapitalrücklage“ oder „Gewinnrücklagen“ oder im letzten Beschluß über die Verwendung des Jahresergebnisses als Zuführung zu diesen Rücklagen ausgewiesen sein.

(1) The capital reserves and retained earnings that will be converted to capital stock must be entered under “Capital Reserve” (“*Kapitalrücklage*”) or “Retained Earnings” (“*Gewinnrücklagen*”) in the preceding annual balance sheet and, if another balance sheet is relied on for the resolution, also in this balance sheet or, in the preceding resolution on the appropriation of the annual profit or loss, as an allocation to these reserves.

(2) Die Rücklagen können nicht umgewandelt werden, soweit in der zugrunde gelegten Bilanz ein Verlust, einschließlich eines Verlustvortrags, ausgewiesen ist.

(2) The reserves may not be converted, insofar as a loss, including a loss carried forward, is entered in the balance sheet being relied on.

(3) Andere Gewinnrücklagen, die einem bestimmten Zweck zu dienen bestimmt sind, dürfen nur umgewandelt werden, soweit dies mit ihrer Zweckbestimmung vereinbar ist.

(3) Other retained earnings that are designated to serve a certain purpose may only be converted, insofar as this is consistent with their designated purpose.

§ 57e Zugrundelegung der letzten Jahresbilanz; Prüfung

§ 57e Relying on the Preceding Annual Balance Sheet; Audit

(1) Dem Beschluß kann die letzte Jahresbilanz zugrunde gelegt werden, wenn die Jahresbilanz geprüft und die festgestellte Jahresbilanz mit dem uneingeschränkten Bestätigungsvermerk der Abschlußprüfer versehen ist und wenn ihr Stichtag höchstens acht Monate vor der Anmeldung des Beschlusses zur Eintragung in das Handelsregister liegt.

(1) The preceding annual balance sheet may be relied on for the resolution if the annual balance sheet is audited and the adopted annual balance sheet is provided with the unqualified audit opinion of the auditor, and if its reference date is no more than eight months before the registration of the resolution for entry in the commercial register (*Handelsregister*).

(2) Bei Gesellschaften, die nicht große im Sinne des § 267 Abs. 3 des Handelsgesetzbuchs sind, kann die Prüfung auch durch vereidigte Buchprüfer erfolgen; die Abschlußprüfer müssen von der Versammlung der Gesellschafter gewählt sein.

(2) The audit may also be effected by certified public accountants for companies that are not large within the meaning of § 267(3) of the Commercial Code (*Handelsgesetzbuch*); the auditors must be selected by the meeting of the members.

§ 57f Anforderungen an die Bilanz

§ 57f Requirements for the Balance Sheet

(1) Wird dem Beschluß nicht die letzte Jahresbilanz zugrunde gelegt, so muß die Bilanz den Vorschriften über die Gliederung der Jahresbilanz und über die Wertansätze in der Jahresbilanz entsprechen. Der Stichtag der Bilanz darf höchstens acht Monate vor der Anmeldung des Beschlusses zur Eintragung in das Handelsregister liegen.

(1) If the preceding annual balance sheet is not relied on for the resolution, then the balance sheet must be in accordance with the provisions on the layout of the annual balance sheet and on the valuation methods in the annual balance sheet. The reference date of the balance sheet may be no more than eight months before the registration of the resolution for entry in the commercial register (*Handelsregister*).

(2) Die Bilanz ist, bevor über die Erhöhung des Stammkapitals Beschluß gefaßt wird, durch einen oder mehrere Prüfer darauf zu prüfen, ob sie dem Absatz 1 entspricht. Sind nach dem abschließenden Ergebnis der Prüfung keine Einwendungen zu erheben, so haben die Prüfer dies durch einen Vermerk zu bestätigen. Die Erhöhung des Stammkapitals kann nicht ohne diese Bestätigung der Prüfer beschlossen werden.

(2) Before a resolution on the increase of the capital stock is adopted, the balance sheet is to be audited by one or more auditors to determine whether it accords with Subsection 1. If, according to the final results of the audit, no objections are to be raised, then the auditors must certify this through an audit opinion. The increase of the capital stock may not be resolved upon without this certification of the auditors.

(3) Die Prüfer werden von den Gesellschaftern gewählt; falls nicht andere Prüfer gewählt werden, gelten die Prüfer als gewählt, die für die Prüfung des letzten Jahresabschlusses von den Gesellschaftern gewählt oder vom Gericht bestellt worden sind. Im übrigen sind, soweit sich aus der Besonderheit des Prüfungsauftrags nichts anderes ergibt, § 318 Abs. 1 Satz 2, § 319 Abs. 1 bis 4, § 319a Abs. 1, § 319b Abs. 1, § 320 Abs. 1 Satz 2, Abs. 2 und die §§ 321 und 323 des Handelsgesetzbuchs anzuwenden. Bei Gesellschaften, die nicht große im Sinne des § 267 Abs. 3 des Handels-

(3) The auditors are selected by the members; if other auditors are not selected, then the auditors that have been selected by the members or appointed by the court for the audit of the preceding annual financial statements are regarded as being selected. Apart from that, § 318(1), Sentence 2, § 319(1) to (4), § 319a(1), § 319b(1), § 320(1), Sentence 2, (2) and §§ 321 and 323 of the Commercial Code (*Handelsgesetzbuch*) are to be applied, insofar as the distinctiveness of the audit engagement does not demand otherwise. Certified public accountants may also be appointed as

gesetzbuchs sind, können auch vereidigte Buchprüfer zu Prüfern bestellt werden.

auditors for companies that are not large within the meaning of § 267(3) of the Commercial Code (*Handelsgesetzbuch*).

§ 57g Vorherige Bekanntgabe des Jahresabschlusses

Die Bestimmungen des Gesellschaftsvertrags über die vorherige Bekanntgabe des Jahresabschlusses an die Gesellschafter sind in den Fällen des § 57f entsprechend anzuwenden.

§ 57g Prior Disclosure of the Annual Financial Statements

The provisions of the articles of association on the prior disclosure of the annual financial statements to the members are to be applied accordingly in the cases of § 57f.

§ 57h Arten der Kapitalerhöhung

(1) Die Kapitalerhöhung kann vorbehaltlich des § 57l Abs. 2 durch Bildung neuer Geschäftsanteile oder durch Erhöhung des Nennbetrags der Geschäftsanteile ausgeführt werden. Die neuen Geschäftsanteile und die Geschäftsanteile, deren Nennbetrag erhöht wird, müssen auf einen Betrag gestellt werden, der auf volle Euro lautet.

(2) Der Beschluß über die Erhöhung des Stammkapitals muß die Art der Erhöhung angeben. Soweit die Kapitalerhöhung durch Erhöhung des Nennbetrags der Geschäftsanteile ausgeführt werden soll, ist sie so zu bemessen, daß durch sie auf keinen Geschäftsanteil, dessen Nennbetrag erhöht wird, Beträge entfallen, die durch die Erhöhung des Nennbetrags des Geschäftsanteils nicht gedeckt werden können.

§ 57h Types of Capital Increase

(1) The capital increase may be carried out, subject to § 57l(2), through the creation of new membership interests or through an increase of the par value of the membership interests. The new membership interests and the membership interests for which the par value is increased must be set at an amount that is denominated in whole euros.

(2) The resolution on the increase of the capital stock must state the type of increase. Insofar as the capital increase will be carried out through an increase of the par value of the membership interests, it is to be calculated in such a way that, through it, amounts that cannot be covered through the increase of the par value of the membership interest are not allotted to any membership interest for which the par value is increased.

§ 57i Anmeldung und Eintragung des Erhöhungsbeschlusses

(1) Der Anmeldung des Beschlusses über die Erhöhung des Stammkapitals zur Eintragung in das Handelsregister ist die der Kapitalerhöhung zugrunde gelegte, mit dem Bestätigungsvermerk der Prüfer versehene Bilanz, in den Fällen des § 57f außerdem die letzte Jahresbilanz, sofern sie noch nicht nach § 325 Abs. 1 des Handelsgesetzbuchs eingereicht ist, beizufügen. Die Anmeldenden haben dem Registergericht gegenüber zu

§ 57i Registration and Entry of the Resolution on the Increase

(1) The balance sheet that was relied on for the capital increase and that was provided with the audit opinion of the auditor and, in the cases of § 57f, also the preceding annual balance sheet, insofar as it is not yet filed according to § 325(1) of the Commercial Code (*Handelsgesetzbuch*), are to be appended to the registration of the resolution on the increase of the capital stock for entry in the commercial register (*Handelsregister*). The registrants must

erklären, daß nach ihrer Kenntnis seit dem Stichtag der zugrunde gelegten Bilanz bis zum Tag der Anmeldung keine Vermögensminderung eingetreten ist, die der Kapitalerhöhung entgegenstünde, wenn sie am Tag der Anmeldung beschlossen worden wäre.

declare to the court of registry that, according to their knowledge, since the reference date of the balance sheet being relied on up to the day of the registration, no reduction of assets has occurred that would conflict with the capital increase if it were to be resolved upon on the day of the registration.

(2) Das Registergericht darf den Beschluß nur eintragen, wenn die der Kapitalerhöhung zugrunde gelegte Bilanz für einen höchstens acht Monate vor der Anmeldung liegenden Zeitpunkt aufgestellt und eine Erklärung nach Absatz 1 Satz 2 abgegeben worden ist.

(2) The court of registry may only enter the resolution if the balance sheet that was relied on for the capital increase was drawn up at a time occurring no more than eight months before the registration and a declaration according to Subsection 1, Sentence 2 has been given.

(3) Zu der Prüfung, ob die Bilanzen den gesetzlichen Vorschriften entsprechen, ist das Gericht nicht verpflichtet.

(3) The court is not obligated to verify whether the balance sheets are in accordance with the statutory provisions.

(4) Bei der Eintragung des Beschlusses ist anzugeben, daß es sich um eine Kapitalerhöhung aus Gesellschaftsmitteln handelt.

(4) Upon the entry of the resolution, it is to be stated that it concerns a capital increase from company funds.

§ 57j Verteilung der Geschäftsanteile

§ 57j Allocation of Membership Interests

Die neuen Geschäftsanteile stehen den Gesellschaftern im Verhältnis ihrer bisherigen Geschäftsanteile zu. Ein entgegenstehender Beschluß der Gesellschafter ist nichtig.

The new membership interests belong to the members in proportion to their preexisting membership interests. A conflicting resolution of the members is void.

§ 57k Teilrechte; Ausübung der Rechte

§ 57k Partial Rights; Exercise of Rights

(1) Führt die Kapitalerhöhung dazu, daß auf einen Geschäftsanteil nur ein Teil eines neuen Geschäftsanteils entfällt, so ist dieses Teilrecht selbständig veräußerlich und vererblich.

(1) If a capital increase leads to only a portion of a new membership interest being allotted to a membership interest, then this partial right is independently transferable and inheritable.

(2) Die Rechte aus einem neuen Geschäftsanteil, einschließlich des Anspruchs auf Ausstellung einer Urkunde über den neuen Geschäftsanteil, können nur ausgeübt werden, wenn Teilrechte, die zusammen einen vollen Geschäftsanteil ergeben, in einer Hand vereinigt sind oder wenn sich mehrere Berechtigte,

(2) The rights of a new membership interest, including the claim to issuance of a certificate concerning the new membership interest, may only be exercised if partial rights that, in the aggregate, result in a whole membership interest are united in one person's possession, or if multiple entitled persons whose partial

deren Teilrechte zusammen einen vollen Geschäftsanteil ergeben, zur Ausübung der Rechte (§ 18) zusammenschließen.

rights, in the aggregate, result in a whole membership interest join for the exercise of the rights (§ 18).

§ 57l Teilnahme an der Erhöhung des Stammkapitals

(1) Eigene Geschäftsanteile nehmen an der Erhöhung des Stammkapitals teil.

(2) Teileingezahlte Geschäftsanteile nehmen entsprechend ihrem Nennbetrag an der Erhöhung des Stammkapitals teil. Bei ihnen kann die Kapitalerhöhung nur durch Erhöhung des Nennbetrags der Geschäftsanteile ausgeführt werden. Sind neben teileingezahlten Geschäftsanteilen vollständig eingezahlte Geschäftsanteile vorhanden, so kann bei diesen die Kapitalerhöhung durch Erhöhung des Nennbetrags der Geschäftsanteile und durch Bildung neuer Geschäftsanteile ausgeführt werden. Die Geschäftsanteile, deren Nennbetrag erhöht wird, können auf jeden Betrag gestellt werden, der auf volle Euro lautet.

§ 57l Participation in the Increase of the Capital Stock

(1) Membership interests held by the company participate in the increase of the capital stock.

(2) Partially paid-in membership interests participate in the increase of the capital stock according to their par value. For them, the capital increase may only be carried out through an increase of the par value of the membership interests. If there are fully paid-in membership interests in addition to partially paid-in membership interests, then the capital increase for the fully paid-in membership interests may be carried out through an increase of the par value of the membership interests and through the creation of new membership interests. The membership interests for which the par value is increased may be set at any amount that is denominated in whole euros.

§ 57m Verhältnis der Rechte; Beziehungen zu Dritten

(1) Das Verhältnis der mit den Geschäftsanteilen verbundenen Rechte zueinander wird durch die Kapitalerhöhung nicht berührt.

(2) Soweit sich einzelne Rechte teileingezahlter Geschäftsanteile, insbesondere die Beteiligung am Gewinn oder das Stimmrecht, nach der je Geschäftsanteil geleisteten Einlage bestimmen, stehen diese Rechte den Gesellschaftern bis zur Leistung der noch ausstehenden Einlagen nur nach der Höhe der geleisteten Einlage, erhöht um den auf den Nennbetrag des Stammkapitals berechneten Hundertsatz der Erhöhung des Stammkapitals, zu. Werden weitere Einzahlungen geleistet, so erweitern sich diese Rechte entsprechend.

§ 57m Proportion of the Rights; Relationships to Third Parties

(1) The proportion of the rights associated with the membership interests to one another is not affected by the capital increase.

(2) Insofar as individual rights of partially paid-in membership interests, in particular the participation in the profits or the right to vote, are determined according to the contributions rendered per membership interest, these rights belong to the members before the rendering of still-outstanding contributions only according to the amount of the contribution rendered, increased by the percentage of the increase of the capital stock calculated with regard to the par value of the capital stock. If further payments are rendered, then these rights expand accordingly.

(3) Der wirtschaftliche Inhalt vertraglicher Beziehungen der Gesellschaft zu Dritten, die von der Gewinnausschüttung der Gesellschaft, dem Nennbetrag oder Wert ihrer Geschäftsanteile oder ihres Stammkapitals oder in sonstiger Weise von den bisherigen Kapital- oder Gewinnverhältnissen abhängen, wird durch die Kapitalerhöhung nicht berührt.

(3) The economic contents of contractual relationships of the company to third parties that depend on the distribution of profits of the company, on the par value or value of its membership interests, or on its capital stock or in another manner on the preexisting capital or profit proportions, are not affected by the capital increase.

§ 57n Gewinnbeteiligung der neuen Geschäftsanteile

(1) Die neuen Geschäftsanteile nehmen, wenn nichts anderes bestimmt ist, am Gewinn des ganzen Geschäftsjahres teil, in dem die Erhöhung des Stammkapitals beschlossen worden ist.

(2) Im Beschluß über die Erhöhung des Stammkapitals kann bestimmt werden, daß die neuen Geschäftsanteile bereits am Gewinn des letzten vor der Beschlußfassung über die Kapitalerhöhung abgelaufenen Geschäftsjahrs teilnehmen. In diesem Fall ist die Erhöhung des Stammkapitals abweichend von § 57c Abs. 2 zu beschließen, bevor über die Ergebnisverwendung für das letzte vor der Beschlußfassung abgelaufene Geschäftsjahr Beschluß gefaßt worden ist. Der Beschluß über die Ergebnisverwendung für das letzte vor der Beschlußfassung über die Kapitalerhöhung abgelaufene Geschäftsjahr wird erst wirksam, wenn das Stammkapital erhöht worden ist. Der Beschluß über die Erhöhung des Stammkapitals und der Beschluß über die Ergebnisverwendung für das letzte vor der Beschlußfassung über die Kapitalerhöhung abgelaufene Geschäftsjahr sind nichtig, wenn der Beschluß über die Kapitalerhöhung nicht binnen drei Monaten nach der Beschlußfassung in das Handelsregister eingetragen worden ist; der Lauf der Frist ist gehemmt, solange eine Anfechtungs- oder Nichtigkeitsklage rechtshängig ist.

§ 57n Profit Participation of the New Membership Interests

(1) The new membership interests participate in the profits of the entire fiscal year in which the increase of the capital stock has been resolved upon, if not determined otherwise.

(2) In the resolution on the increase of the capital stock, it may be determined that the new membership interests already participate in the profits of the preceding fiscal year elapsing before the adoption of the resolution on the capital increase. In this case, the increase of the capital stock is to be resolved upon, § 57c(2) notwithstanding, before the resolution on the appropriation of profit or loss has been adopted for the preceding fiscal year elapsing before the adoption of the resolution. The resolution on the appropriation of profit or loss for the preceding fiscal year elapsing before the adoption of the resolution on the capital increase becomes first effective when the capital stock has been increased. The resolution on the increase of the capital stock and the resolution on the appropriation of profit or loss for the preceding fiscal year elapsing before the adoption of the resolution on the capital increase are void if the resolution on the capital increase has not been entered in the commercial register (*Handelsregister*) within three months after the adoption of the resolution; the running of the period is tolled as long as an action for rescission or an action for a declaration of voidness is pending.

§ 57o Anschaffungskosten

Als Anschaffungskosten der vor der Erhöhung des Stammkapitals erworbenen Geschäftsanteile und der auf sie entfallenden neuen Geschäftsanteile gelten die Beträge, die sich für die einzelnen Geschäftsanteile ergeben, wenn die Anschaffungskosten der vor der Erhöhung des Stammkapitals erworbenen Geschäftsanteile auf diese und auf die auf sie entfallenden neuen Geschäftsanteile nach dem Verhältnis der Nennbeträge verteilt werden. Der Zuwachs an Geschäftsanteilen ist nicht als Zugang auszuweisen.

§ 57o Acquisition Costs

The amounts that result for the individual membership interests are regarded as acquisition costs of the membership interests that are acquired before the increase of the capital stock and as acquisition costs of the new membership interests allotted to them, if the acquisition costs of the membership interests that are acquired before the increase of the capital stock are apportioned to the membership interests acquired before the capital increase as well as to the new membership interests allotted to them according to the proportion of the par values. The increase in membership interests is not to be entered as an accrual.

§ 58 Herabsetzung des Stammkapitals

(1) Eine Herabsetzung des Stammkapitals kann nur unter Beobachtung der nachstehenden Bestimmungen erfolgen:

1. der Beschluß auf Herabsetzung des Stammkapitals muß von den Geschäftsführern in den Gesellschaftsblättern bekanntgemacht werden; in dieser Bekanntmachung sind zugleich die Gläubiger der Gesellschaft aufzufordern, sich bei derselben zu melden; die aus den Handelsbüchern der Gesellschaft ersichtlichen oder in anderer Weise bekannten Gläubiger sind durch besondere Mitteilung zur Anmeldung aufzufordern;

2. die Gläubiger, welche sich bei der Gesellschaft melden und der Herabsetzung nicht zustimmen, sind wegen der erhobenen Ansprüche zu befriedigen oder sicherzustellen;

3. die Anmeldung des Herabsetzungsbeschlusses zur Eintragung in das Handelsregister erfolgt nicht vor Ablauf eines Jahres seit dem Tage, an welchem die Aufforderung der Gläubiger in den Gesellschaftsblättern stattgefunden hat;

4. mit der Anmeldung ist die Bekanntmachung des Beschlusses einzu-

§ 58 Reduction of the Capital Stock

(1) A reduction of the capital stock may only be effected under adherence to the following provisions:

1. the resolution on the reduction of the capital stock must be published by the managing directors in the company bulletins; in this publication the creditors of the company are to be simultaneously requested to contact the company; the creditors that appear in the accounting books of the company or that are known in another way are to be requested to make contact through a special notification;

2. the creditors that contact the company and do not consent to the reduction are to be satisfied or provided with security concerning the claims lodged;

3. the registration of the reduction resolution for entry in the commercial register (*Handelsregister*) is not effected before the expiration of one year from the day on which the request to the creditors in the company bulletins took place;

4. the publication of the resolution is to be filed with the registration; the man-

reichen; zugleich haben die Geschäftsführer die Versicherung abzugeben, daß die Gläubiger, welche sich bei der Gesellschaft gemeldet und der Herabsetzung nicht zugestimmt haben, befriedigt oder sichergestellt sind.

aging directors must simultaneously give the assertion that the creditors that have contacted the company and have not consented to the reduction have been satisfied or provided with security.

(2) Die Bestimmung in § 5 Abs. 1 über den Mindestbetrag des Stammkapitals bleibt unberührt. Erfolgt die Herabsetzung zum Zweck der Zurückzahlung von Einlagen oder zum Zweck des Erlasses zu leistender Einlagen, dürfen die verbleibenden Nennbeträge der Geschäftsanteile nicht unter den in § 5 Abs. 2 und 3 bezeichneten Betrag herabgehen.

(2) The provision in § 5(1) on the minimum capital stock amount remains unaffected. If the reduction is effected for the purpose of repaying contributions or for the purpose of exempting persons from contributions to be rendered, then the remaining par values of the membership interests may not fall below the amount designated in § 5(2) and (3).

§ 58a Vereinfachte Kapitalherabsetzung

(1) Eine Herabsetzung des Stammkapitals, die dazu dienen soll, Wertminderungen auszugleichen oder sonstige Verluste zu decken, kann als vereinfachte Kapitalherabsetzung vorgenommen werden.

(2) Die vereinfachte Kapitalherabsetzung ist nur zulässig, nachdem der Teil der Kapital- und Gewinnrücklagen, der zusammen über zehn vom Hundert des nach der Herabsetzung verbleibenden Stammkapitals hinausgeht, vorweg aufgelöst ist. Sie ist nicht zulässig, solange ein Gewinnvortrag vorhanden ist.

(3) Im Beschluß über die vereinfachte Kapitalherabsetzung sind die Nennbeträge der Geschäftsanteile dem herabgesetzten Stammkapital anzupassen. Die Geschäftsanteile müssen auf einen Betrag gestellt werden, der auf volle Euro lautet.

(4) Das Stammkapital kann unter den in § 5 Abs. 1 bestimmten Mindestnennbetrag herabgesetzt werden, wenn dieser durch eine Kapitalerhöhung wieder erreicht wird, die zugleich mit der Kapitalherabsetzung beschlossen ist und bei der Sacheinlagen nicht festgesetzt sind. Die Beschlüsse sind nichtig, wenn sie nicht binnen drei Monaten nach der Beschluß-

§ 58a Simplified Capital Reduction

(1) A reduction of the capital stock that will serve to compensate for a decrease in value or to cover other loses may be performed as a simplified capital reduction.

(2) The simplified capital reduction is only permissible after the portion of the capital reserves and retained earnings that, in the aggregate, exceeds ten percent of the capital stock remaining after the reduction, has previously been released. It is not permissible as long as there is a profit carried forward.

(3) In the resolution on the simplified capital reduction, the par values of the membership interests are to be adjusted to the reduced capital stock. The membership interests must be set at an amount that is denominated in whole euros.

(4) The capital stock may be reduced below the minimum par value provided in § 5(1) if the minimum par value is reached again through a capital increase that is resolved upon simultaneously with the capital reduction and for which no in-kind contributions are determined. The resolutions are void if they have not been entered in the commercial register (*Handelsregis-*

fassung in das Handelsregister eingetragen worden sind. Der Lauf der Frist ist gehemmt, solange eine Anfechtungs- oder Nichtigkeitsklage rechtshängig ist. Die Beschlüsse sollen nur zusammen in das Handelsregister eingetragen werden.

ter) within three months after the adoption of the resolution. The running of the period is tolled as long as an action for rescission or an action for a declaration of voidness is pending. The resolutions shall only be entered in the commercial register (*Handelsregister*) together.

(5) Neben den §§ 53 und 54 über die Abänderung des Gesellschaftsvertrags gelten die §§ 58b bis 58f.

(5) In addition to §§ 53 and 54 on the amendment of the articles of association, §§ 58b to 58f apply.

§ 58b Beträge aus Rücklagenauflösung und Kapitalherabsetzung

§ 58b Amounts from Release of Reserves and Capital Reduction

(1) Die Beträge, die aus der Auflösung der Kapital- oder Gewinnrücklagen und aus der Kapitalherabsetzung gewonnen werden, dürfen nur verwandt werden, um Wertminderungen auszugleichen und sonstige Verluste zu decken.

(1) The amounts that are obtained from the release of the capital reserves or retained earnings and from the capital reduction may only be used to compensate for decreases in value and to cover other losses.

(2) Daneben dürfen die gewonnenen Beträge in die Kapitalrücklage eingestellt werden, soweit diese zehn vom Hundert des Stammkapitals nicht übersteigt. Als Stammkapital gilt dabei der Nennbetrag, der sich durch die Herabsetzung ergibt, mindestens aber der nach § 5 Abs. 1 zulässige Mindestnennbetrag.

(2) In addition thereto, the obtained amounts may be allocated to the capital reserve, insofar as the capital reserve does not exceed ten percent of the capital stock. In this regard, the capital stock is regarded as the par value that results from the reduction, but no less than the permissible minimum par value according to § 5(1).

(3) Ein Betrag, der auf Grund des Absatzes 2 in die Kapitalrücklage eingestellt worden ist, darf vor Ablauf des fünften nach der Beschlußfassung über die Kapitalherabsetzung beginnenden Geschäftsjahrs nur verwandt werden

(3) Before the expiration of the fifth fiscal year beginning after the adoption of the resolution on the capital reduction, an amount that has been allocated to the capital reserve based on Subsection 2 may only be used

1. zum Ausgleich eines Jahresfehlbetrags, soweit er nicht durch einen Gewinnvortrag aus dem Vorjahr gedeckt ist und nicht durch Auflösung von Gewinnrücklagen ausgeglichen werden kann;

1. to compensate for an annual deficit, insofar as it is not covered by a profit carried forward from the previous year and cannot be compensated for through the release of retained earnings;

2. zum Ausgleich eines Verlustvortrags aus dem Vorjahr, soweit er nicht durch einen Jahresüberschuß gedeckt ist und nicht durch Auflösung von Gewinnrücklagen ausgeglichen werden kann;

2. to compensate for a loss carried forward from the previous year, insofar as it is not covered by an annual net profit and cannot be compensated for through the release of retained earnings;

3. zur Kapitalerhöhung aus Gesellschaftsmitteln.

3. for a capital increase from company funds.

§ 58c Nichteintritt angenommener Verluste

Ergibt sich bei Aufstellung der Jahresbilanz für das Geschäftsjahr, in dem der Beschluß über die Kapitalherabsetzung gefaßt wurde, oder für eines der beiden folgenden Geschäftsjahre, daß Wertminderungen und sonstige Verluste in der bei der Beschlußfassung angenommenen Höhe tatsächlich nicht eingetreten oder ausgeglichen waren, so ist der Unterschiedsbetrag in die Kapitalrücklage einzustellen. Für einen nach Satz 1 in die Kapitalrücklage eingestellten Betrag gilt § 58b Abs. 3 sinngemäß.

§ 58c Non-occurrence of Assumed Losses

If, upon drawing up the annual balance sheet for the fiscal year in which the resolution on the capital reduction was adopted, or for one of the two following fiscal years, it appears that decreases in value and other losses in the amount assumed upon the adoption of the resolution did not actually occur or were compensated for, then the amount of the difference is to be allocated to the capital reserve. § 58b(3) applies accordingly to an amount allocated to the capital reserve according to Sentence 1.

§ 58d Gewinnausschüttung

(1) Gewinn darf vor Ablauf des fünften nach der Beschlußfassung über die Kapitalherabsetzung beginnenden Geschäftsjahrs nur ausgeschüttet werden, wenn die Kapital- und Gewinnrücklagen zusammen zehn vom Hundert des Stammkapitals erreichen. Als Stammkapital gilt dabei der Nennbetrag, der sich durch die Herabsetzung ergibt, mindestens aber der nach § 5 Abs. 1 zulässige Mindestnennbetrag.

(2) Die Zahlung eines Gewinnanteils von mehr als vier vom Hundert ist erst für ein Geschäftsjahr zulässig, das später als zwei Jahre nach der Beschlußfassung über die Kapitalherabsetzung beginnt. Dies gilt nicht, wenn die Gläubiger, deren Forderungen vor der Bekanntmachung der Eintragung des Beschlusses begründet worden waren, befriedigt oder sichergestellt sind, soweit sie sich binnen sechs Monaten nach der Bekanntmachung des Jahresabschlusses, auf Grund dessen die Gewinnverteilung beschlossen ist, zu diesem Zweck gemeldet haben. Einer Sicherstellung der Gläubiger bedarf es nicht, die im Fall des Insolvenzverfahrens ein Recht auf vorzugsweise Befriedigung aus einer Deckungsmasse haben, die nach gesetzlicher Vorschrift

§ 58d Distribution of Profit

(1) Profit may only be distributed before the expiration of the fifth fiscal year beginning after the adoption of the resolution on the capital reduction if the capital reserves and retained earnings reach, in the aggregate, ten percent of the capital stock. In this regard, the capital stock is regarded as the par value that results from the reduction, but no less than the permissible minimum par value according to § 5(1).

(2) The payment of a share of profit of more than four percent is first permissible for a fiscal year that begins later than two years after the adoption of the resolution on the capital reduction. This does not apply if the creditors whose claims have been established before the publication of the entry of the resolution are satisfied or provided with security, insofar as they have made contact for this purpose within six months after the publication of the annual financial statements based on which the profit distribution is resolved upon. A provision of security is not required for the creditors that, in the case of an insolvency proceeding, have a right to preferential satisfaction from a cover pool that is founded for their protection according to statutory provisions and is moni-

zu ihrem Schutz errichtet und staatlich überwacht ist. Die Gläubiger sind in der Bekanntmachung nach § 325 Abs. 2 des Handelsgesetzbuchs auf die Befriedigung oder Sicherstellung hinzuweisen.

tored by the state. The creditors are to be advised of the satisfaction or the provision of security in the publication according to § 325(2) of the Commercial Code (*Handelsgesetzbuch*).

§ 58e Beschluss über die Kapitalherabsetzung

§ 58e Resolution on the Capital Reduction

(1) Im Jahresabschluß für das letzte vor der Beschlußfassung über die Kapitalherabsetzung abgelaufene Geschäftsjahr können das Stammkapital sowie die Kapital- und Gewinnrücklagen in der Höhe ausgewiesen werden, in der sie nach der Kapitalherabsetzung bestehen sollen. Dies gilt nicht, wenn der Jahresabschluß anders als durch Beschluß der Gesellschafter festgestellt wird.

(1) In the annual financial statements for the preceding fiscal year elapsing before the adoption of the resolution on the capital reduction, the capital stock as well as the capital reserves and retained earnings may be entered in the amount in which they will exist after the capital reduction. This does not apply if the annual financial statements are adopted other than through a resolution of the members.

(2) Der Beschluß über die Feststellung des Jahresabschlusses soll zugleich mit dem Beschluß über die Kapitalherabsetzung gefaßt werden.

(2) The resolution on the adoption of the annual financial statements shall be adopted simultaneously with the resolution on the capital reduction.

(3) Die Beschlüsse sind nichtig, wenn der Beschluß über die Kapitalherabsetzung nicht binnen drei Monaten nach der Beschlußfassung in das Handelsregister eingetragen worden ist. Der Lauf der Frist ist gehemmt, solange eine Anfechtungs- oder Nichtigkeitsklage rechtshängig ist.

(3) The resolutions are void if the resolution on the capital reduction has not been entered in the commercial register (*Handelsregister*) within three months after the adoption of the resolution. The running of the period is tolled as long as an action for rescission or an action for a declaration of voidness is pending.

(4) Der Jahresabschluß darf nach § 325 des Handelsgesetzbuchs erst nach Eintragung des Beschlusses über die Kapitalherabsetzung offengelegt werden.

(4) The annual financial statements may first be published according to § 325 of the Commercial Code (*Handelsgesetzbuch*) after entry of the resolution on the capital reduction.

§ 58f Kapitalherabsetzung bei gleichzeitiger Erhöhung des Stammkapitals

§ 58f Capital Reduction upon Simultaneous Increase of the Capital Stock

(1) Wird im Fall des § 58e zugleich mit der Kapitalherabsetzung eine Erhöhung des Stammkapitals beschlossen, so kann auch die Kapitalerhöhung in dem Jahresabschluß als vollzogen berücksichtigt werden. Die Beschlussfassung ist nur zulässig, wenn die neuen Geschäftsantei-

(1) If, in the case of § 58e, an increase of the capital stock is resolved upon simultaneously with the capital reduction, then the capital increase may also be accounted for in the annual financial statements as having been completed. The adoption of the resolution is only

le übernommen, keine Sacheinlagen festgesetzt sind und wenn auf jeden neuen Geschäftsanteil die Einzahlung geleistet ist, die nach § 56a zur Zeit der Anmeldung der Kapitalerhöhung bewirkt sein muss. Die Übernahme und die Einzahlung sind dem Notar nachzuweisen, der den Beschluß über die Erhöhung des Stammkapitals beurkundet.

permissible if the new membership interests are accepted, if no in-kind contributions are determined, and if, for each new membership interest, the payment that must be made has been rendered, according to § 56a, by the time of the registration of the capital increase. The acceptance and the payment are to be proved before the notary (*Notar*) who certifies the resolution on the increase of the capital stock.

(2) Sämtliche Beschlüsse sind nichtig, wenn die Beschlüsse über die Kapitalherabsetzung und die Kapitalerhöhung nicht binnen drei Monaten nach der Beschlußfassung in das Handelsregister eingetragen worden sind. Der Lauf der Frist ist gehemmt, solange eine Anfechtungs- oder Nichtigkeitsklage rechtshängig ist. Die Beschlüsse sollen nur zusammen in das Handelsregister eingetragen werden.

(2) All resolutions are void if the resolutions on the capital reduction and on the capital increase have not been entered in the commercial register (*Handelsregister*) within three months after the adoption of the resolution. The running of the period is tolled as long as an action for rescission or an action for a declaration of voidness is pending. The resolutions shall only be entered in the commercial register (*Handelsregister*) together.

(3) Der Jahresabschluß darf nach § 325 des Handelsgesetzbuchs erst offengelegt werden, nachdem die Beschlüsse über die Kapitalherabsetzung und Kapitalerhöhung eingetragen worden sind.

(3) The annual financial statements may first be published according to § 325 of the Commercial Code (*Handelsgesetzbuch*) after the resolutions on the capital reduction and on the capital increase have been entered.

§ 59 (weggefallen)

§ 59 (repealed)

Abschnitt 5 Auflösung und Nichtigkeit der Gesellschaft

Chapter 5 Dissolution and Voidness of the Company

§ 60 Auflösungsgründe

§ 60 Reasons for Dissolution

(1) Die Gesellschaft mit beschränkter Haftung wird aufgelöst:

(1) The company with limited liability is dissolved:

1. durch Ablauf der im Gesellschaftsvertrag bestimmten Zeit;

1. upon the expiration of the time provided in the articles of association;

2. durch Beschluß der Gesellschafter; derselbe bedarf, sofern im Gesellschaftsvertrag nicht ein anderes bestimmt ist, einer Mehrheit von drei Vierteilen der abgegebenen Stimmen;

2. through the resolution of the members; the resolution requires a majority of three-fourths of the votes cast, if not otherwise provided in the articles of association;

3. durch gerichtliches Urteil oder durch Entscheidung des Verwaltungsgerichts oder der Verwaltungsbehörde in den Fällen der §§ 61 und 62;

4. durch die Eröffnung des Insolvenzverfahrens; wird das Verfahren auf Antrag des Schuldners eingestellt oder nach der Bestätigung eines Insolvenzplans, der den Fortbestand der Gesellschaft vorsieht, aufgehoben, so können die Gesellschafter die Fortsetzung der Gesellschaft beschließen;

5. mit der Rechtskraft des Beschlusses, durch den die Eröffnung des Insolvenzverfahrens mangels Masse abgelehnt worden ist;

6. mit der Rechtskraft einer Verfügung des Registergerichts, durch welche nach § 399 des Gesetzes über das Verfahren in Familiensachen und in den Angelegenheiten der freiwilligen Gerichtsbarkeit ein Mangel des Gesellschaftsvertrags festgestellt worden ist;

7. durch die Löschung der Gesellschaft wegen Vermögenslosigkeit nach § 394 des Gesetzes über das Verfahren in Familiensachen und in den Angelegenheiten der freiwilligen Gerichtsbarkeit.

(2) Im Gesellschaftsvertrag können weitere Auflösungsgründe festgesetzt werden.

3. through a court judgment or through a decision of an administrative court or of an administrative agency in the cases of §§ 61 and 62;

4. through the initiation of an insolvency proceeding; if the proceeding is discontinued upon the petition of the debtor or is terminated according to the confirmation of an insolvency plan that provides for the continuance of the company, then the members may resolve upon the continuation of the company;

5. when the order through which the initiation of the insolvency proceeding is refused for lack of funds becomes res judicata;

6. when the decree of the court of registry through which a defect in the articles of association is ascertained according to § 399 of the Act on Proceedings in Family Matters and in Matters of Non-contentious Jurisdiction (*Gesetz über das Verfahren in Familiensachen und in den Angelegenheiten der freiwilligen Gerichtsbarkeit*) becomes res judicata.

7. through the deregistration of the company because of a lack of assets according to § 394 of the Act on Proceedings in Family Matters and in Matters of Non-contentious Jurisdiction (*Gesetz über das Verfahren in Familiensachen und in den Angelegenheiten der freiwilligen Gerichtsbarkeit*).

(2) Further reasons for dissolution may be determined in the articles of association.

§ 61 Auflösung durch Urteil

(1) Die Gesellschaft kann durch gerichtliches Urteil aufgelöst werden, wenn die Erreichung des Gesellschaftszweckes unmöglich wird, oder wenn andere, in den Verhältnissen der Gesellschaft liegende, wichtige Gründe für die Auflösung vorhanden sind.

§ 61 Dissolution through Judgment

(1) The company may be dissolved through a court judgment if the accomplishment of the company purpose becomes impossible, or if there are other important reasons in the affairs of the company for the dissolution.

(2) Die Auflösungsklage ist gegen die Gesellschaft zu richten. Sie kann nur von Gesellschaftern erhoben werden, deren Geschäftsanteile zusammen mindestens dem zehnten Teil des Stammkapitals entsprechen.

(3) Für die Klage ist das Landgericht ausschließlich zuständig, in dessen Bezirk die Gesellschaft ihren Sitz hat.

(2) The action for dissolution is to be directed against the company. It may only be brought by members whose membership interests correspond, in the aggregate, to at least one-tenth of the capital stock.

(3) The state court of the district in which the company has its registered office has exclusive jurisdiction over the action.

§ 62 Auflösung durch eine Verwaltungsbehörde

(1) Wenn eine Gesellschaft das Gemeinwohl dadurch gefährdet, daß die Gesellschafter gesetzwidrige Beschlüsse fassen oder gesetzwidrige Handlungen der Geschäftsführer wissentlich geschehen lassen, so kann sie aufgelöst werden, ohne daß deshalb ein Anspruch auf Entschädigung stattfindet.

(2) Das Verfahren und die Zuständigkeit der Behörden richtet sich nach den für streitige Verwaltungssachen *landesgesetzlich* geltenden Vorschriften.

§ 62 Dissolution by an Administrative Agency

(1) If a company endangers the common welfare in that the members adopt illegal resolutions or knowingly allow illegal acts of the managing directors to occur, then it may be dissolved without a claim to compensation arising therefrom.

(2) The proceeding and the jurisdiction of the agencies are governed by the *state law* provisions applicable to contentious administrative matters.

§ 63 (weggefallen)

§ 63 (repealed)

§ 64 Haftung für Zahlungen nach Zahlungsunfähigkeit oder Überschuldung

Die Geschäftsführer sind der Gesellschaft zum Ersatz von Zahlungen verpflichtet, die nach Eintritt der Zahlungsunfähigkeit der Gesellschaft oder nach Feststellung ihrer Überschuldung geleistet werden. Dies gilt nicht von Zahlungen, die auch nach diesem Zeitpunkt mit der Sorgfalt eines ordentlichen Geschäftsmanns vereinbar sind. Die gleiche Verpflichtung trifft die Geschäftsführer für Zahlungen an Gesellschafter, soweit diese zur Zahlungsunfähigkeit der Gesellschaft führen mussten, es sei denn, dies war auch bei Beachtung der in Satz 2 bezeichneten Sorgfalt nicht erkennbar. Auf den Ersatzanspruch finden die Bestimmungen in § 43 Abs. 3 und 4 entsprechende Anwendung.

§ 64 Liability for Payments after Illiquidity or Over-indebtedness

The managing directors are obligated to the company to compensate payments that were made after the occurrence of the company's illiquidity or after the ascertainment of its over-indebtedness. This does not apply to payments that are, even after this time, consistent with the care of a prudent businessman. The same obligation exists for the managing directors with respect to payments to members, insofar as the payments must have led to the illiquidity of the company, unless this was not recognizable even by observance of the care designated in Sentence 2. The provisions in § 43(3) and (4) apply accordingly to the claim to compensation.

§ 65 Anmeldung und Eintragung der Auflösung

(1) Die Auflösung der Gesellschaft ist zur Eintragung in das Handelsregister anzumelden. Dies gilt nicht in den Fällen der Eröffnung oder der Ablehnung der Eröffnung des Insolvenzverfahrens und der gerichtlichen Feststellung eines Mangels des Gesellschaftsvertrags. In diesen Fällen hat das Gericht die Auflösung und ihren Grund von Amts wegen einzutragen. Im Falle der Löschung der Gesellschaft (§ 60 Abs. 1 Nr. 7) entfällt die Eintragung der Auflösung.

(2) Die Auflösung ist von den Liquidatoren in den Gesellschaftsblättern bekanntzumachen. Durch die Bekanntmachung sind zugleich die Gläubiger der Gesellschaft aufzufordern, sich bei derselben zu melden.

§ 65 Registration and Entry of the Dissolution

(1) The dissolution of the company is to be registered for entry in the commercial register (*Handelsregister*). This does not apply in the cases of the initiation or the refusal of the initiation of the insolvency proceeding and of a court ascertainment of a defect in the articles of association. In these cases, the court must enter the dissolution and its reason on its own accord. In the case of the deregistration of the company (§ 60(1), No. 7), there is no entry of the dissolution.

(2) The dissolution is to be published in the company bulletins by the liquidators. Also, the creditors of the company are to be requested in this publication to contact the company.

§ 66 Liquidatoren

(1) In den Fällen der Auflösung außer dem Fall des Insolvenzverfahrens erfolgt die Liquidation durch die Geschäftsführer, wenn nicht dieselbe durch den Gesellschaftsvertrag oder durch Beschluß der Gesellschafter anderen Personen übertragen wird.

(2) Auf Antrag von Gesellschaftern, deren Geschäftsanteile zusammen mindestens dem zehnten Teil des Stammkapitals entsprechen, kann aus wichtigen Gründen die Bestellung von Liquidatoren durch das Gericht erfolgen.

(3) Die Abberufung von Liquidatoren kann durch das Gericht unter derselben Voraussetzung wie die Bestellung stattfinden. Liquidatoren, welche nicht vom Gericht ernannt sind, können auch durch Beschluß der Gesellschafter vor Ablauf des Zeitraums, für welchen sie bestellt sind, abberufen werden.

(4) Für die Auswahl der Liquidatoren findet § 6 Abs. 2 Satz 2 und 3 entsprechende Anwendung.

§ 66 Liquidators

(1) In the cases of dissolution other than in the case of an insolvency proceeding, the liquidation is carried out by the managing directors, unless it is assigned to other persons through the articles of association or through a resolution of the members.

(2) Upon the petition of members whose membership interests correspond, in the aggregate, to at least one-tenth of the capital stock, the appointment of liquidators may, for important reasons, be effected by the court.

(3) The dismissal of liquidators by the court may take place under the same conditions as the appointment. Liquidators who are not appointed by the court may also be dismissed through a resolution of the members before expiration of the time period for which they were appointed.

(4) § 6(2), Sentences 2 and 3 apply accordingly to the selection of liquidators.

(5) Ist die Gesellschaft durch Löschung wegen Vermögenslosigkeit aufgelöst, so findet eine Liquidation nur statt, wenn sich nach der Löschung herausstellt, daß Vermögen vorhanden ist, das der Verteilung unterliegt. Die Liquidatoren sind auf Antrag eines Beteiligten durch das Gericht zu ernennen.

(5) If the company is dissolved through deregistration because of a lack of assets, then a liquidation only takes place if it becomes apparent, after the deregistration, that there are assets that are subject to distribution. The liquidators are to be appointed by the court upon the petition of an interested party.

§ 67 Anmeldung der Liquidatoren

§ 67 Registration of the Liquidators

(1) Die ersten Liquidatoren sowie ihre Vertretungsbefugnis sind durch die Geschäftsführer, jeder Wechsel der Liquidatoren und jede Änderung ihrer Vertretungsbefugnis sind durch die Liquidatoren zur Eintragung in das Handelsregister anzumelden.

(1) The first liquidators as well as their power of representation are to be registered by the managing directors, and each replacement of the liquidators and each change in their power of representation are to be registered by the liquidators, for entry in the commercial register (*Handelsregister*).

(2) Der Anmeldung sind die Urkunden über die Bestellung der Liquidatoren oder über die Änderung in den Personen derselben in Urschrift oder öffentlich beglaubigter Abschrift beizufügen.

(2) The documents for the appointment of the liquidators, or for the change in the persons who are the liquidators, are to be appended to the registration in original or as a publicly authenticated copy.

(3) In der Anmeldung haben die Liquidatoren zu versichern, daß keine Umstände vorliegen, die ihrer Bestellung nach § 66 Abs. 4 in Verbindung mit § 6 Abs. 2 Satz 2 Nr. 2 und 3 sowie Satz 3 entgegenstehen, und daß sie über ihre unbeschränkte Auskunftspflicht gegenüber dem Gericht belehrt worden sind. § 8 Abs. 3 Satz 2 ist anzuwenden.

(3) The liquidators must assert in the registration that no circumstances exist that conflict with their appointment according to § 66(4) in connection with § 6(2), Sentence 2, No. 2 and 3, as well as Sentence 3, and that they have been instructed on their unlimited duty of disclosure to the court. § 8(3), Sentence 2 is to be applied.

(4) Die Eintragung der gerichtlichen Ernennung oder Abberufung der Liquidatoren geschieht von Amts wegen.

(4) The entry of the court appointment or dismissal of the liquidators occurs on the court's own accord.

(5) (weggefallen)

(5) (repealed)

§ 68 Zeichnung der Liquidatoren

§ 68 Signing of the Liquidators

(1) Die Liquidatoren haben in der bei ihrer Bestellung bestimmten Form ihre Willenserklärungen kundzugeben und für die Gesellschaft zu zeichnen. Ist nichts darüber bestimmt, so muß die Erklärung und Zeichnung durch sämtliche Liquidatoren erfolgen.

(1) The liquidators must make their declarations of intent and sign for the company in the form determined upon their appointment. If not otherwise determined, the declaration and signing must be effected by all liquidators.

(2) Die Zeichnungen geschehen in der Weise, daß die Liquidatoren der bisherigen, nunmehr als Liquidationsfirma zu bezeichnenden Firma ihre Namensunterschrift beifügen.

(2) The signing occurs in the manner such that the liquidators append their signature to the preexisting company name, now to be designated as the liquidation company name.

§ 69 Rechtsverhältnisse von Gesellschaft und Gesellschaftern

§ 69 Legal Relationships of the Company and Members

(1) Bis zur Beendigung der Liquidation kommen ungeachtet der Auflösung der Gesellschaft in bezug auf die Rechtsverhältnisse derselben und der Gesellschafter die Vorschriften des zweiten und dritten Abschnitts zur Anwendung, soweit sich aus den Bestimmungen des gegenwärtigen Abschnitts und aus dem Wesen der Liquidation nicht ein anderes ergibt.

(1) Until the termination of the liquidation, the provisions of the Second and of the Third Chapters become applicable, regardless of the dissolution of the company, in relation to the legal relationships of the company and of the members, insofar as the provisions of the present Chapter and the character of the liquidation do not demand otherwise.

(2) Der Gerichtsstand, welchen die Gesellschaft zur Zeit ihrer Auflösung hatte, bleibt bis zur vollzogenen Verteilung des Vermögens bestehen.

(2) The place of jurisdiction that the company had up to the time of its dissolution persists until the completed distribution of the assets.

§ 70 Aufgaben der Liquidatoren

§ 70 Responsibilities of the Liquidators

Die Liquidatoren haben die laufenden Geschäfte zu beendigen, die Verpflichtungen der aufgelösten Gesellschaft zu erfüllen, die Forderungen derselben einzuziehen und das Vermögen der Gesellschaft in Geld umzusetzen; sie haben die Gesellschaft gerichtlich und außergerichtlich zu vertreten. Zur Beendigung schwebender Geschäfte können die Liquidatoren auch neue Geschäfte eingehen.

The liquidators must terminate current transactions, fulfill the obligations of the dissolved company, collect on the claims of the company, and convert the assets of the company to cash; they must represent the company in and out of court. The liquidators may also enter into new transactions for the termination of pending transactions.

§ 71 Eröffnungsbilanz; Rechte und Pflichten

§ 71 Opening Balance Sheet; Rights and Duties

(1) Die Liquidatoren haben für den Beginn der Liquidation eine Bilanz (Eröffnungsbilanz) und einen die Eröffnungsbilanz erläuternden Bericht sowie für den Schluß eines jeden Jahres einen Jahresabschluß und einen Lagebericht aufzustellen.

(1) The liquidators must draw up a balance sheet (opening balance sheet) and a report explaining the opening balance sheet at the beginning of the liquidation as well as, for the conclusion of each year, annual financial statements and a management report.

(2) Die Gesellschafter beschließen über die Feststellung der Eröffnungsbilanz und des Jahresabschlusses sowie

(2) The members resolve upon the adoption of the opening balance sheet and of the annual financial statements, as

über die Entlastung der Liquidatoren. Auf die Eröffnungsbilanz und den erläuternden Bericht sind die Vorschriften über den Jahresabschluß entsprechend anzuwenden. Vermögensgegenstände des Anlagevermögens sind jedoch wie Umlaufvermögen zu bewerten, soweit ihre Veräußerung innerhalb eines übersehbaren Zeitraums beabsichtigt ist oder diese Vermögensgegenstände nicht mehr dem Geschäftsbetrieb dienen; dies gilt auch für den Jahresabschluß.

well as upon the discharge of the liquidators. The provisions on the annual financial statements are to be applied accordingly to the opening balance sheet and the explanatory report. However, items of non-current assets are to be valued as current assets, insofar as their disposal is intended within a foreseeable time period or these items no longer serve business operations; this also applies for the annual financial statements.

(3) Das Gericht kann von der Prüfung des Jahresabschlusses und des Lageberichts durch einen Abschlußprüfer befreien, wenn die Verhältnisse der Gesellschaft so überschaubar sind, daß eine Prüfung im Interesse der Gläubiger und der Gesellschafter nicht geboten erscheint. Gegen die Entscheidung ist die Beschwerde zulässig.

(3) The court may release the liquidators from the audit of the annual financial statements and of the management report by an auditor if the affairs of the company are so clear that an audit does not appear necessary in the interest of the creditors and the members. An appeal of the decision is permissible.

(4) Im übrigen haben sie die aus §§ 37, 41, 43 Abs. 1, 2 und 4, § 49 Abs. 1 und 2, § 64 sich ergebenden Rechte und Pflichten der Geschäftsführer.

(4) Apart from that, they have the rights and duties of the managing directors resulting from §§ 37, 41, 43(1), (2) and (4), § 49(1) and (2), and § 64.

(5) Auf den Geschäftsbriefen ist anzugeben, dass sich die Gesellschaft in Liquidation befindet; im Übrigen gilt § 35a entsprechend.

(5) It is to be stated in the business letters that the company is in liquidation; apart from that, § 35a applies accordingly.

§ 72 Vermögensverteilung

Das Vermögen der Gesellschaft wird unter die Gesellschafter nach Verhältnis ihrer Geschäftsanteile verteilt. Durch den Gesellschaftsvertrag kann ein anderes Verhältnis für die Verteilung bestimmt werden.

§ 72 Distribution of Assets

The assets of the company are distributed to the members in proportion to their membership interests. Another proportion for the distribution may be provided in the articles of association.

§ 73 Sperrjahr

(1) Die Verteilung darf nicht vor Tilgung oder Sicherstellung der Schulden der Gesellschaft und nicht vor Ablauf eines Jahres seit dem Tage vorgenommen werden, an welchem die Aufforderung an die Gläubiger (§ 65 Abs. 2) in den Gesellschaftsblättern erfolgt ist.

§ 73 Restrictive Year

(1) The distribution may not be performed before the paying-off of, or the provision of security for, the debts of the company, and not before the expiration of one year from the day on which the request to the creditors (§ 65(2)) in the company bulletins is effected.

(2) Meldet sich ein bekannter Gläubiger nicht, so ist der geschuldete Betrag, wenn die Berechtigung zur Hinterlegung vorhanden ist, für den Gläubiger zu hinterlegen. Ist die Berichtigung einer Verbindlichkeit zur Zeit nicht ausführbar oder ist eine Verbindlichkeit streitig, so darf die Verteilung des Vermögens nur erfolgen, wenn dem Gläubiger Sicherheit geleistet ist.

(2) If a known creditor does not make contact, then the amount owed is to be deposited for the creditor, if the deposit is permissible. If the adjustment of a liability at the time is not practicable or if a liability is disputed, then the distribution of the assets may only be effected if security is provided to the creditor.

(3) Liquidatoren, welche diesen Vorschriften zuwiderhandeln, sind zum Ersatz der verteilten Beträge solidarisch verpflichtet. Auf den Ersatzanspruch finden die Bestimmungen in § 43 Abs. 3 und 4 entsprechende Anwendung.

(3) Liquidators who act contrary to these provisions are jointly and severally liable for compensation of the distributed amounts. The provisions in § 43(3) and (4) apply to the claim to compensation accordingly.

§ 74 Schluss der Liquidation

§ 74 Closure of the Liquidation

(1) Ist die Liquidation beendet und die Schlußrechnung gelegt, so haben die Liquidatoren den Schluß der Liquidation zur Eintragung in das Handelsregister anzumelden. Die Gesellschaft ist zu löschen.

(1) If the liquidation is terminated and the final account is rendered, then the liquidators must register the closure of the liquidation for entry in the commercial register (*Handelsregister*). The company is to be deregistered.

(2) Nach Beendigung der Liquidation sind die Bücher und Schriften der Gesellschaft für die Dauer von zehn Jahren einem der Gesellschafter oder einem Dritten in Verwahrung zu geben. Der Gesellschafter oder der Dritte wird in Ermangelung einer Bestimmung des Gesellschaftsvertrags oder eines Beschlusses der Gesellschafter durch das Gericht bestimmt.

(2) After termination of the liquidation, the books and records of the company are to be given to one of the members or a third party for storage for the duration of ten years. The member or the third party is determined by the court in the absence of a provision of the articles of association or of a resolution of the members.

(3) Die Gesellschafter und deren Rechtsnachfolger sind zur Einsicht der Bücher und Schriften berechtigt. Gläubiger der Gesellschaft können von dem Gericht zur Einsicht ermächtigt werden.

(3) The members and their successors in interest are entitled to inspect the books and records. Creditors of the company may be authorized to inspect by the court.

§ 75 Nichtigkeitsklage

§ 75 Action for a Declaration of Voidness

(1) Enthält der Gesellschaftsvertrag keine Bestimmungen über die Höhe des Stammkapitals oder über den Gegenstand des Unternehmens oder sind die Best-

(1) If the articles of association contain no provisions on the amount of the capital stock or on the purpose of the business, or if the provisions of the articles of

immungen des Gesellschaftsvertrags über den Gegenstand des Unternehmens nichtig, so kann jeder Gesellschafter, jeder Geschäftsführer und, wenn ein Aufsichtsrat bestellt ist, jedes Mitglied des Aufsichtsrats im Wege der Klage beantragen, daß die Gesellschaft für nichtig erklärt werde.

(2) Die Vorschriften der §§ 246 bis 248 des Aktiengesetzes finden entsprechende Anwendung.

association on the purpose of the business are void, then each member, each managing director and, if a supervisory board is appointed, each member of the supervisory board may petition, by means of an action, that the company be declared void.

(2) The provisions of §§ 246 to 248 of the Stock Corporation Act (*Aktiengesetz*) apply accordingly.

§ 76 Heilung von Mängeln durch Gesellschafterbeschluss

Ein Mangel, der die Bestimmungen über den Gegenstand des Unternehmens betrifft, kann durch einstimmigen Beschluß der Gesellschafter geheilt werden.

§ 76 Remedy of Defects through a Member Resolution

A defect that pertains to the provisions on the purpose of the business may be remedied through a unanimous resolution of the members.

§ 77 Wirkung der Nichtigkeit

(1) Ist die Nichtigkeit einer Gesellschaft in das Handelsregister eingetragen, so finden zum Zwecke der Abwicklung ihrer Verhältnisse die für den Fall der Auflösung geltenden Vorschriften entsprechende Anwendung.

(2) Die Wirksamkeit der im Namen der Gesellschaft mit Dritten vorgenommenen Rechtsgeschäfte wird durch die Nichtigkeit nicht berührt.

(3) Die Gesellschafter haben die versprochenen Einzahlungen zu leisten, soweit es zur Erfüllung der eingegangenen Verbindlichkeiten erforderlich ist.

§ 77 Effect of the Voidness

(1) If the voidness of a company is entered in the commercial register (*Handelsregister*), then the provisions applicable in the case of dissolution apply accordingly for the purpose of winding up its affairs.

(2) The effectiveness of the legal transactions performed in the name of the company with third parties is not affected by the voidness.

(3) The members must render the promised payments, insofar as it is necessary for the fulfillment of the liabilities entered into.

Abschnitt 6 Ordnungs-, Straf- und Bußgeldvorschriften

Chapter 6 Administrative, Criminal, and Civil Fine Provisions

§ 78 Anmeldepflichtige

Die in diesem Gesetz vorgesehenen Anmeldungen zum Handelsregister sind durch die Geschäftsführer oder die Liquidatoren, die in § 7 Abs. 1, § 57 Abs. 1, § 57i Abs. 1, § 58 Abs. 1 Nr. 3

§ 78 Parties Obligated to Register

The registrations in the commercial register (*Handelsregister*) provided for in this Act are to be effectuated by the managing directors or the liquidators, and the registrations provided for in § 7(1), vorgesehenen Anmeldungen sind durch sämtliche Geschäftsführer zu bewirken.

§ 57(1), § 57i(1), § 58(1), No. 3 are to be effectuated by all managing directors.

§ 79 Zwangsgelder

(1) Geschäftsführer oder Liquidatoren, die §§ 35a, 71 Abs. 5 nicht befolgen, sind hierzu vom Registergericht durch Festsetzung von Zwangsgeld anzuhalten; § 14 des Handelsgesetzbuchs bleibt unberührt. Das einzelne Zwangsgeld darf den Betrag von fünftausend Euro nicht übersteigen.

(2) In Ansehung der in §§ 7, 54, 57 Abs. 1, § 58 Abs. 1 Nr. 3 bezeichneten Anmeldungen zum Handelsregister findet, soweit es sich um die Anmeldung zum Handelsregister des Sitzes der Gesellschaft handelt, eine Festsetzung von Zwangsgeld nach § 14 des Handelsgesetzbuchs nicht statt.

§ 79 Coercive Fines

(1) Managing directors or liquidators who do not abide by §§ 35a and 71(5) are to be compelled to do so by the court of registry through the determination of a coercive fine; § 14 of the Commercial Code (*Handelsgesetzbuch*) remains unaffected. A single coercive fine may not exceed the amount of five thousand euros.

(2) With respect to the registrations in the commercial register (*Handelsregister*) designated in §§ 7, 54, 57(1), § 58(1), No. 3, a determination of a coercive fine according to § 14 of the Commercial Code (*Handelsgesetzbuch*) will not take place, insofar as it concerns the registration in the commercial register (*Handelsregister*) for the registered office of the company.

§ 80 (weggefallen)

§ 81 (weggefallen)

§ 80 (repealed)

§ 81 (repealed)

§ 82 Falsche Angaben

(1) Mit Freiheitsstrafe bis zu drei Jahren oder mit Geldstrafe wird bestraft, wer

1. als Gesellschafter oder als Geschäftsführer zum Zweck der Eintragung der Gesellschaft über die Übernahme der Geschäftsanteile, die Leistung der Einlagen, die Verwendung eingezahlter Beträge, über Sondervorteile, Gründungsaufwand und Sacheinlagen,

2. als Gesellschafter im Sachgründungsbericht,

3. als Geschäftsführer zum Zweck der Eintragung einer Erhöhung des Stammkapitals über die Zeichnung oder Einbringung des neuen Kapitals oder über Sacheinlagen,

4. als Geschäftsführer in der in § 57i Abs. 1 Satz 2 vorgeschriebenen Erklärung oder

§ 82 False Information

(1) A person who gives false information

1. as a member or as a managing director, for the purpose of entering the company, on the acceptance of the membership interests, on the rendering of contributions, on the use of amounts paid in, on special benefits, on incorporation expenses, and on in-kind contributions,

2. as a member in the report on the incorporation using in-kind contributions,

3. as a managing director for the purpose of entering an increase of the capital stock on the subscription or contribution of the new capital or on in-kind contributions,

4. as a managing director in the declaration prescribed in § 57i(1), Sentence 2, or

5. als Geschäftsführer einer Gesellschaft mit beschränkter Haftung oder als Geschäftsleiter einer ausländischen juristischen Person in der nach § 8 Abs. 3 Satz 1 oder § 39 Abs. 3 Satz 1 abzugebenden Versicherung oder als Liquidator in der nach § 67 Abs. 3 Satz 1 abzugebenden Versicherung

falsche Angaben macht.

(2) Ebenso wird bestraft, wer

1. als Geschäftsführer zum Zweck der Herabsetzung des Stammkapitals über die Befriedigung oder Sicherstellung der Gläubiger eine unwahre Versicherung abgibt oder

2. als Geschäftsführer, Liquidator, Mitglied eines Aufsichtsrats oder ähnlichen Organs in einer öffentlichen Mitteilung die Vermögenslage der Gesellschaft unwahr darstellt oder verschleiert, wenn die Tat nicht in § 331 Nr. 1 oder Nr. 1a des Handelsgesetzbuchs mit Strafe bedroht ist.

§ 83 (weggefallen)

§ 84 Verletzung der Verlustanzeigepflicht

(1) Mit Freiheitsstrafe bis zu drei Jahren oder mit Geldstrafe wird bestraft, wer es als Geschäftsführer unterläßt, den Gesellschaftern einen Verlust in Höhe der Hälfte des Stammkapitals anzuzeigen.

(2) Handelt der Täter fahrlässig, so ist die Strafe Freiheitsstrafe bis zu einem Jahr oder Geldstrafe.

§ 85 Verletzung der Geheimhaltungspflicht

(1) Mit Freiheitsstrafe bis zu einem Jahr oder mit Geldstrafe wird bestraft,

5. as a managing director of a company with limited liability, or as an executive of a foreign legal person, in the assertion to be given under § 8(3), Sentence 1 or § 39(3), Sentence 1 or as a liquidator in the assertion to be given according to § 67(3), Sentence 1

will be punished with a term of imprisonment of up to three years or with a fine.

(2) A person who

1. as a managing director, for the purpose of reducing the capital stock, gives an untrue assertion about the satisfaction of, or the provision of security to, the creditors, or

2. as a managing director, liquidator, or member of a supervisory board or a similar body, falsely presents or conceals the financial situation of the company in a public notification, if the offense is not punishable under § 331, No. 1 or No. 1a of the Commercial Code (*Handelsgesetzbuch*)

will be punished in the same way.

§ 83 (repealed)

§ 84 Breach of the Duty to Notify of a Loss

(1) A person who, as a managing director, fails to notify the members of a loss in the amount of half of the capital stock will be punished with a term of imprisonment of up to three years or with a fine.

(2) If the offender acts negligently, then the punishment is a term of imprisonment of up to one year or a fine.

§ 85 Breach of the Duty to Observe Secrecy

(1) A person who, without authority, reveals a secret of the company, particu-

wer ein Geheimnis der Gesellschaft, namentlich ein Betriebs- oder Geschäftsgeheimnis, das ihm in seiner Eigenschaft als Geschäftsführer, Mitglied des Aufsichtsrats oder Liquidator bekanntgeworden ist, unbefugt offenbart.

(2) Handelt der Täter gegen Entgelt oder in der Absicht, sich oder einen anderen zu bereichern oder einen anderen zu schädigen, so ist die Strafe Freiheitsstrafe bis zu zwei Jahren oder Geldstrafe. Ebenso wird bestraft, wer ein Geheimnis der in Absatz 1 bezeichneten Art, namentlich ein Betriebs- oder Geschäftsgeheimnis, das ihm unter den Voraussetzungen des Absatzes 1 bekanntgeworden ist, unbefugt verwertet.

(3) Die Tat wird nur auf Antrag der Gesellschaft verfolgt. Hat ein Geschäftsführer oder ein Liquidator die Tat begangen, so sind der Aufsichtsrat und, wenn kein Aufsichtsrat vorhanden ist, von den Gesellschaftern bestellte besondere Vertreter antragsberechtigt. Hat ein Mitglied des Aufsichtsrats die Tat begangen, so sind die Geschäftsführer oder die Liquidatoren antragsberechtigt.

§ 86 Verletzung der Pflichten bei Abschlussprüfungen

(1) Mit Freiheitsstrafe bis zu einem Jahr oder mit Geldstrafe wird bestraft, wer als Mitglied eines Aufsichtsrats oder als Mitglied eines Prüfungsausschusses einer Gesellschaft, die kapitalmarktorientiert im Sinne des § 264d des Handelsgesetzbuchs, die CRR-Kreditinstitut im Sinne des § 1 Absatz 3d Satz 1 des Kreditwesengesetzes, mit Ausnahme der in § 2 Absatz 1 Nummer 1 und 2 des Kreditwesengesetzes genannten Institute, oder die Versicherungsunternehmen ist im Sinne des Artikels 2 Absatz 1 der Richtlinie 91/674/EWG des Rates vom 19. Dezember 1991 über den Jahresab-

larly a trade or business secret, that became known to him in his role as a managing director, member of the supervisory board, or liquidator, will be punished with a term of imprisonment of up to one year or with a fine.

(2) If the offender acts in exchange for consideration or with the intent to enrich himself or another or to injure another, then the punishment is a term of imprisonment of up to two years or a fine. A person who, without authority, exploits a secret of the type designated in Subsection 1, particularly a trade or business secret that became known to him under the conditions of Subsection 1, will be punished in the same way.

(3) The offense is only prosecuted upon the petition of the company. If a managing director or a liquidator committed the offense, then the supervisory board and, if there is no supervisory board, special representatives appointed by the members are entitled to file the petition. If a member of the supervisory board committed the offense, then the managing directors or the liquidators are entitled to file the petition.

§ 86 Breach of Duties in Connection with Audits of the Financial Statements

(1) Whoever, as a member of a supervisory board or member of an audit committee of a company that is capital markets-oriented within the meaning of § 264d of the Commercial Code (*Handelsgesetzbuch*), a CRR-credit institution within the meaning of § 1(3d), Sentence 1 of the Banking Act (*Kreditwesengesetz*), except for the institutions specified in § 2(1), No. 1 and 2 of the Banking Act (*Kreditwesengesetz*), or an insurance undertaking within the meaning of Article 2(1) of Council Directive 91/674/EEC of December 19, 1991, on the annual accounts and consolidated

schluß und den konsolidierten Abschluß von Versicherungsunternehmen (ABl. L 374 vom 31.12.1991, S. 7), die zuletzt durch die Richtlinie 2006/46/EG (ABl. L 224 vom 16.8.2006, S. 1) geändert worden ist,

1. eine in § 87 Absatz 1 bezeichnete Handlung begeht und dafür einen Vermögensvorteil erhält oder sich versprechen lässt oder

2. eine in § 87 Absatz 1 bezeichnete Handlung beharrlich wiederholt.

(2) Ebenso wird bestraft, wer als Mitglied eines Aufsichtsrats oder als Mitglied eines Prüfungsausschusses einer Gesellschaft, die kapitalmarktorientiert im Sinne des § 264d des Handelsgesetzbuchs oder die CRR-Kreditinstitut ist im Sinne des § 1 Absatz 3d Satz 1 des Kreditwesengesetzes, mit Ausnahme der in § 2 Absatz 1 Nummer 1 und 2 des Kreditwesengesetzes genannten Institute,

1. eine in § 87 Absatz 2 oder 3 bezeichnete Handlung begeht und dafür einen Vermögensvorteil erhält oder sich versprechen lässt oder

2. eine in § 87 Absatz 2 oder 3 bezeichnete Handlung beharrlich wiederholt.

§ 87 Bußgeldvorschriften

(1) Ordnungswidrig handelt, wer als Mitglied eines Aufsichtsrats oder als Mitglied eines Prüfungsausschusses einer Gesellschaft, die kapitalmarktorientiert im Sinne des § 264d des Handelsgesetzbuchs, die CRR-Kreditinstitut im Sinne des § 1 Absatz 3d Satz 1 des Kreditwesengesetzes, mit Ausnahme der in § 2 Absatz 1 Nummer 1 und 2 des Kreditwesengesetzes genannten Institute, oder die

accounts of insurance undertakings (OJ L 374, 31.12.1991, page 7), as last amended by Directive 2006/46/EC (OJ L 224, 16.8.2006, page 1)),

1. commits an act referred to in § 87(1) and obtains a financial advantage or accepts a promise therefor or

2. persistently repeats an act referred to in § 87(1)

will be punished with a term of imprisonment of up to one year or with a fine.

(2) Whoever, as a member of a supervisory board or member of an audit committee of a company that is capital markets-oriented within the meaning of § 264d of the Commercial Code (*Handelsgesetzbuch*), or a CRR-credit institution within the meaning of § 1(3d), Sentence 1 of the Banking Act (*Kreditwesengesetz*), except for the institutions specified in § 2(1), No. 1 and 2 of the Banking Act (*Kreditwesengesetz*),

1. commits an act referred to in § 87(2) or (3) and obtains a financial advantage or accepts a promise therefor or

2. persistently repeats an act referred to in § 87(2) or (3)

will be likewise punished.

§ 87 Civil Fine Provisions

(1) Whoever, as a member of a supervisory board or member of an audit committee of a company that is capital markets-oriented within the meaning of § 264d of the Commercial Code (*Handelsgesetzbuch*), a CRR-credit institution within the meaning of § 1(3d), Sentence 1 of the Banking Act (*Kreditwesengesetz*), except for the institutions specified in § 2(1), No. 1 and 2 of the

Versicherungsunternehmen ist im Sinne des Artikels 2 Absatz 1 der Richtlinie 91/674/EWG des Rates vom 19. Dezember 1991 über den Jahresabschluß und den konsolidierten Abschluß von Versicherungsunternehmen (ABl. L 374 vom 31.12.1991, S. 7), die zuletzt durch die Richtlinie 2006/46/EG (ABl. L 224 vom 16.8.2006, S. 1) geändert worden ist,

1. die Unabhängigkeit des Abschlussprüfers oder der Prüfungsgesellschaft nicht nach Maßgabe des Artikels 4 Absatz 3 Unterabsatz 2, des Artikels 5 Absatz 4 Unterabsatz 1 Satz 1 oder des Artikels 6 Absatz 2 der Verordnung (EU) Nr. 537/2014 des Europäischen Parlaments und des Rates vom 16. April 2014 über spezifische Anforderungen an die Abschlussprüfung bei Unternehmen von öffentlichem Interesse und zur Aufhebung des Beschlusses 2005/909/EG der Kommission (ABl. L 158 vom 27.5.2014, S. 77, L 170 vom 11.6.2014, S. 66) überwacht oder

2. eine Empfehlung für die Bestellung eines Abschlussprüfers oder einer Prüfungsgesellschaft vorlegt, die nicht auf einem Verlangen der Aufsichtsbehörde nach § 36 Absatz 1 Satz 2 des Versicherungsaufsichtsgesetzes beruht und

a) die den Anforderungen nach Artikel 16 Absatz 2 Unterabsatz 2 oder 3 der Verordnung (EU) Nr. 537/2014 nicht entspricht oder

b) der ein Auswahlverfahren nach Artikel 16 Absatz 3 Unterabsatz 1 der Verordnung (EU) Nr. 537/2014 nicht vorangegangen ist.

(2) Ordnungswidrig handelt, wer als Mitglied eines Aufsichtsrats, der einen Prüfungsausschuss nicht bestellt hat, einer Gesellschaft, die kapitalmarktorientiert im Sinne des § 264d des Handelsgesetzbuchs oder die CRR-Kreditinstitut ist

Banking Act (*Kreditwesengesetz*), or an insurance undertaking within the meaning of Article 2(1) of Council Directive 91/674/EEC of December 19, 1991, on the annual accounts and consolidated accounts of insurance undertakings (OJ L 374, 31.12.1991, page 7), as last amended by Directive 2006/46/EC (OJ L 224, 16.8.2006, page 1),

1. fails to monitor the independence of the auditor or audit firm in compliance with Article 4(3)(2), Article 5(4)(1), Sentence 1, or Article 6(2) of Regulation (EU) No. 537/2014 of the European Parliament and of the Council of April 16, 2014, on specific requirements regarding statutory audit of public-interest entities and repealing Commission Decision 2005/909/EC (OJ L 158, 27.5.2014, page 77, L 170, 11.6.2014, page 66) or

2. submits a recommendation for the appointment of an auditor or an audit firm that is not based on a demand by the supervisory authority pursuant to § 36(1), Sentence 2 of the Insurance Supervision Act (*Versicherungsaufsichtsgesetz*) and

a) that does not comply with the requirements of Article 16(2)(2) or (3) of Regulation (EU) No. 537/2014 or

b) that has not been preceded by a selection procedure in accordance with Article 16(3)(1) of Regulation (EU) No. 537/2014

commits an administrative offense.

(2) Whoever, as a member of a supervisory board that has not appointed an audit committee of a company that is capital markets-oriented within the meaning of § 264d of the Commercial Code (*Handelsgesetzbuch*) or a CRR-

im Sinne des § 1 Absatz 3d Satz 1 des Kreditwesengesetzes, mit Ausnahme der in § 2 Absatz 1 Nummer 1 und 2 des Kreditwesengesetzes genannten Institute, den Gesellschaftern einen Vorschlag für die Bestellung eines Abschlussprüfers oder einer Prüfungsgesellschaft vorlegt, der den Anforderungen nach Artikel 16 Absatz 5 Unterabsatz 1 der Verordnung (EU) Nr. 537/2014 nicht entspricht.

credit institution within the meaning of § 1(3d), Sentence 1 of the Banking Act (*Kreditwesengesetz*), except for the institutions specified in § 2(1), No. 1 and 2 of the Banking Act (*Kreditwesengesetz*), submits a proposal to the members for the appointment of an auditor or audit firm that does not comply with the requirements of Article 16(5)(1) of Regulation (EU) No. 537/2014, commits an administrative offense.

(3) Ordnungswidrig handelt, wer als Mitglied eines Aufsichtsrats, der einen Prüfungsausschuss bestellt hat, einer in Absatz 2 genannten Gesellschaft den Gesellschaftern einen Vorschlag für die Bestellung eines Abschlussprüfers oder einer Prüfungsgesellschaft vorlegt, der den Anforderungen nach Artikel 16 Absatz 5 Unterabsatz 1 oder Unterabsatz 2 Satz 1 oder Satz 2 der Verordnung (EU) Nr. 537/2014 nicht entspricht.

(3) Whoever, as a member of a supervisory board that has appointed an audit committee of a company specified in Subsection 2, submits a proposal to the members for the appointment of an auditor or audit firm that does not comply with the requirements of Article 16(5)(1) or (2), Sentence 1 or Sentence 2, of Regulation (EU) No. 537/2014, commits an administrative offense.

(4) Die Ordnungswidrigkeit kann mit einer Geldbuße bis zu fünfzigtausend Euro geahndet werden.

(4) The administrative offense can be punished with a fine of up to 50,000 euros.

(5) Verwaltungsbehörde im Sinne des § 36 Absatz 1 Nummer 1 des Gesetzes über Ordnungswidrigkeiten ist bei CRR-Kreditinstituten im Sinne des § 1 Absatz 3d Satz 1 des Kreditwesengesetzes, mit Ausnahme der in § 2 Absatz 1 Nummer 1 und 2 des Kreditwesengesetzes genannten Institute, und bei Versicherungsunternehmen im Sinne des Artikels 2 Absatz 1 der Richtlinie 91/674/EWG die Bundesanstalt für Finanzdienstleistungsaufsicht, im Übrigen das Bundesamt für Justiz.

(5) The administrative agency within the meaning of § 36(1), No. 1 of the Administrative Offenses Act (*Gesetz über Ordnungswidrigkeiten*) is, in the case of CRR-credit institutions within the meaning of § 1(3d), Sentence 1 of the Banking Act (*Kreditwesengesetz*), except for the institutions specified in § 2(1), No. 1 and 2 of the Banking Act (*Kreditwesengesetz*), and in the case of insurance undertakings within the meaning of Article 2(1) of Council Directive 91/674/EEC, the Federal Financial Supervisory Authority (*Bundesanstalt für Finanzdienstleistungsaufsicht*) and in all other cases the Federal Office of Justice (*Bundesamt für Justiz*).

§ 88 Mitteilungen an die Abschlussprüferaufsichtsstelle

§ 88 Notifications to the Auditor Oversight Body

(1) Die nach § 87 Absatz 5 zuständige Verwaltungsbehörde übermittelt der Ab-

(1) The responsible administrative agency according to § 87(5) will transmit

schlussprüferaufsichtsstelle beim Bundesamt für Wirtschaft und Ausfuhrkontrolle alle Bußgeldentscheidungen nach § 87 Absatz 1 bis 3.

all decisions on civil fines according to § 87(1) to (3) to the Auditor Oversight Body (*Abschlussprüferaufsichtsstelle*) of the Federal Office for Economic Affairs and Export Control (*Bundesamt für Wirtschaft und Ausfuhrkontrolle*).

(2) In Strafverfahren, die eine Straftat nach § 86 zum Gegenstand haben, übermittelt die Staatsanwaltschaft im Falle der Erhebung der öffentlichen Klage der Abschlussprüferaufsichtsstelle die das Verfahren abschließende Entscheidung. Ist gegen die Entscheidung ein Rechtsmittel eingelegt worden, ist die Entscheidung unter Hinweis auf das eingelegte Rechtsmittel zu übermitteln.

(2) In criminal proceedings, the subject matter of which is a criminal offense according to § 86, the Public Prosecutor's Office (*Staatsanwaltschaft*) will, in case public charges are filed, transmit the final decision in the proceedings to the Auditor Oversight Body (*Abschlussprüferaufsichtsstelle*). If an appeal is filed against the decision, then the decision is to be transmitted with a reference to the appeal filed.

Anlage (zu § 2 Abs. 1a)

a)

Musterprotokoll
für die Gründung einer Einpersonengesellschaft

UR. Nr. ....

Heute, den .... ,

erschien vor mir, ... ,

Notar/in mit dem Amtssitz in

.... ,

Herr/Frau[1)] ....[2)].

1. Der Erschienene errichtet hiermit nach § 2 Abs. 1a GmbHG eine Gesellschaft mit beschränkter Haftung unter der Firma ....

   ....

   mit dem Sitz in ....

2. Gegenstand des Unternehmens ist ....

3. Das Stammkapital der Gesellschaft beträgt .... € (i. W. .... Euro) und wird vollständig von Herrn/Frau[1)] .... (Geschäftsanteil Nr. 1) übernommen. Die Einlage ist in Geld zu erbringen, und zwar sofort in voller Höhe/zu 50 Prozent sofort, im Übrigen sobald die Gesellschafterversammlung ihre Einforderung beschließt[3)].

4. Zum Geschäftsführer der Gesellschaft wird Herr/Frau[4)] .... geboren am .... , wohnhaft in

   ....

   , bestellt. Der Geschäftsführer ist von den Beschränkungen des § 181 des Bürgerlichen Gesetzbuchs befreit.

5. Die Gesellschaft trägt die mit der Gründung verbundenen Kosten bis zu einem Gesamtbetrag von 300 €, höchstens jedoch bis zum Betrag ihres Stammkapitals. Darüber hinausgehende Kosten trägt der Gesellschafter.

6. Von dieser Urkunde erhält eine Ausfertigung der Gesellschafter, beglaubigte Ablichtungen die Gesellschaft und das Registergericht (in elektronischer Form) sowie eine einfache Abschrift das Finanzamt – Körperschaftsteuerstelle –.

7. Der Erschienene wurde vom Notar/von der Notarin insbesondere auf Folgendes hingewiesen: ....

Hinweise:

[1]) Nicht Zutreffendes streichen. Bei juristischen Personen ist die Anrede Herr/Frau wegzulassen.

[2]) Hier sind neben der Bezeichnung des Gesellschafters und den Angaben zur notariellen Identitätsfeststellung ggf. der Güterstand und die Zustimmung des Ehegatten sowie die Angaben zu einer etwaigen Vertretung zu vermerken.

[3]) Nicht Zutreffendes streichen. Bei der Unternehmergesellschaft muss die zweite Alternative gestrichen werden.

[4]) Nicht Zutreffendes streichen.

Appendix (to § 2(1a))

a) **Model Protocol**
for the Incorporation of a One-person Company

Doc., No. …………

Today, the ……………………………………………………………………………,

appears before me, ……………………………………………………………………,
notary (*Notar*), with office at
………………………………………………………………………………………….,

Mr./Ms.[1)]
……………………………………………………………………………………………
……………………………………………………………………………………………
……………………………………………………………………………………………[2)].

1. The appearing person hereby founds a company with limited liability according to § 2(1a) of the GmbH Act with the company name ………………………… , ……………………………………………………………………………………… with registered office at ………………………………………………………… .

2. The purpose of the business is …………………………………………………… .

3. The capital stock of the company amounts to € ………………………………… (in words ……………………………… euros) and will be entirely accepted by Mr./Ms.[1]) ………………………………………………………………………… (membership interest No. 1). The contribution is to be rendered in cash immediately in the full amount/immediately to 50 percent of it, and the rest as soon as the meeting of the members resolves to call it in[3]).

4. Mr./Ms.[4]) …………………………………………………………………………… …………………………………………………………………………………… , born on ……………, resident at …………………………………………… ………………………………………………, will be appointed managing director. The managing director is released from the limitations of § 181 of the Civil Code (*Bürgerliches Gesetzbuch*).

5. The company bears the costs associated with the incorporation up to a total amount of € 300, but no more than the amount of its capital stock. Costs beyond that are born by the member.

6. Of this certificate, the member receives an executed copy, the company and the court of registry (in electronic form) receive authenticated photocopies, and the Tax and Revenue Office, Corporate Tax Department (*Finanzamt, Körperschaftsteuerstelle*) receives a simple copy.

7. The appearing person was particularly advised of the following by the notary (*Notar*):

   ……………………………………………………………………………………… .

Instructions:

[1]) Strike if inapplicable. For legal persons, the title Mr./Ms. is to be omitted.

[2]) Here, in addition to the form of address of the member and the information for the notarial determination of identity, the matrimonial property regime and the consent of the spouse, as well as the information on a possible representative is to be noted, where applicable.

[3]) Strike if inapplicable. For an entrepreneurial company, the second alternative must be stricken.

[4]) Strike if inapplicable.

b)

Musterprotokoll für die Gründung einer Mehrpersonengesellschaft mit bis zu drei Gesellschaftern

UR. Nr. ....

Heute, den ....,

erschienen vor mir,
....,
Notar/in mit dem Amtssitz in
....,

Herr/Frau[1)]
....
....
....[2)],

Herr/Frau[1)]
....
....
....[2)],
Herr/Frau[1)]
....
....
....[2)].

1. Die Erschienenen errichten hiermit nach § 2 Abs. 1a GmbHG eine Gesellschaft mit beschränkter Haftung unter der Firma ....
....,
mit dem Sitz in ....

2. Gegenstand des Unternehmens ist ....

3. Das Stammkapital der Gesellschaft beträgt .... € (i. W. .... Euro) und wird wie folgt übernommen:

   Herr/Frau[1)] .... übernimmt einen Geschäftsanteil mit einem Nennbetrag in Höhe von .... € (i. W. .... Euro) (Geschäftsanteil Nr. 1),

   Herr/Frau[1)] .... übernimmt einen Geschäftsanteil mit einem Nennbetrag in Höhe von .... € (i. W. .... Euro) (Geschäftsanteil Nr. 2),

   Herr/Frau[1)] .... übernimmt einen Geschäftsanteil mit einem Nennbetrag in Höhe von .... € (i. W. .... Euro) (Geschäftsanteil Nr. 3).

Die Einlagen sind in Geld zu erbringen, und zwar sofort in voller Höhe/zu 50 Prozent sofort, im Übrigen sobald die Gesellschafterversammlung ihre Einforderung beschließt[3)].

4. Zum Geschäftsführer der Gesellschaft wird Herr/Frau[4)].................................... .... , geboren am ...., wohnhaft in ...., bestellt. Der Geschäftsführer ist von den Beschränkungen des § 181 des Bürgerlichen Gesetzbuchs befreit.

5. Die Gesellschaft trägt die mit der Gründung verbundenen Kosten bis zu einem Gesamtbetrag von 300 €, höchstens jedoch bis zum Betrag ihres Stammkapitals. Darüber hinausgehende Kosten tragen die Gesellschafter im Verhältnis der Nennbeträge ihrer Geschäftsanteile.

6. Von dieser Urkunde erhält eine Ausfertigung jeder Gesellschafter, beglaubigte Ablichtungen die Gesellschaft und das Registergericht (in elektronischer Form) sowie eine einfache Abschrift das Finanzamt – Körperschaftsteuerstelle –.

7. Die Erschienenen wurden vom Notar/von der Notarin insbesondere auf Folgendes hingewiesen: ....

Hinweise:

[1]) Nicht Zutreffendes streichen. Bei juristischen Personen ist die Anrede Herr/Frau wegzulassen.

[2]) Hier sind neben der Bezeichnung des Gesellschafters und den Angaben zur notariellen Identitätsfeststellung ggf. der Güterstand und die Zustimmung des Ehegatten sowie die Angaben zu einer etwaigen Vertretung zu vermerken.

[3]) Nicht Zutreffendes streichen. Bei der Unternehmergesellschaft muss die zweite Alternative gestrichen werden.

[4]) Nicht Zutreffendes streichen.

b) **Model Protocol**
for the Incorporation of a Multiple-person Company

Doc. No. …………

Today, the ………………………………………………………………………….…,

appear before me, ………………………………………………………………,
notary (*Notar*), with office at
……………………..……………………………………………………………….,

Mr./Ms.[1)]
………………………………………………………………………………………
………………………………………………………………………………………
……………………………………………………………………………………[2)],
Mr./Ms.[1)]
………………………………………………………………………………………
………………………………………………………………………………………
……………………………………………………………………………………[2)],
Mr./Ms.[1)]
………………………………………………………………………………………
………………………………………………………………………………………
……………………………………………………………………………………[2)].

1. The appearing persons hereby found a company with limited liability according to § 2(1a) of the GmbH Act with the company name ………………..………., …..………………………………………………………………………………
with registered office at ……………………………………………………….. .

2. The purpose of the business is ………………………………………………… .

3. The capital stock of the company amounts to € ……………………………….. (in words ……………………………….. euros) and will be accepted as follows:

   Mr./Ms.[1]) …………………………………………………………………… accepts a membership interest with a par value in the amount of € ………………………... (in words …………………………………….. euros) (membership interest No. 1),

   Mr./Ms.[1]) …………………………………………………………………… accepts a membership interest with a par value in the amount of € ………………………... (in words …………………………………….. euros) (membership interest No. 2),

   Mr./Ms.[1]) …………………………………………………………………… accepts a membership interest with a par value in the amount of € ………………………... (in words …………………………………….. euros) (membership interest No. 3),

The contributions are to be rendered in cash immediately in the full amount/immediately to 50 percent of it, and the rest as soon as the meeting of the members resolves to call it in[3]).

4. Mr./Ms.[4]) ....
....,
born on.., resident at ....
...., will be appointed managing director. The managing director is released from the limitations of § 181 of the Civil Code (*Bürgerliches Gesetzbuch*).

5. The company bears the costs associated with the incorporation up to a total amount of € 300, but no more than the amount of its capital stock. Costs beyond that are born by the members in proportion to the par values of their membership interests.

6. Of this certificate, every member receives an executed copy, the company and the court of registry (in electronic form) receive authenticated photocopies, and the Tax and Revenue Office, Corporate Tax Department (*Finanzamt, Körperschaftsteuerstelle*) receives a simple copy.

7. The appearing persons were particularly advised of the following by the notary (*Notar*):
....

Instructions:

[1]) Strike if inapplicable. For legal persons, the title Mr./Ms. is to be omitted.

[2]) Here, in addition to the form of address of the member and the information for the notarial determination of identity, the matrimonial property regime and the consent of the spouse, as well as the information on a possible representative is to be noted, where applicable.

[3]) Strike if inapplicable. For an entrepreneurial company, the second alternative must be stricken.

[4]) Strike if inapplicable.

B. Introductory Act to the Act pertaining to Companies with Limited Liability

Einführungsgesetz zum Gesetz betreffend die Gesellschaften mit beschränkter Haftung

§ 1 Umstellung auf Euro

(1) Gesellschaften, die vor dem 1. Januar 1999 in das Handelsregister eingetragen worden sind, dürfen ihr auf Deutsche Mark lautendes Stammkapital beibehalten; Entsprechendes gilt für Gesellschaften, die vor dem 1. Januar 1999 zur Eintragung in das Handelsregister angemeldet und bis zum 31. Dezember 2001 eingetragen worden sind. Für Mindestbetrag und Teilbarkeit von Kapital, Einlagen und Geschäftsanteilen sowie für den Umfang des Stimmrechts bleiben bis zu einer Kapitaländerung nach Satz 4 die bis dahin gültigen Beträge weiter maßgeblich. Dies gilt auch, wenn die Gesellschaft ihr Kapital auf Euro umgestellt hat; das Verhältnis der mit den Geschäftsanteilen verbundenen Rechte zueinander wird durch Umrechnung zwischen Deutscher Mark und Euro nicht berührt. Eine Änderung des Stammkapitals darf nach dem 31. Dezember 2001 nur eingetragen werden, wenn das Kapital auf Euro umgestellt wird.

(2) Bei Gesellschaften, die zwischen dem 1. Januar 1999 und dem 31. Dezember 2001 zum Handelsregister angemeldet und in das Register eingetragen worden sind, dürfen Stammkapital und Stammeinlagen auch auf Deutsche Mark lauten. Für Mindestbetrag und Teilbarkeit von Kapital, Einlagen und Geschäftsanteilen sowie für den Umfang des Stimmrechts gelten die zu dem vom Rat der Europäischen Union nach Artikel 123 Abs. 4 Satz 1 des Vertrages zur Gründung der Europäischen Gemeinschaft unwiderruflich festgelegten Um-

Introductory Act to the Act pertaining to Companies with Limited Liability

§ 1 Redenomination to Euros

(1) Companies that have been entered in the commercial register (*Handelsregister*) before January 1, 1999, may retain their capital stock denominated in German marks (*Deutsche Mark*); the same applies to companies that have been registered for entry in the commercial register (*Handelsregister*) before January 1, 1999, and have been entered before December 31, 2001. For the minimum amount and the divisibility of capital, contributions, and membership interests, as well as for the extent of the right to vote, the theretofore valid amounts continue to remain authoritative until a change in capital according to Sentence 4. This also applies if the company has redenominated its capital to euros; the proportion of the rights associated with the membership interests to one another is not affected by conversion between German marks (*Deutsche Mark*) and euros. After December 31, 2001, a change of the capital stock may only be entered if the capital is redenominated to euros.

(2) For companies that have been registered in the commercial register (*Handelsregister*) and entered in the register between January 1, 1999, and December 31, 2001, the capital stock and initial contributions may also be denominated in German marks (*Deutsche Mark*). For the minimum amount and the divisibility of capital, contributions, and membership interests, as well as for the extent of the right to vote, the amounts of the Act in the version effective from January 1, 1999, in German marks (*Deutsche Mark*), as converted at the conversion

rechnungskurs in Deutsche Mark umzurechnenden Beträge des Gesetzes in der ab dem 1. Januar 1999 geltenden Fassung.

(3) Die Umstellung des Stammkapitals und der Geschäftsanteile sowie weiterer satzungsmäßiger Betragsangaben auf Euro zu dem nach Artikel 123 Abs. 4 Satz 1 des Vertrages zur Gründung der Europäischen Gemeinschaft unwiderruflich festgelegten Umrechnungskurs erfolgt durch Beschluss der Gesellschafter mit einfacher Stimmenmehrheit nach § 47 des Gesetzes betreffend die Gesellschaften mit beschränkter Haftung; § 53 Abs. 2 Satz 1 des Gesetzes betreffend die Gesellschaften mit beschränkter Haftung ist nicht anzuwenden. Auf die Anmeldung und Eintragung der Umstellung in das Handelsregister ist § 54 Abs. 1 Satz 2 und Abs. 2 Satz 2 des Gesetzes betreffend die Gesellschaften mit beschränkter Haftung nicht anzuwenden. Werden mit der Umstellung weitere Maßnahmen verbunden, insbesondere das Kapital verändert, bleiben die hierfür geltenden Vorschriften unberührt; auf eine Herabsetzung des Stammkapitals, mit der die Nennbeträge der Geschäftsanteile auf einen Betrag nach Absatz 1 Satz 4 gestellt werden, ist jedoch § 58 Abs. 1 des Gesetzes betreffend die Gesellschaften mit beschränkter Haftung nicht anzuwenden, wenn zugleich eine Erhöhung des Stammkapitals gegen Bareinlagen beschlossen und diese in voller Höhe vor der Anmeldung zum Handelsregister geleistet werden.

§ 2 Übergangsvorschriften zum Transparenz- und Publizitätsgesetz

§ 42a Abs. 4 des Gesetzes betreffend die Gesellschaften mit beschränkter Haftung in der Fassung des Artikels 3 Abs. 3 des Transparenz- und Publizitäts-

rate irrevocably determined by the Council of the European Union according to Article 123(4), Sentence 1 of the Treaty on the Foundation of the European Community, are applicable.

(3) The redenomination of the capital stock and of the membership interests, as well as of further amounts in the articles of association to euros at the conversion rate irrevocably determined according to Article 123(4), Sentence 1 of the Treaty on the Foundation of the European Community is effected by resolution of the members with a simple majority of votes according to § 47 of the Act pertaining to Companies with Limited Liability; § 53(2), Sentence 1 of the Act pertaining to Companies with Limited Liability is not to be applied. § 54(1), Sentence 2 and (2), Sentence 2 of the Act pertaining to Companies with Limited Liability is not to be applied to the registration and entry of the redenomination in the commercial register (*Handelsregister*). If further measures are connected with the redenomination, in particular if the capital is changed, then the applicable provisions therefor remain unaffected; however, § 58(1) of the Act pertaining to Companies with Limited Liability is not to be applied to a reduction of the capital stock, with which the par values of the membership interests are set at an amount according to Subsection 1, Sentence 4, if an increase of the capital stock for cash contributions is simultaneously resolved upon and if these are rendered in the full amount before the registration in the commercial register (*Handelsregister*).

§ 2 Transitional Provisions regarding the Transparency and Public Disclosure Act

§ 42a(4) of the Act pertaining to Companies with Limited Liability in the version of Article 3(3) of the Transparency and Public Disclosure Act (*Transparenz-*

gesetzes vom 19. Juli 2002 (BGBl. I S. 2681) ist erstmals auf den Konzernabschluss und den Konzernlagebericht für das nach dem 31. Dezember 2001 beginnende Geschäftsjahr anzuwenden.

und Publizitätsgesetz) of July 19, 2002 (Federal Law Bulletin, Part I, page 2681), is to be applied, for the first time, to the consolidated financial statements and the group management report for the fiscal year beginning after December 31, 2001.

§ 3 Übergangsvorschriften zum Gesetz zur Modernisierung des GmbH-Rechts und zur Bekämpfung von Missbräuchen

(1) Die Pflicht, die inländische Geschäftsanschrift bei dem Gericht nach § 8 des Gesetzes betreffend die Gesellschaften mit beschränkter Haftung in der ab dem Inkrafttreten des Gesetzes vom 23. Oktober 2008 (BGBl. I S. 2026) am 1. November 2008 geltenden Fassung zur Eintragung in das Handelsregister anzumelden, gilt auch für Gesellschaften, die zu diesem Zeitpunkt bereits in das Handelsregister eingetragen sind, es sei denn, die inländische Geschäftsanschrift ist dem Gericht bereits nach § 24 Abs. 2 der Handelsregisterverordnung mitgeteilt worden und hat sich anschließend nicht geändert. In diesen Fällen ist die inländische Geschäftsanschrift mit der ersten die eingetragene Gesellschaft betreffenden Anmeldung zum Handelsregister ab dem 1. November 2008, spätestens aber bis zum 31. Oktober 2009 anzumelden. Wenn bis zum 31. Oktober 2009 keine inländische Geschäftsanschrift zur Eintragung in das Handelsregister angemeldet worden ist, trägt das Gericht von Amts wegen und ohne Überprüfung kostenfrei die ihm nach § 24 Abs. 2 der Handelsregisterverordnung bekannte inländische Anschrift als Geschäftsanschrift in das Handelsregister ein; in diesem Fall gilt die mitgeteilte Anschrift zudem unabhängig von dem Zeitpunkt ihrer tatsächlichen Eintragung ab dem 31. Oktober 2009 als eingetragene inländische Geschäftsanschrift der Gesellschaft, wenn sie im elektronischen In-

§ 3 Transitional Provisions regarding the Act on the Modernization of GmbH Law and on the Combating of Abuses

(1) The duty to register, according to § 8 of the Act pertaining to Companies with Limited Liability in the version effective from the entry into force of the Act of October 23, 2008 (Federal Law Bulletin, Part I, page 2681), on November 1, 2008, the domestic business address at the court for entry in the commercial register (*Handelsregister*) also applies to companies that are, prior to this point in time, already entered in the commercial register (*Handelsregister*), unless the domestic business address has already been communicated to the court according to § 24(2) of the Commercial Register Regulation (*Handelsregisterverordnung*), and has not been subsequently changed. In these cases, the domestic business address is to be registered together with the first registration pertaining to the entered company in the commercial register (*Handelsregister*) after November 1, 2008, but no later than October 31, 2009. If, by October 31, 2009, no domestic business address has been registered for entry in the commercial register (*Handelsregister*), then the court, on its own accord and without verification, enters, free of charge, the domestic address known to the court according to § 24(2) of the Commercial Register Regulation (*Handelsregisterverordnung*) as the business address in the commercial register (*Handelsregister*); in this case, the address communicated is, effective from October 31,

formations- und Kommunikationssystem nach § 9 Abs. 1 des Handelsgesetzbuchs abrufbar ist. Ist dem Gericht keine Mitteilung im Sinne des § 24 Abs. 2 der Handelsregisterverordnung gemacht worden, ist ihm aber in sonstiger Weise eine inländische Geschäftsanschrift bekannt geworden, so gilt Satz 3 mit der Maßgabe, dass diese Anschrift einzutragen ist, wenn sie im elektronischen Informations- und Kommunikationssystem nach § 9 Abs. 1 des Handelsgesetzbuchs abrufbar ist. Dasselbe gilt, wenn eine in sonstiger Weise bekannt gewordene inländische Anschrift von einer früher nach § 24 Abs. 2 der Handelsregisterverordnung mitgeteilten Anschrift abweicht. Eintragungen nach den Sätzen 3 bis 5 werden abweichend von § 10 des Handelsgesetzbuchs nicht bekannt gemacht.

2009, furthermore regarded as the entered domestic business address of the company, regardless of the point in time of its actual entry, if it is accessible in the electronic information and communication system according to § 9(1) of the Commercial Code (*Handelsgesetzbuch*). If no notification within the meaning of § 24(2) of the Commercial Register Regulation (*Handelsregisterverordnung*) has been given to the court, but a domestic business address has become known to the court in another manner, then Sentence 3 applies, with the modification that this address is only to be entered if it is accessible in the electronic information and communication system according to § 9(1) of the Commercial Code (*Handelsgesetzbuch*). The same applies if a domestic address that has become known in another manner differs from an address communicated earlier according to § 24(2) of the Commercial Register Regulation (*Handelsregisterverordnung*). Entries according to Sentences 3 to 5 are not published, notwithstanding § 10 of the Commercial Code (*Handelsgesetzbuch*).

(2) § 6 Abs. 2 Satz 2 Nr. 3 Buchstabe a, c, d und e des Gesetzes betreffend die Gesellschaften mit beschränkter Haftung in der ab dem 1. November 2008 geltenden Fassung ist auf Personen, die vor dem 1. November 2008 zum Geschäftsführer bestellt worden sind, nicht anzuwenden, wenn die Verurteilung vor dem 1. November 2008 rechtskräftig geworden ist. Entsprechendes gilt für § 6 Abs. 2 Satz 3 des Gesetzes betreffend die Gesellschaften mit beschränkter Haftung in der ab dem 1. November 2008 geltenden Fassung, soweit die Verurteilung wegen einer Tat erfolgte, die den Straftaten im Sinne des Satzes 1 vergleichbar ist.

(2) § 6(2), Sentence 2, No. 3, letters a, c, d and e of the Act pertaining to Companies with Limited Liability in the version effective from 1 November 2008 is not to be applied to persons that were appointed as managing director before November 1, 2008, if the conviction became res judicata before November 1, 2008. The same applies to § 6(2), Sentence 3 of the Act pertaining to Companies with Limited Liability in the version effective from November 1, 2008, insofar as the conviction resulted from an offense that is comparable to the criminal offenses within the meaning of Sentence 1.

(3) Bei Gesellschaften, die vor dem 1. November 2008 gegründet worden sind, findet § 16 Abs. 3 des Gesetzes

(3) For companies that were incorporated before November 1, 2008, § 16(3) of the Act pertaining to Companies with

betreffend die Gesellschaften mit beschränkter Haftung in der ab dem 1. November 2008 geltenden Fassung für den Fall, dass die Unrichtigkeit in der Gesellschafterliste bereits vor dem 1. November 2008 vorhanden und dem Berechtigten zuzurechnen ist, hinsichtlich des betreffenden Geschäftsanteils frühestens auf Rechtsgeschäfte nach dem 1. Mai 2009 Anwendung. Ist die Unrichtigkeit dem Berechtigten im Fall des Satzes 1 nicht zuzurechnen, so ist abweichend von dem 1. Mai 2009 der 1. November 2011 maßgebend.

Limited Liability in the version effective from November 1, 2008, applies for cases in which the incorrectness in the list of members already existed before November 1, 2008, and is attributable to the entitled person, at the earliest to legal transactions after May 1, 2009, with respect to the affected membership interest. If the incorrectness in the case of Sentence 1 is not attributable to the entitled person, then November 1, 2011, is applicable instead of May, 1, 2009.

(4) § 19 Abs. 4 und 5 des Gesetzes betreffend die Gesellschaften mit beschränkter Haftung in der ab dem 1. November 2008 geltenden Fassung gilt auch für Einlagenleistungen, die vor diesem Zeitpunkt bewirkt worden sind, soweit sie nach der vor dem 1. November 2008 geltenden Rechtslage wegen der Vereinbarung einer Einlagenrückgewähr oder wegen einer verdeckten Sacheinlage keine Erfüllung der Einlagenverpflichtung bewirkt haben. Dies gilt nicht, soweit über die aus der Unwirksamkeit folgenden Ansprüche zwischen der Gesellschaft und dem Gesellschafter bereits vor dem 1. November 2008 ein rechtskräftiges Urteil ergangen oder eine wirksame Vereinbarung zwischen der Gesellschaft und dem Gesellschafter getroffen worden ist; in diesem Fall beurteilt sich die Rechtslage nach den bis zum 1. November 2008 geltenden Vorschriften.

(4) § 19(4) and (5) of the Act pertaining to Companies with Limited Liability in the version effective from November 1, 2008, also applies to renderings of contributions that have been made before this time, insofar as they have not effectuated the fulfillment of the contribution obligation according to the legal situation applicable before November 1, 2008, due to an agreement on a repayment of a contribution or due to an undisclosed in-kind contribution. This does not apply insofar as a final judgment has been issued or an effective agreement has already been reached between the company and the member on the claims between the company and the member resulting from the ineffectiveness before November 1, 2008; in this case, the legal situation is assessed according to the provisions applicable until November 1, 2008.

§ 4 Übergangsvorschrift zum Bilanzrechtsmodernisierungsgesetz

§ 52 Abs. 1 Satz 1 des Gesetzes betreffend die Gesellschaften mit beschränkter Haftung in Verbindung mit § 100 Abs. 5 und § 107 Abs. 4 des Aktiengesetzes in der Fassung des Bilanzrechtsmodernisierungsgesetzes vom 25. Mai 2009 (BGBl. I S. 1102) findet keine Anwendung, solange alle Mitglieder des Auf-

§ 4 Transitional Provision regarding the Accounting Law Modernization Act

§ 52(1), Sentence 1 of the Law pertaining to Companies with Limited Liability in connection with § 100(5) and § 107(4) of the Stock Corporation Act (*Aktiengesetz*), as amended by the Accounting Law Modernization Act of May 25, 2009 (Federal Law Bulletin, Part I, page 1102), does not apply as long as all sichtsrats und des Prüfungsausschusses vor dem 29. Mai 2009 bestellt worden sind.

members of the supervisory board and the audit committee have been appointed before May 29, 2009.

§ 5 Übergangsvorschrift zu dem Gesetz für die gleichberechtigte Teilhabe von Frauen und Männern an Führungspositionen in der Privatwirtschaft und im öffentlichen Dienst

Die Festlegungen nach § 36 Satz 1 und 3 sowie § 52 Absatz 2 Satz 1, 2 und 4 des Gesetzes betreffend die Gesellschaften mit beschränkter Haftung haben erstmals bis spätestens 30. September 2015 zu erfolgen. Die nach § 36 Satz 3 und § 52 Absatz 2 Satz 4 des Gesetzes betreffend die Gesellschaften mit beschränkter Haftung erstmals festzulegende Frist darf nicht länger als bis zum 30. Juni 2017 dauern.

§ 5 Transitional Provision regarding the Act for the Equal Participation of Women and Men in Leadership Positions in the Private Economy and in Public Service

The determinations according to § 36, Sentence 1 and 3, as well as § 52(2), Sentence 1, 2 and 4 of the Act pertaining to Companies with Limited Liability, shall be applied for the first time by September 30, 2015, at the latest. The period to be determined for the first time according to § 36, Sentence 3, and § 52(2), Sentence 4, of the Act pertaining to Companies with Limited Liability may not last later than June 30, 2017.

§ 6 Übergangsvorschriften zum Bilanzrichtlinie-Umsetzungsgesetz

§ 29 des Gesetzes betreffend die Gesellschaften mit beschränkter Haftung in der Fassung des Bilanzrichtlinie-Umsetzungsgesetzes vom 17. Juli 2015 (BGBl. I S. 1245) ist erstmals auf Jahres- und Konzernabschlüsse für ein nach dem 31. Dezember 2015 beginnendes Geschäftsjahr anzuwenden. Auf Jahres- und Konzernabschlüsse für ein vor dem 1. Januar 2016 beginnendes Geschäftsjahr bleibt § 29 des Gesetzes betreffend die Gesellschaften mit beschränkter Haftung in der bis zum 22. Juli 2015 geltenden Fassung anwendbar.

§ 6 Transitional Provisions regarding the Accounting Directive Implementation Act

§ 29 of the Act pertaining to Companies with Limited Liability, as amended by the Accounting Directive Implementation Act of July 17, 2015 (Federal Law Bulletin, Part I, page 1245), is to be applied for the first time for annual financial statements and consolidated financial statements for a fiscal year beginning after December 31, 2015. For annual financial statements and consolidated financial statements for a fiscal year beginning before January 1, 2016, § 29 of the Act pertaining to Companies with Limited Liability, as in force until July 22, 2015, remains applicable.

§ 7 Übergangsvorschrift zum Abschlussprüfungsreformgesetz

§ 52 Absatz 1 des Gesetzes betreffend die Gesellschaften mit beschränkter Haftung in Verbindung mit § 100 Absatz 5 und § 107 Absatz 4 des Aktiengesetzes, jeweils in der Fassung des Abschlussprü-

§ 7 Transitional Provision regarding the Audit Reform Act

§ 52(1) of the Act pertaining to Companies with Limited Liability in connection with § 100(5) and § 107(4) of the Stock Corporation Act (*Aktiengesetz*), in each case as amended by the Audit Reform fungsreformgesetzes vom 10. Mai 2016 (BGBl. I S. 1142) müssen so lange nicht angewandt werden, wie alle Mitglieder des Aufsichtsrats und des Prüfungsausschusses vor dem 17. Juni 2016 bestellt worden sind.

Act (*Abschlussprüfungsreformgesetz*) of May 10, 2016 (Federal Law Bulletin, Part I, page 1142), do not have to be applied as long as all members of the supervisory board and the audit committee were appointed before June 17, 2016.

§ 8 Übergangsvorschrift zum Gesetz zur Umsetzung der Vierten EU-Geldwäscherichtlinie, zur Ausführung der EU-Geldtransferverordnung und zur Neuorganisation der Zentralstelle für Finanztransaktionsuntersuchungen

§ 8 Absatz 1 Nummer 3 und § 40 Absatz 1 Satz 1 bis 3 des Gesetzes betreffend die Gesellschaften mit beschränkter Haftung in der Fassung des Gesetzes zur Umsetzung der Vierten EU-Geldwäscherichtlinie, zur Ausführung der EU-Geldtransferverordnung und zur Neuorganisation der Zentralstelle für Finanztransaktionsuntersuchungen vom 23. Juni 2017 (BGBl. I S. 1822) finden auf Gesellschaften mit beschränkter Haftung, die am 26. Juni 2017 in das Handelsregister eingetragen sind, mit der Maßgabe Anwendung, dass die geänderten Anforderungen an den Inhalt der Liste der Gesellschafter erst dann zu beachten sind, wenn aufgrund einer Veränderung nach § 40 Absatz 1 Satz 1 des Gesetzes betreffend die Gesellschaften mit beschränkter Haftung in der vor dem 26. Juni 2017 geltenden Fassung eine Liste einzureichen ist.

§ 8 Transitional Provision regarding the Act for Implementation of the Fourth EU Money Laundering Directive, for the Implementation of the EU Funds Transfer Regulation and for the Re-organization of the Financial Intelligence Unit

§ 8(1), No. 3 and § 40(1), Sentence 1 to 3 of the Act pertaining to Companies with Limited Liability, as amended by the Act for Implementation of the Fourth EU Money Laundering Directive, for the Implementation of the EU Funds Transfer Regulation and for the Re-organization of the Financial Intelligence Unit of June 23, 2017 (Federal Law Bulletin, Part I, page 1822), apply to companies with limited liability already entered in the commercial register (*Handelsregister*) on June 26, 2017, provided that the changed requirements for the contents of the list of the members must first be observed when a list has to be filed due to a change pursuant to § 40(1), Sentence 1 of the Act pertaining to Companies with Limited Liability as in force before June 26, 2017.

C. Commercial Code (*Handelsgesetzbuch*) (Excerpt)

§ 242 Pflicht zur Aufstellung

(1) Der Kaufmann hat zu Beginn seines Handelsgewerbes und für den Schluß eines jeden Geschäftsjahrs einen das Verhältnis seines Vermögens und seiner Schulden darstellenden Abschluß (Eröffnungsbilanz, Bilanz) aufzustellen. Auf die Eröffnungsbilanz sind die für den Jahresabschluß geltenden Vorschriften entsprechend anzuwenden, soweit sie sich auf die Bilanz beziehen.

(2) Er hat für den Schluß eines jeden Geschäftsjahrs eine Gegenüberstellung der Aufwendungen und Erträge des Geschäftsjahrs (Gewinn- und Verlustrechnung) aufzustellen.

(3) Die Bilanz und die Gewinn- und Verlustrechnung bilden den Jahresabschluß.

[…]

§ 264 Pflicht zur Aufstellung; Befreiung

(1) Die gesetzlichen Vertreter einer Kapitalgesellschaft haben den Jahresabschluß (§ 242) um einen Anhang zu erweitern, der mit der Bilanz und der Gewinn- und Verlustrechnung eine Einheit bildet, sowie einen Lagebericht aufzustellen. Die gesetzlichen Vertreter einer kapitalmarktorientierten Kapitalgesellschaft, die nicht zur Aufstellung eines Konzernabschlusses verpflichtet ist, haben den Jahresabschluss um eine Kapitalflussrechnung und einen Eigenkapitalspiegel zu erweitern, die mit der Bilanz, Gewinn- und Verlustrechnung und dem Anhang eine Einheit bilden; sie können den Jahresabschluss um eine Segmentberichterstattung erweitern. Der Jahresabschluß

§ 242 Duty to Draw up the Financial Statements

(1) At the beginning of his commercial enterprise and for the conclusion of each fiscal year, the merchant must draw up financial statements showing the relationship of his assets and of his debts (opening balance sheet, balance sheet). The provisions applicable to the annual financial statements are to be applied to the opening balance sheet accordingly, insofar as they relate to the balance sheet.

(2) He must draw up a comparison of the expenditures and the income of the fiscal year (profit and loss statement) for the conclusion of each fiscal year.

(3) The balance sheet and profit and loss statement constitute the annual financial statements.

[…]

§ 264 Duty to Draw up the Notes, etc.; Exemption

(1) The statutory representatives of an incorporated legal entity must supplement the annual financial statements (§ 242) with notes that, together with the balance sheet and the profit and loss statement, compose a unit, and must draw up a management report. The statutory representatives of a capital markets-oriented incorporated legal entity that is not obligated to draw up consolidated financial statements must supplement the annual financial statements with a cash flow statement and a statement of shareholders' equity, which, together with the balance sheet, the profit and loss statement, and the notes, compose a unit; they may supplement the financial statements with seg-

und der Lagebericht sind von den gesetzlichen Vertretern in den ersten drei Monaten des Geschäftsjahrs für das vergangene Geschäftsjahr aufzustellen. Kleine Kapitalgesellschaften (§ 267 Abs. 1) brauchen den Lagebericht nicht aufzustellen; sie dürfen den Jahresabschluß auch später aufstellen, wenn dies einem ordnungsgemäßen Geschäftsgang entspricht, jedoch innerhalb der ersten sechs Monate des Geschäftsjahres. Kleinstkapitalgesellschaften (§ 267a) brauchen den Jahresabschluss nicht um einen Anhang zu erweitern, wenn sie

1. die in § 268 Absatz 7 genannten Angaben,

2. die in § 285 Nummer 9 Buchstabe c genannten Angaben und

3. im Falle einer Aktiengesellschaft die in § 160 Absatz 3 Satz 2 des Aktiengesetzes genannten Angaben

unter der Bilanz angeben.

(1a) In dem Jahresabschluss sind die Firma, der Sitz, das Registergericht und die Nummer, unter der die Gesellschaft in das Handelsregister eingetragen ist, anzugeben. Befindet sich die Gesellschaft in Liquidation oder Abwicklung, ist auch diese Tatsache anzugeben.

(2) Der Jahresabschluß der Kapitalgesellschaft hat unter Beachtung der Grundsätze ordnungsmäßiger Buchführung ein den tatsächlichen Verhältnissen entsprechendes Bild der Vermögens-, Finanz- und Ertragslage der Kapitalgesellschaft zu vermitteln. Führen besondere Umstände dazu, daß der Jahresabschluß ein den tatsächlichen Verhältnissen entsprechendes Bild im Sinne des Satzes 1 nicht vermittelt, so sind im Anhang zusätzliche Angaben zu machen. [...] Macht eine Kleinstkapitalgesellschaft von der Erleichterung nach Absatz 1 Satz 5 Gebrauch, sind nach Satz 2 erforderliche

ment reporting. The annual financial statements and the management report for the previous fiscal year are to be drawn up by the statutory representatives within the first three months of the fiscal year. Small incorporated legal entities (§ 267(1)) need not draw up the management report; if this accords with a proper course of business, then they may also draw up the financial statements later, but in any case within the first six months of the fiscal year. The smallest incorporated legal entities (§ 267a) do not need to supplement the annual financial statements with notes if they state below the balance sheet

1. the information specified in § 268(7),

2. the information specified in § 285, No. 9(c), and

3. in the case of a stock corporation, the information specified in § 160(3), Sentence 2.

(1a) The company name, the registered office, the court of registry and the number under which the company is entered in the commercial register (*Handelsregister*) must be stated in the annual financial statements. If the company is in liquidation or winding up, this fact must also be stated.

(2) The annual financial statements of the incorporated legal entity must present a picture of the assets, financial and earnings position of the group corresponding to the actual situation, in observance of the principles of proper accounting. If special circumstances result in the annual financial statements not providing a picture corresponding to the actual situation within the meaning of Sentence 1, then additional information is to be given in the notes. [...] If a smallest incorporated legal entity makes use of the relief according to Subsection 1, Sentence 5, then additional information required according to

zusätzliche Angaben unter der Bilanz zu machen. Es wird vermutet, dass ein unter Berücksichtigung der Erleichterungen für Kleinstkapitalgesellschaften aufgestellter Jahresabschluss den Erfordernissen des Satzes 1 entspricht.

(3) Eine Kapitalgesellschaft, die als Tochterunternehmen in den Konzernabschluss eines Mutterunternehmens mit Sitz in einem Mitgliedstaat der Europäischen Union oder einem anderen Vertragsstaat des Abkommens über den Europäischen Wirtschaftsraum einbezogen ist, braucht die Vorschriften dieses Unterabschnitts und des Dritten und Vierten Unterabschnitts dieses Abschnitts nicht anzuwenden, wenn alle folgenden Voraussetzungen erfüllt sind:

1. alle Gesellschafter des Tochterunternehmens haben der Befreiung für das jeweilige Geschäftsjahr zugestimmt;

2. das Mutterunternehmen hat sich bereit erklärt, für die von dem Tochterunternehmen bis zum Abschlussstichtag eingegangenen Verpflichtungen im folgenden Geschäftsjahr einzustehen;

3. der Konzernabschluss und der Konzernlagebericht des Mutterunternehmens sind nach den Rechtsvorschriften des Staates, in dem das Mutterunternehmen seinen Sitz hat, und im Einklang mit folgenden Richtlinien aufgestellt und geprüft worden:

a) Richtlinie 2013/34/EU des Europäischen Parlaments und des Rates vom 26. Juni 2013 über den Jahresabschluss, den konsolidierten Abschluss und damit verbundene Berichte von Unternehmen bestimmter Rechtsformen und zur Änderung der Richtlinie 2006/43/EG des Europäischen Parlaments und des Rates und zur Aufhebung der Richtlinien 78/660/EWG und 83/349/EWG des Rates (ABl. L 182 vom 29.6.2013, S. 19), die zuletzt durch die Richtlinie 2014/102/EU (ABl. L 334 vom 21.11.2014, S. 86) geändert worden ist,

Sentence 2 must be provided below the balance sheet. It is assumed that annual financial statements prepared taking into account the relief granted to smallest incorporated legal entities meet the requirements of Sentence 1.

(3) An incorporated legal entity included as a daughter company in the consolidated financial statements of a parent company with registered office in a Member State of the European Union or in another state party to the Agreement on the European Economic Area does not need to apply the provisions of this sub-chapter or the third or fourth sub-chapters of this chapter if all of the following requirements are fulfilled:

1. all members of the daughter company have consented to the exemption for the respective fiscal year;

2. the parent company has agreed to be responsible for the obligations entered into by the daughter company by the balance sheet date in the following financial year;

3. the consolidated financial statements and the consolidated management report of the parent company are prepared and audited according to the legal provisions of the state in which the parent company has its registered office, and in accordance with the following directives:

a) Directive 2013/34/EU of the European Parliament and of the Council of June 26, 2013, on the annual financial statements, consolidated financial statements and related reports of certain types of undertakings, amending Directive 2006/43/EC of the European Parliament and of the Council and repealing Council Directives 78/660/EEC and 83/349/EEC (OJ L 182, 29.6.2013, page 19), as last amended by Directive 2014/102/EU (OJ L 334, 21.11.2014, page 86),

b) Richtlinie 2006/43/EG des Europäischen Parlaments und des Rates vom 17. Mai 2006 über Abschlussprüfungen von Jahresabschlüssen und konsolidierten Abschlüssen, zur Änderung der Richtlinien 78/660/EWG und 83/349/EWG des Rates und zur Aufhebung der Richtlinie 84/253/EWG des Rates (ABl. L 157 vom 9.6.2006, S. 87), die durch die Richtlinie 2013/34/EU (ABl. L 182 vom 29.6.2013, S. 19) geändert worden ist;

4. die Befreiung des Tochterunternehmens ist im Anhang des Konzernabschlusses des Mutterunternehmens angegeben und

5. für das Tochterunternehmen sind nach § 325 Absatz 1 bis 1b offengelegt worden:

a) der Beschluss nach Nummer 1,

b) die Erklärung nach Nummer 2,

c) der Konzernabschluss,

d) der Konzernlagebericht und

e) der Bestätigungsvermerk zum Konzernabschluss und Konzernlagebericht des Mutterunternehmens nach Nummer 3.

Hat bereits das Mutterunternehmen einzelne oder alle der in Satz 1 Nummer 5 bezeichneten Unterlagen offengelegt, braucht das Tochterunternehmen die betreffenden Unterlagen nicht erneut offenzulegen, wenn sie im Bundesanzeiger unter dem Tochterunternehmen auffindbar sind; § 326 Absatz 2 ist auf diese Offenlegung nicht anzuwenden. Satz 2 gilt nur dann, wenn das Mutterunternehmen die betreffende Unterlage in deutscher oder in englischer Sprache offengelegt hat oder das Tochterunternehmen zusätzlich eine beglaubigte Übersetzung dieser Unterlage in deutscher Sprache nach § 325 Absatz 1 bis 1b offenlegt.

b) Directive 2006/43/EC of the European Parliament and of the Council of May 17, 2006, on statutory audits of annual accounts and consolidated accounts, amending Council Directives 78/660/EEC and 83/349/EEC and repealing Council Directive 84/253/EEC (OJ L 157, 9.6.2006, page 87), as amended by Directive 2013/34/EU (OJ L 182, 29.6.2013, page 19);

4. the exemption of the daughter company is stated in the notes to the consolidated financial statements of the parent company and

5. for the daughter company

a) the resolution according to No. 1,

b) the declaration according to No. 2,

c) the consolidated financial statements,

d) the consolidated management report and

e) the audit opinion on the consolidated financial statements and consolidated management report of the parent company according to No. 3

have been published according to § 325(1) to (1b).

If the parent company has already published some or all of the documents specified in Sentence 1, No. 5, then the daughter company does not need to disclose the documents concerned again if they can be found in the Federal Gazette (*Bundesanzeiger*) under the daughter company; § 326(2) shall not apply to this disclosure. Sentence 2 shall only apply if the parent company has published the relevant document in German or in English or if the daughter company additionally publishes a certified translation of this document in German in accordance with § 325(1) to (1b).

(4) Absatz 3 ist nicht anzuwenden, wenn eine Kapitalgesellschaft das Tochterunternehmen eines Mutterunternehmens ist, das einen Konzernabschluss nach den Vorschriften des Publizitätsgesetzes aufgestellt hat, und wenn in diesem Konzernabschluss von dem Wahlrecht des § 13 Absatz 3 Satz 1 des Publizitätsgesetzes Gebrauch gemacht worden ist; § 314 Absatz 3 bleibt unberührt.

(4) Subsection 3 is not to be applied if an incorporated legal entity is a daughter company of a parent company that has prepared consolidated financial statements according to the provisions of the Public Disclosure Act (*Publizitätsgesetz*), and if, in these consolidated financial statements, use has been made of the option in § 13(3), Sentence 1, of the Public Disclosure Act (*Publizitätsgesetz*); § 314(3) remains unaffected.

§ 266 Gliederung der Bilanz

(1) Die Bilanz ist in Kontoform aufzustellen. Dabei haben mittelgroße und große Kapitalgesellschaften (§ 267 Absatz 2 und 3) auf der Aktivseite die in Absatz 2 und auf der Passivseite die in Absatz 3 bezeichneten Posten gesondert und in der vorgeschriebenen Reihenfolge auszuweisen. Kleine Kapitalgesellschaften (§ 267 Abs. 1) brauchen nur eine verkürzte Bilanz aufzustellen, in die nur die in den Absätzen 2 und 3 mit Buchstaben und römischen Zahlen bezeichneten Posten gesondert und in der vorgeschriebenen Reihenfolge aufgenommen werden. Kleinstkapitalgesellschaften (§ 267a) brauchen nur eine verkürzte Bilanz aufzustellen, in die nur die in den Absätzen 2 und 3 mit Buchstaben bezeichneten Posten gesondert und in der vorgeschriebenen Reihenfolge aufgenommen werden.

(2) Aktivseite

A. Anlagevermögen:

I. Immaterielle Vermögensgegenstände:

1. Selbst geschaffene gewerbliche Schutzrechte und ähnliche Rechte und Werte;
2. entgeltlich erworbene Konzessionen, gewerbliche Schutzrechte und ähnliche Rechte und Werte sowie Lizenzen an solchen Rechten und Werten;
3. Geschäfts- oder Firmenwert;

§ 266 Layout of the Balance Sheet

(1) The balance sheet is to be drawn up in account form. In this regard, midsize and large incorporated legal entities (§ 267(2) and (3)) must enter, separately and in the prescribed order, the items designated in Subsection 2 on the assets side and the items designated in Subsection 3 on the liabilities side. Small incorporated legal entities (§ 267(1)) need only to draw up a condensed balance sheet, in which only the items designated in Subsections 2 and 3 with letters and Roman numerals, separately and in the prescribed order, are recorded. The smallest incorporated legal entities (§ 267a) only need to prepare a condensed balance sheet, in which only the items designated in Subsections 2 and 3 with letters, separately and in the prescribed order, are recorded.

(2) Assets side

A. Non-current assets:

I. Intangible assets:

1. self-created industrial property rights and similar rights and assets;
2. non-gratuitously acquired concessions, industrial property rights, and similar rights and assets, as well as licenses to such rights and assets;
3. goodwill;

4. geleistete Anzahlungen;	4. advances paid;
II. Sachanlagen:	II. Tangible assets:
1. Grundstücke, grundstücksgleiche Rechte und Bauten einschließlich der Bauten auf fremden Grundstücken;	1. real property, rights equivalent to real property, and buildings, including buildings on third-party real property;
2. technische Anlagen und Maschinen;	2. technical equipment and machinery;
3. andere Anlagen, Betriebs- und Geschäftsausstattung;	3. office, factory, and other equipment;
4. geleistete Anzahlungen und Anlagen im Bau;	4. advances paid and construction in progress;
III. Finanzanlagen:	III. Financial assets:
1. Anteile an verbundenen Unternehmen;	1. equity interests in affiliated undertakings;
2. Ausleihungen an verbundene Unternehmen;	2. lending to affiliated undertakings;
3. Beteiligungen;	3. shareholdings;
4. Ausleihungen an Unternehmen, mit denen ein Beteiligungsverhältnis besteht;	4. lending to undertakings, with which a shareholding relationship exists;
5. Wertpapiere des Anlagevermögens;	5. securities held as non-current assets;
6. sonstige Ausleihungen.	6. other lending.
B. Umlaufvermögen:	B. Current assets:
I. Vorräte:	I. Inventory:
1. Roh-, Hilfs- und Betriebsstoffe;	1. raw materials, auxiliary material, and supplies;
2. unfertige Erzeugnisse, unfertige Leistungen;	2. unfinished products, unfinished work;
3. fertige Erzeugnisse und Waren;	3. finished products and goods;
4. geleistete Anzahlungen;	4. advances paid;
II. Forderungen und sonstige Vermögensgegenstände:	II. Claims and other assets:
1. Forderungen aus Lieferungen und Leistungen;	1. trade receivables;
2. Forderungen gegen verbundene Unternehmen;	2. claims against affiliated undertakings;

3. Forderungen gegen Unternehmen, mit denen ein Beteiligungsverhältnis besteht;

4. sonstige Vermögensgegenstände;

III. Wertpapiere:

1. Anteile an verbundenen Unternehmen;

2. sonstige Wertpapiere;

IV. Kassenbestand, Bundesbankguthaben, Guthaben bei Kreditinstituten und Schecks.

C. Rechnungsabgrenzungsposten.

D. Aktive latente Steuern.

E. Aktiver Unterschiedsbetrag aus der Vermögensverrechnung.

(3) Passivseite

A. Eigenkapital:

I. Gezeichnetes Kapital;

II. Kapitalrücklage;

III. Gewinnrücklagen:

1. gesetzliche Rücklage;

2. Rücklage für Anteile an einem herrschenden oder mehrheitlich beteiligten Unternehmen;

3. satzungsmäßige Rücklagen;

4. andere Gewinnrücklagen;

IV. Gewinnvortrag/Verlustvortrag;

V. Jahresüberschuß/Jahresfehlbetrag.

B. Rückstellungen:

1. Rückstellungen für Pensionen und ähnliche Verpflichtungen;

2. Steuerrückstellungen;

3. sonstige Rückstellungen.

3. claims against undertakings, with which a shareholding relationship exists;

4. other assets;

III. Securities:

1. equity interests in affiliated undertakings;

2. other securities;

IV. Cash on hand, balance with the Federal Bank (*Bundesbank*), balance with banks, checks.

C. Deferred charges and prepaid expenses.

D. Deferred tax assets.

E. Positive difference from the offsetting of assets and liabilities.

(3) Liabilities side

A. Equity:

I. Capital subscribed;

II. Capital reserve;

III. Retained earnings:

1. statutory reserve;

2. reserve for equity interests in a controlling or majority-held undertaking;

3. reserves required by the articles of association;

4. other retained earnings;

IV. Profit carried forward/Loss carried forward;

V. Annual net profit/annual deficit.

B. Provisions:

1. provisions for pensions and similar obligations;

2. tax provisions;

3. other provisions.

C. Verbindlichkeiten:

1. Anleihen
davon konvertibel;

2. Verbindlichkeiten gegenüber Kreditinstituten;

3. erhaltene Anzahlungen auf Bestellungen;

4. Verbindlichkeiten aus Lieferungen und Leistungen;

5. Verbindlichkeiten aus der Annahme gezogener Wechsel und der Ausstellung eigener Wechsel;

6. Verbindlichkeiten gegenüber verbundenen Unternehmen;

7. Verbindlichkeiten gegenüber Unternehmen, mit denen ein Beteiligungsverhältnis besteht;

8. sonstige Verbindlichkeiten,
davon aus Steuern,
davon im Rahmen der sozialen Sicherheit.

D. Rechnungsabgrenzungsposten.

E. Passive latente Steuern.

§ 267 Umschreibung der Größenklassen

(1) Kleine Kapitalgesellschaften sind solche, die mindestens zwei der drei nachstehenden Merkmale nicht überschreiten:

1. 6 000 000 Euro Bilanzsumme.

2. 12 000 000 Euro Umsatzerlöse in den zwölf Monaten vor dem Abschlußstichtag.

3. Im Jahresdurchschnitt fünfzig Arbeitnehmer.

(2) Mittelgroße Kapitalgesellschaften sind solche, die mindestens zwei der drei in Absatz 1 bezeichneten Merkmale

C. Liabilities:

1. bond issues
those that are convertible;

2. liabilities to banks;

3. received advances for orders;

4. trade payables;

5. liabilities from the acceptance of drawn bills of exchange and the issuance of the company's own bills of exchange;

6. liabilities to affiliated undertakings;

7. liabilities to undertakings, with which a shareholding relationship exists;

8. other liabilities,
those from taxes,
those relating to social security.

D. Deferred income.

E. Deferred tax liabilities.

§ 267 Description of the Size Categories

(1) Small incorporated legal entities are those that do not surpass at least two of the three following thresholds:

1. A balance sheet total of 6,000,000 euros.

2. Revenues of 12,000,000 euros in the twelve months before the reference date of the financial statements.

3. An annual average of fifty employees.

(2) Mid-size incorporated legal entities are those that surpass at least two of the three thresholds designated in Subsec-

überschreiten und jeweils mindestens zwei der drei nachstehenden Merkmale nicht überschreiten:

1. 20 000 000 Euro Bilanzsumme.

2. 40 000 000 Euro Umsatzerlöse in den zwölf Monaten vor dem Abschlußstichtag.

3. Im Jahresdurchschnitt zweihundertfünfzig Arbeitnehmer.

(3) Große Kapitalgesellschaften sind solche, die mindestens zwei der drei in Absatz 2 bezeichneten Merkmale überschreiten. Eine Kapitalgesellschaft im Sinn des § 264d gilt stets als große.

[...]

(4a) Die Bilanzsumme setzt sich aus den Posten zusammen, die in den Buchstaben A bis E des § 266 Absatz 2 aufgeführt sind. Ein auf der Aktivseite ausgewiesener Fehlbetrag (§ 268 Absatz 3) wird nicht in die Bilanzsumme einbezogen.

[…]

§ 268 Vorschriften zu einzelnen Posten der Bilanz. Bilanzvermerke

[…]

(3) Ist das Eigenkapital durch Verluste aufgebraucht und ergibt sich ein Überschuß der Passivposten über die Aktivposten, so ist dieser Betrag am Schluß der Bilanz auf der Aktivseite gesondert unter der Bezeichnung „Nicht durch Eigenkapital gedeckter Fehlbetrag“ auszuweisen.

[…]

§ 272 Eigenkapital

(1) Gezeichnetes Kapital ist mit dem Nennbetrag anzusetzen. Die nicht eingeforderten ausstehenden Einlagen auf das gezeichnete Kapital sind von dem Posten

tion 1, and do not surpass at least two of the three following thresholds:

1. A balance sheet total of 20,000,000 euros.

2. Revenues of 40,000,000 euros in the twelve months before the reference date of the financial statements.

3. An annual average of two hundred and fifty employees.

(3) Large incorporated legal entities are those that surpass at least two of the three thresholds designated in Subsection 2. An incorporated legal entity within the meaning of § 264d is always regarded as large.

[…]

(4a) The balance sheet total comprises the aggregate of items that are specified under letters A to E of § 266(2). A deficit entered on the assets side of the balance sheet (§ 268(3)) is not taken into account in the balance sheet total.

[…]

§ 268 Provisions on Individual Items of the Balance Sheet. Footnotes to the Balance Sheet

[…]

(3) If the equity has been depleted through losses and there is an excess of liability items over asset items, then this amount is to be separately entered at the end of the balance sheet on the assets side under the designation “Deficit not covered by equity”.

[…]

§ 272 Equity

(1) Capital subscribed is to be entered with the par value. The outstanding contributions to the capital subscribed that have not been called in are to be clearly

„Gezeichnetes Kapital" offen abzusetzen; der verbleibende Betrag ist als Posten „Eingefordertes Kapital" in der Hauptspalte der Passivseite auszuweisen; der eingeforderte, aber noch nicht eingezahlte Betrag ist unter den Forderungen gesondert auszuweisen und entsprechend zu bezeichnen.

[...]

(2) Als Kapitalrücklage sind auszuweisen

1. der Betrag, der bei der Ausgabe von Anteilen einschließlich von Bezugsanteilen über den Nennbetrag oder, falls ein Nennbetrag nicht vorhanden ist, über den rechnerischen Wert hinaus erzielt wird;

2. der Betrag, der bei der Ausgabe von Schuldverschreibungen für Wandlungsrechte und Optionsrechte zum Erwerb von Anteilen erzielt wird;

3. der Betrag von Zuzahlungen, die Gesellschafter gegen Gewährung eines Vorzugs für ihre Anteile leisten;

4. der Betrag von anderen Zuzahlungen, die Gesellschafter in das Eigenkapital leisten.

(3) Als Gewinnrücklagen dürfen nur Beträge ausgewiesen werden, die im Geschäftsjahr oder in einem früheren Geschäftsjahr aus dem Ergebnis gebildet worden sind. Dazu gehören aus dem Ergebnis zu bildende gesetzliche oder auf Gesellschaftsvertrag oder Satzung beruhende Rücklagen und andere Gewinnrücklagen.

[...]

§ 297 Inhalt

(1) Der Konzernabschluss besteht aus der Konzernbilanz, der Konzern-Gewinn- und Verlustrechnung, dem Konzernanhang, der Kapitalflussrechnung und dem Eigenkapitalspiegel. Er kann um eine Segmentberichterstattung erweitert werden.

deducted from the item "Capital Subscribed"; the remaining amount is to be entered in the main column of the liabilities side as the item "Called-in Capital"; the called-in, but not yet paid-in amount is to be entered separately under the claims and designated accordingly.

[...]

(2) The following are to be entered as capital reserves:

1. the amount that is obtained by issuing equity interests, including preemptive rights, beyond the par value or, if a par value does not exist, beyond the calculated value;

2. the amount that is obtained by issuing bonds for conversion rights and options for the acquisition of equity interests;

3. the amount of additional payments that members render for the granting of a preference for their equity interests;

4. the amount of other additional payments that members render into the equity.

(3) Only amounts that have been accumulated from the profit or loss during the fiscal year or an earlier fiscal year may be entered as retained earnings. Such amounts include reserves to be accumulated from the profit or loss according to statute or based on the articles of association, as well as other retained earnings.

[...]

§ 297 Contents

(1) The consolidated financial statements consist of the consolidated balance sheet, the consolidated profit and loss statement, the consolidated notes, the cash flow statement, and the statement of shareholder's equity. It may be supplemented by segment reporting.

(1a) Im Konzernabschluss sind die Firma, der Sitz, das Registergericht und die Nummer, unter der das Mutterunternehmen in das Handelsregister eingetragen ist, anzugeben. Befindet sich das Mutterunternehmen in Liquidation oder Abwicklung, ist auch diese Tatsache anzugeben.

(2) Der Konzernabschluß ist klar und übersichtlich aufzustellen. Er hat unter Beachtung der Grundsätze ordnungsmäßiger Buchführung ein den tatsächlichen Verhältnissen entsprechendes Bild der Vermögens-, Finanz- und Ertragslage des Konzerns zu vermitteln. […]

(3) Im Konzernabschluß ist die Vermögens-, Finanz- und Ertragslage der einbezogenen Unternehmen so darzustellen, als ob diese Unternehmen insgesamt ein einziges Unternehmen wären. Die auf den vorhergehenden Konzernabschluß angewandten Konsolidierungsmethoden sind beizubehalten. Abweichungen von Satz 2 sind in Ausnahmefällen zulässig. Sie sind im Konzernanhang anzugeben und zu begründen. Ihr Einfluß auf die Vermögens-, Finanz- und Ertragslage des Konzerns ist anzugeben.

[...]

§ 313 Erläuterung der Konzernbilanz und der Konzern-Gewinn- und Verlustrechnung. Angaben zum Beteiligungsbesitz

(1) In den Konzernanhang sind diejenigen Angaben aufzunehmen, die zu einzelnen Posten der Konzernbilanz oder der Konzern-Gewinn- und Verlustrechnung vorgeschrieben sind; diese Angaben sind in der Reihenfolge der einzelnen Posten der Konzernbilanz und der Konzern-Gewinn- und Verlustrechnung darzustellen. Im Konzernanhang sind auch die Angaben zu machen, die in Ausübung eines Wahlrechts nicht in die Konzernbilanz oder in die Konzern-Gewinn- und Verlustrechnung aufge-

(1a) The company name, registered office, court of registry, and number under which the parent company is entered in the commercial register (*Handelsregister*) are to be stated in the consolidated financial statements. If the parent company is in liquidation or winding up, this fact must also be stated.

(2) The consolidated financial statements are to be clearly and concisely prepared. They have to present a picture of the assets, financial and earnings position of the group corresponding to the actual situation, in observance of the principles of proper accounting. […]

(3) The assets, financial and earnings position of the consolidated undertakings is to be presented in the consolidated financial statements as if these undertakings together were one undertaking. The methods of consolidation applied to the preceding consolidated financial statements are to be retained. Deviations from Sentence 2 are permissible in exceptional cases. They are to be stated and justified in the notes. Their influence on the assets, financial and earnings position of the group of companies is to be stated.

[…]

§ 313 Explanation of the Consolidated Balance Sheet and the Consolidated Profit and Loss Statement. Information on Shareholdings

(1) In the consolidated notes, such information is to be included that is prescribed for individual items in the consolidated balance sheet or in the consolidated profit and loss statement; this information is to be presented in the order of the individual items in the consolidated balance sheet and the consolidated profit and loss statement. Information that was, in the exercise of the company's option, not recorded in the consolidated balance sheet or in the consolidated profit and loss statement is also to be

nommen wurden. Im Konzernanhang müssen

1. die auf die Posten der Konzernbilanz und der Konzern-Gewinn- und Verlustrechnung angewandten Bilanzierungs- und Bewertungsmethoden angegeben werden;

2. Abweichungen von Bilanzierungs-, Bewertungs- und Konsolidierungsmethoden angegeben und begründet werden; deren Einfluß auf die Vermögens-, Finanz- und Ertragslage des Konzerns ist gesondert darzustellen.

[...]

included in the consolidated notes. In the consolidated notes,

1. the accounting and valuation methods applied to the items of the consolidated balance sheet and of the consolidated profit and loss statement must be stated;

2. deviations from accounting methods, valuation methods, and consolidation methods must be stated and justified; their influence on the assets, financial, and earnings position of the group of companies is to be presented separately.

[...]

§ 325 Offenlegung

(1) Die Mitglieder des vertretungsberechtigten Organs von Kapitalgesellschaften haben für die Gesellschaft folgende Unterlagen in deutscher Sprache offenzulegen:

1. den festgestellten oder gebilligten Jahresabschluss, den Lagebericht und den Bestätigungsvermerk oder den Vermerk über dessen Versagung sowie

2. den Bericht des Aufsichtsrats und die nach § 161 des Aktiengesetzes vorgeschriebene Erklärung.

Die Unterlagen sind elektronisch beim Betreiber des Bundesanzeigers in einer Form einzureichen, die ihre Bekanntmachung ermöglicht.

(1a) Die Unterlagen nach Absatz 1 Satz 1 sind spätestens ein Jahr nach dem Abschlussstichtag des Geschäftsjahrs einzureichen, auf das sie sich beziehen. Liegen die Unterlagen nach Absatz 1 Satz 1 Nummer 2 nicht innerhalb der Frist vor, sind sie unverzüglich nach ihrem Vorliegen nach Absatz 1 offenzulegen.

(1b) Wird der Jahresabschluss oder der Lagebericht geändert, so ist auch die

§ 325 Publication

(1) The members of the body authorized to represent incorporated legal entities have to publish the following documents in the German language for the company:

1. the adopted or approved annual financial statements, the management report and the audit opinion or the report on the denial thereof, as well as

2. the report of the supervisory board and the declaration prescribed by § 161 of the Stock Corporation Act (*Aktiengesetz*).

The documents are to be filed electronically with the operator of the Federal Gazette (*Bundesanzeiger*) in a form that allows their publication.

(1a) The documents under Subsection 1, Sentence 1 are to be filed no later than one year following the reference date of the financial statements of the fiscal year to which they relate. If the documents under Subsection 1, Sentence 1, No. 2 are not available within the period, then they are to be published without undue delay following their availability according to Subsection 1.

(1b) If the annual financial statements or the management report are amended,

Änderung nach Absatz 1 Satz 1 offenzulegen. Ist im Jahresabschluss nur der Vorschlag für die Ergebnisverwendung enthalten, ist der Beschluss über die Ergebnisverwendung nach seinem Vorliegen nach Absatz 1 Satz 1 offenzulegen.

then the amendment is also to be published according to Subsection 1, Sentence 1. If only the proposal for the appropriation of profit or loss is contained in the annual financial statements, then the resolution on the appropriation of profit or loss is to be published according to Subsection 1, Sentence 1 once it is available.

(2) Die Mitglieder des vertretungsberechtigten Organs der Kapitalgesellschaft haben für diese die in Absatz 1 bezeichneten Unterlagen jeweils unverzüglich nach der Einreichung im Bundesanzeiger bekannt machen zu lassen.

(2) The members of the body authorized to represent the incorporated legal entity must publish any documentation designated in Subsection 1 in the Federal Gazette (*Bundesanzeiger*) without undue delay after the filing.

[...]

[...]

(5) Auf Gesetz, Gesellschaftsvertrag oder Satzung beruhende Pflichten der Gesellschaft, den Jahresabschluss, den Einzelabschluss nach Absatz 2a, den Lagebericht, den Konzernabschluss oder den Konzernlagebericht in anderer Weise bekannt zu machen, einzureichen oder Personen zugänglich zu machen, bleiben unberührt.

(5) Duties of the company based on statute or the articles of association to publish, to file, or to make accessible to persons the annual financial statements, the individual financial statements according to Subsection 2a, the management report, the consolidated financial statements, or the consolidated management report in another way remain unaffected.

[...]

[...]

D. Stock Corporation Act (*Aktiengesetz*) (Excerpt)

§ 17 Abhängige und herrschende Unternehmen

(1) Abhängige Unternehmen sind rechtlich selbständige Unternehmen, auf die ein anderes Unternehmen (herrschendes Unternehmen) unmittelbar oder mittelbar einen beherrschenden Einfluß ausüben kann.

(2) Von einem in Mehrheitsbesitz stehenden Unternehmen wird vermutet, daß es von dem an ihm mit Mehrheit beteiligten Unternehmen abhängig ist.

§ 17 Controlled and Controlling Undertakings

(1) Controlled undertakings are legally independent undertakings over which another undertaking (controlling undertaking) can directly or indirectly exercise a controlling influence.

(2) It is presumed that a majority-held undertaking is controlled by the undertaking holding a majority interest in it.

§ 291 Beherrschungsvertrag. Gewinnabführungsvertrag

(1) Unternehmensverträge sind Verträge, durch die eine Aktiengesellschaft oder Kommanditgesellschaft auf Aktien die Leitung ihrer Gesellschaft einem anderen Unternehmen unterstellt (Beherrschungsvertrag) oder sich verpflichtet, ihren ganzen Gewinn an ein anderes Unternehmen abzuführen (Gewinnabführungsvertrag). Als Vertrag über die Abführung des ganzen Gewinns gilt auch ein Vertrag, durch den eine Aktiengesellschaft oder Kommanditgesellschaft auf Aktien es übernimmt, ihr Unternehmen für Rechnung eines anderen Unternehmens zu führen.

(2) Stellen sich Unternehmen, die voneinander nicht abhängig sind, durch Vertrag unter einheitliche Leitung, ohne daß dadurch eines von ihnen von einem anderen vertragschließenden Unternehmen abhängig wird, so ist dieser Vertrag kein Beherrschungsvertrag.

[...]

§ 291 Control Agreement. Profit Transfer Agreement

(1) Affiliation agreements are agreements through which a stock corporation or a partnership limited by shares subjects the governance of its company to another undertaking (control agreement), or obligates itself to transfer its entire profit to another undertaking (profit transfer agreement). An agreement through which a stock corporation or partnership limited by shares undertakes to manage its undertaking for the account of another undertaking is also regarded as an agreement on the transfer of the entire profit.

(2) If undertakings that are not dependent on each other subject themselves to unified governance without one of them thereby becoming dependent on another contracting undertaking, then this agreement is not a control agreement.

[...]

§ 296 Aufhebung

(1) Ein Unternehmensvertrag kann nur zum Ende des Geschäftsjahrs oder des

§ 296 Cancellation

(1) An affiliation agreement can only be cancelled at the end of the fiscal year

sonst vertraglich bestimmten Abrechnungszeitraums aufgehoben werden. Eine rückwirkende Aufhebung ist unzulässig. Die Aufhebung bedarf der schriftlichen Form.

or other contractually determined accounting period. A retroactive cancellation is impermissible. The cancellation must be in writing.

[...]

[...]

§ 302 Verlustübernahme

§ 302 Assumption of Losses

(1) Besteht ein Beherrschungs- oder ein Gewinnabführungsvertrag, so hat der andere Vertragsteil jeden während der Vertragsdauer sonst entstehenden Jahresfehlbetrag auszugleichen, soweit dieser nicht dadurch ausgeglichen wird, daß den anderen Gewinnrücklagen Beträge entnommen werden, die während der Vertragsdauer in sie eingestellt worden sind.

(1) If there is a control or a profit transfer agreement, then the other contracting party has to compensate each annual deficit during the term of the contract, insofar as this is not compensated with amounts taken from other retained earnings that were allocated to them during the term of the contract.

[...]

[...]

§ 304 Angemessener Ausgleich

§ 304 Adequate Compensation

(1) Ein Gewinnabführungsvertrag muß einen angemessenen Ausgleich für die außenstehenden Aktionäre durch eine auf die Anteile am Grundkapital bezogene wiederkehrende Geldleistung (Ausgleichszahlung) vorsehen. Ein Beherrschungsvertrag muß, wenn die Gesellschaft nicht auch zur Abführung ihres ganzen Gewinns verpflichtet ist, den außenstehenden Aktionären als angemessenen Ausgleich einen bestimmten jährlichen Gewinnanteil nach der für die Ausgleichszahlung bestimmten Höhe garantieren. Von der Bestimmung eines angemessenen Ausgleichs kann nur abgesehen werden, wenn die Gesellschaft im Zeitpunkt der Beschlußfassung ihrer Hauptversammlung über den Vertrag keinen außenstehenden Aktionär hat.

(1) A profit transfer agreement must provide for adequate compensation for the outside shareholders through a recurring cash payment based on the shares of the share capital (compensation payment). A control agreement must, if the company is not also obligated to transfer its entire profit, guarantee a certain annual share of the profit based on the amount determined for the compensation payment to the outside shareholders as adequate compensation. A determination of adequate compensation may only be disregarded if the company does not have any outside shareholders at the point in time of the resolution of its shareholder meeting on the agreement.

(2) Als Ausgleichszahlung ist mindestens die jährliche Zahlung des Betrags zuzusichern, der nach der bisherigen Ertragslage der Gesellschaft und ihren künftigen Ertragsaussichten unter Berücksichtigung angemessener Abschreibungen und Wertberichtigungen, jedoch ohne Bildung anderer Gewinnrücklagen, voraussicht-

(2) As compensation payment, at least the annual payment of the amount must be ensured that prospectively could be distributed to the individual shares as an average share of the profits according to the previous earnings position of the company and its future earnings prospects, considering adequate write-offs

lich als durchschnittlicher Gewinnanteil auf die einzelne Aktie verteilt werden könnte.

[...]

§ 305 Abfindung

(1) Außer der Verpflichtung zum Ausgleich nach § 304 muß ein Beherrschungs- oder ein Gewinnabführungsvertrag die Verpflichtung des anderen Vertragsteils enthalten, auf Verlangen eines außenstehenden Aktionärs dessen Aktien gegen eine im Vertrag bestimmte angemessene Abfindung zu erwerben.

[...]

§ 308 Leitungsmacht

(1) Besteht ein Beherrschungsvertrag, so ist das herrschende Unternehmen berechtigt, dem Vorstand der Gesellschaft hinsichtlich der Leitung der Gesellschaft Weisungen zu erteilen. Bestimmt der Vertrag nichts anderes, so können auch Weisungen erteilt werden, die für die Gesellschaft nachteilig sind, wenn sie den Belangen des herrschenden Unternehmens oder der mit ihm und der Gesellschaft konzernverbundenen Unternehmen dienen.

(2) Der Vorstand ist verpflichtet, die Weisungen des herrschenden Unternehmens zu befolgen. Er ist nicht berechtigt, die Befolgung einer Weisung zu verweigern, weil sie nach seiner Ansicht nicht den Belangen des herrschenden Unternehmens oder der mit ihm und der Gesellschaft konzernverbundenen Unternehmen dient, es sei denn, daß sie offensichtlich nicht diesen Belangen dient.

(3) Wird der Vorstand angewiesen, ein Geschäft vorzunehmen, das nur mit Zustimmung des Aufsichtsrats der Gesellschaft vorgenommen werden darf, und wird diese Zustimmung nicht innerhalb einer angemessenen Frist erteilt, so hat der

and value adjustments, but without the accumulation of other retained earnings.

[...]

§ 305 Compensation

(1) Other than the obligation to compensate according to § 304, a control or profit transfer agreement must contain an obligation of the other contracting party, upon demand of an outside shareholder, to acquire his shares against payment of adequate compensation determined in the agreement.

[...]

§ 308 Power to Instruct

(1) If there is a control agreement, then the controlling undertaking is authorized to issue instructions to the management board of the company in relation to the management of the company. If the agreement does not provide otherwise, then instructions that are detrimental to the company can also be issued if they serve the interests of the controlling undertaking or of undertakings affiliated with the same group as the controlling undertaking and the company.

(2) The management board is obligated to follow the instructions of the controlling undertaking. It is not authorized to refuse to follow an instruction because, in its opinion, the instruction does not serve the interests of the controlling undertaking or of undertakings affiliated with the same group as the controlling undertaking and the company, unless it obviously does not serve these interests.

(3) If the management board is instructed to carry out a transaction that may only be made with the consent of the supervisory board, and if this consent is not given within a reasonable period, then the management board has to notify

Vorstand dies dem herrschenden Unternehmen mitzuteilen. Wiederholt das herrschende Unternehmen nach dieser Mitteilung die Weisung, so ist die Zustimmung des Aufsichtsrats nicht mehr erforderlich; die Weisung darf, wenn das herrschende Unternehmen einen Aufsichtsrat hat, nur mit dessen Zustimmung wiederholt werden.

the controlling undertaking of this. If, following this notification, the controlling undertaking repeats the instruction, then the consent of the supervisory board is not required; if the controlling undertaking has a supervisory board, then the instruction may only be repeated with its consent.

§ 311 Schranken des Einflusses

(1) Besteht kein Beherrschungsvertrag, so darf ein herrschendes Unternehmen seinen Einfluß nicht dazu benutzen, eine abhängige Aktiengesellschaft oder Kommanditgesellschaft auf Aktien zu veranlassen, ein für sie nachteiliges Rechtsgeschäft vorzunehmen oder Maßnahmen zu ihrem Nachteil zu treffen oder zu unterlassen, es sei denn, daß die Nachteile ausgeglichen werden.

[...]

§ 311 Limits of Influence

(1) If there is no control agreement, then a controlling undertaking may not use its influence to cause a dependent stock corporation or partnership limited by shares to carry out a detrimental legal transaction or to take or fail to take measures to its detriment, unless the detriment is compensated.

[...]

§ 317 Verantwortlichkeit des herrschenden Unternehmens und seiner gesetzlichen Vertreter

(1) Veranlaßt ein herrschendes Unternehmen eine abhängige Gesellschaft, mit der kein Beherrschungsvertrag besteht, ein für sie nachteiliges Rechtsgeschäft vorzunehmen oder zu ihrem Nachteil eine Maßnahme zu treffen oder zu unterlassen, ohne daß es den Nachteil bis zum Ende des Geschäftsjahrs tatsächlich ausgleicht oder der abhängigen Gesellschaft einen Rechtsanspruch auf einen zum Ausgleich bestimmten Vorteil gewährt, so ist es der Gesellschaft zum Ersatz des ihr daraus entstehenden Schadens verpflichtet. Es ist auch den Aktionären zum Ersatz des ihnen daraus entstehenden Schadens verpflichtet, soweit sie, abgesehen von einem Schaden, der ihnen durch Schädigung der Gesellschaft zugefügt worden ist, geschädigt worden sind.

[...]

§ 317 Responsibility of the controlling undertaking and its statutory representatives

(1) If a controlling undertaking causes a dependent company, with which there is no control agreement, to carry out a legal transaction detrimental to it, or to take or fail to take a measure to its detriment, without actually compensating the detriment before the end of the fiscal year or granting to the dependent company a legal claim to a benefit designated for the compensation, then it is obligated to compensate the company for the damages resulting therefrom. It is also obligated to compensate the shareholders for damages resulting therefrom, insofar as they are damaged, disregarding damage inflicted on them through damages to the company.

[...]

E. Insolvency Code (*Insolvenzordnung*) (Excerpt)

Erster Teil. Allgemeine Vorschriften

§ 1 Ziele des Insolvenzverfahrens

Das Insolvenzverfahren dient dazu, die Gläubiger eines Schuldners gemeinschaftlich zu befriedigen, indem das Vermögen des Schuldners verwertet und der Erlös verteilt oder in einem Insolvenzplan eine abweichende Regelung insbesondere zum Erhalt des Unternehmens getroffen wird. Dem redlichen Schuldner wird Gelegenheit gegeben, sich von seinen restlichen Verbindlichkeiten zu befreien.

§ 3a Gruppen-Gerichtsstand

(1) Auf Antrag eines Schuldners, der einer Unternehmensgruppe im Sinne von § 3e angehört (gruppenangehöriger Schuldner), erklärt sich das angerufene Insolvenzgericht für die Insolvenzverfahren über die anderen gruppenangehörigen Schuldner (Gruppen-Folgeverfahren) für zuständig, wenn in Bezug auf den Schuldner ein zulässiger Eröffnungsantrag vorliegt und der Schuldner nicht offensichtlich von untergeordneter Bedeutung für die gesamte Unternehmensgruppe ist. [...]

§ 3e Unternehmensgruppe

(1) Eine Unternehmensgruppe im Sinne dieses Gesetzes besteht aus rechtlich selbständigen Unternehmen, die den Mittelpunkt ihrer hauptsächlichen Interessen im Inland haben und die unmittelbar oder mittelbar miteinander verbunden sind durch

1. die Möglichkeit der Ausübung eines beherrschenden Einflusses oder

Part One. General Provisions

§ 1 Objectives of the Insolvency Proceeding

The insolvency proceeding serves to satisfy the creditors of the debtor collectively by disposing of the assets of the debtor and distributing the proceeds, or by making a different arrangement in an insolvency plan, particularly for the survival of the business. The honest debtor is given the opportunity to discharge himself from his remaining liabilities.

§ 3a Group Jurisdiction

(1) Upon petition of a debtor that belongs to a group of undertakings within the meaning of § 3e (debtor belonging to the group), the insolvency court seised declares itself competent for the insolvency proceeding of the other debtors belonging to the group (group follow-on proceedings) if, with respect to the debtor, a permissible initiating petition has been presented and the debtor is not obviously of subordinate importance for the entire group of undertakings. [...]

§ 3e Group of Undertakings

(1) A group of undertakings within the meaning of this Act is composed of legally independent undertakings that have the center of their principal interests in Germany and that are directly or indirectly affiliated through

1. the possibility to exercise a controlling influence or

2. eine Zusammenfassung unter einheitlicher Leitung.

(2) Als Unternehmensgruppe im Sinne des Absatzes 1 gelten auch eine Gesellschaft und ihre persönlich haftenden Gesellschafter, wenn zu diesen weder eine natürliche Person noch eine Gesellschaft zählt, an der eine natürliche Person als persönlich haftender Gesellschafter beteiligt ist, oder sich die Verbindung von Gesellschaften in dieser Art fortsetzt.

2. a concentration under common control.

(2) A company and its personally liable members also constitute a group of undertakings within the meaning of Subsection 1 if they do not include a natural person or a company in which a natural person participates as a personally liable member, or the combination of companies proceeds in this way.

Zweiter Teil. Eröffnung des Insolvenzverfahrens. Erfaßtes Vermögen und Verfahrensbeteiligte

Part Two. Initiation of the Insolvency Proceedings. Subject Assets and Parties to the Proceeding

Erster Abschnitt. Eröffnungsvoraussetzungen und Eröffnungsverfahren

Chapter 1. Requirements for Initiation and Initiation Proceeding

§ 11 Zulässigkeit des Insolvenzverfahrens

(1) Ein Insolvenzverfahren kann über das Vermögen jeder natürlichen und jeder juristischen Person eröffnet werden. [...]

[...]

§ 11 Permissibility of the Insolvency Proceeding

(1) An insolvency proceeding may be initiated concerning the assets of each natural person and each legal person. [...]

[...]

§ 13 Eröffnungsantrag

(1) Das Insolvenzverfahren wird nur auf schriftlichen Antrag eröffnet. Antragsberechtigt sind die Gläubiger und der Schuldner. Dem Antrag des Schuldners ist ein Verzeichnis der Gläubiger und ihrer Forderungen beizufügen. Wenn der Schuldner einen Geschäftsbetrieb hat, der nicht eingestellt ist, sollen in dem Verzeichnis besonders kenntlich gemacht werden

1. die höchsten Forderungen,

2. die höchsten gesicherten Forderungen,

3. die Forderungen der Finanzverwaltung,

4. die Forderungen der Sozialversicherungsträger sowie

§ 13 Petition for Initiation

(1) The insolvency proceeding is only initiated upon a written petition. The creditors and the debtor are entitled to file such a petition. A list of the creditors and their claims is to be appended to the debtor's petition. If the debtor has business operations that have not been ceased, then the list shall indicate in particular

1. the highest claims,

2. the highest secured claims,

3. the claims of the fiscal authority,

4. the claims of the social insurance agencies, and

5. die Forderungen aus betrieblicher Altersversorgung.

Der Schuldner hat in diesem Fall auch Angaben zur Bilanzsumme, zu den Umsatzerlösen und zur durchschnittlichen Zahl der Arbeitnehmer des vorangegangenen Geschäftsjahres zu machen. Die Angaben nach Satz 4 sind verpflichtend, wenn

1. der Schuldner Eigenverwaltung beantragt,

2. der Schuldner die Merkmale des § 22a Absatz 1 erfüllt oder

3. die Einsetzung eines vorläufigen Gläubigerausschusses beantragt wurde.

Dem Verzeichnis nach Satz 3 und den Angaben nach den Sätzen 4 und 5 ist die Erklärung beizufügen, dass die enthaltenen Angaben richtig und vollständig sind.

(2) Der Antrag kann zurückgenommen werden, bis das Insolvenzverfahren eröffnet oder der Antrag rechtskräftig abgewiesen ist.

(3) Ist der Eröffnungsantrag unzulässig, so fordert das Insolvenzgericht den Antragsteller unverzüglich auf, den Mangel zu beheben und räumt ihm hierzu eine angemessene Frist ein.

[...]

5. the claims from company pension schemes.

In this case the debtor also has to disclose information on the balance sheet total, revenues and average number of employees in the preceding fiscal year. The information in Sentence 4 is obligatory if

1. the debtor applies for self-administration,

2. the debtor fulfills the requirements of § 22a(1) or

3. the appointment of a preliminary creditor committee was applied for.

A declaration that the included information is correct and complete is to be appended to the list under Sentence 3 and to the information under Sentences 4 and 5.

(2) The petition may be withdrawn until the insolvency proceeding is initiated or a refusal of the petition becomes res judicata.

(3) If the initiating petition is impermissible, then the insolvency court requests without undue delay the petitioner to cure the defect and grants him an appropriate period therefor.

[...]

§ 15 Antragsrecht bei juristischen Personen und Gesellschaften ohne Rechtspersönlichkeit

(1) Zum Antrag auf Eröffnung eines Insolvenzverfahrens über das Vermögen einer juristischen Person oder einer Gesellschaft ohne Rechtspersönlichkeit ist außer den Gläubigern jedes Mitglied des Vertretungsorgans, bei einer Gesellschaft ohne Rechtspersönlichkeit oder bei einer Kommanditgesellschaft auf Aktien jeder persönlich haftende Gesellschafter, sowie jeder Abwickler berechtigt. Bei einer

§ 15 Right to File a Petition with respect to Legal Persons and Companies without Legal Personality

(1) In addition to the creditors, each member of the representative body and, with respect to a company without legal personality or with respect to a partnership limited by shares, each personally liable member, as well as each liquidator, is entitled to file a petition for the initiation of an insolvency proceeding concerning the assets of a legal person or a company without legal personality. With

juristischen Person ist im Fall der Führungslosigkeit auch jeder Gesellschafter, bei einer Aktiengesellschaft oder einer Genossenschaft zudem auch jedes Mitglied des Aufsichtsrats zur Antragstellung berechtigt.

(2) Wird der Antrag nicht von allen Mitgliedern des Vertretungsorgans, allen persönlich haftenden Gesellschaftern, allen Gesellschaftern der juristischen Person, allen Mitgliedern des Aufsichtsrats oder allen Abwicklern gestellt, so ist er zulässig, wenn der Eröffnungsgrund glaubhaft gemacht wird. Zusätzlich ist bei Antragstellung durch Gesellschafter einer juristischen Person oder Mitglieder des Aufsichtsrats auch die Führungslosigkeit glaubhaft zu machen. Das Insolvenzgericht hat die übrigen Mitglieder des Vertretungsorgans, persönlich haftenden Gesellschafter, Gesellschafter der juristischen Person, Mitglieder des Aufsichtsrats oder Abwickler zu hören.

(3) Ist bei einer Gesellschaft ohne Rechtspersönlichkeit kein persönlich haftender Gesellschafter eine natürliche Person, so gelten die Absätze 1 und 2 entsprechend für die organschaftlichen Vertreter und die Abwickler der zur Vertretung der Gesellschaft ermächtigten Gesellschafter. Entsprechendes gilt, wenn sich die Verbindung von Gesellschaften in dieser Art fortsetzt.

§ 15a Antragspflicht bei juristischen Personen und Gesellschaften ohne Rechtspersönlichkeit

(1) Wird eine juristische Person zahlungsunfähig oder überschuldet, haben die Mitglieder des Vertretungsorgans oder die Abwickler ohne schuldhaftes Zögern, spätestens aber drei Wochen nach Eintritt der Zahlungsunfähigkeit oder Überschuldung, einen Eröffnungsantrag zu stellen. Das Gleiche gilt für die organschaftlichen Vertreter der zur Vertretung der Gesellschaft ermächtigten

respect to a legal person, each member and, with respect to a stock corporation or a cooperative society, also each member of the supervisory board, is entitled to file a petition in the case of leadershiplessness.

(2) If the petition is not filed by all members of the representative body, by all personally liable members, by all members of the legal person, by all members of the supervisory board, or by all liquidators, then the petition is permissible if the reason for initiation is credibly shown. Additionally, upon the filing of a petition by members of a legal person or by members of the supervisory board, the leadershiplessness is also to be credibly shown. The insolvency court must hear the remaining members of the representative body, personally liable members, members of the legal person, members of the supervisory board, or liquidators.

(3) If, with respect to a company without legal personality, no personally liable member is a natural person, then Subsections 1 and 2 apply to the representatives belonging to a body and to the liquidators of the members authorized to represent the company accordingly. The same applies if the affiliation of companies persists in such a manner.

§ 15a Duty to File a Petition with respect to Legal Persons and Companies without Legal Personality

(1) If a legal person becomes illiquid or over-indebted, then the members of the representative body or the liquidators must file an initiating petition without undue delay, but no later than three weeks after the occurrence of the illiquidity or over-indebtedness. With respect to a company without legal personality, of which no personally liable member is a natural person, the same

Gesellschafter oder die Abwickler bei einer Gesellschaft ohne Rechtspersönlichkeit, bei der kein persönlich haftender Gesellschafter eine natürliche Person ist; dies gilt nicht, wenn zu den persönlich haftenden Gesellschaftern eine andere Gesellschaft gehört, bei der ein persönlich haftender Gesellschafter eine natürliche Person ist.

(2) Bei einer Gesellschaft im Sinne des Absatzes 1 Satz 2 gilt Absatz 1 sinngemäß, wenn die organschaftlichen Vertreter der zur Vertretung der Gesellschaft ermächtigten Gesellschafter ihrerseits Gesellschaften sind, bei denen kein persönlich haftender Gesellschafter eine natürliche Person ist, oder sich die Verbindung von Gesellschaften in dieser Art fortsetzt.

(3) Im Fall der Führungslosigkeit einer Gesellschaft mit beschränkter Haftung ist auch jeder Gesellschafter, im Fall der Führungslosigkeit einer Aktiengesellschaft oder einer Genossenschaft ist auch jedes Mitglied des Aufsichtsrats zur Stellung des Antrags verpflichtet, es sei denn, diese Person hat von der Zahlungsunfähigkeit und der Überschuldung oder der Führungslosigkeit keine Kenntnis.

(4) Mit Freiheitsstrafe bis zu drei Jahren oder mit Geldstrafe wird bestraft, wer entgegen Absatz 1 Satz 1, auch in Verbindung mit Satz 2 oder Absatz 2 oder Absatz 3, einen Eröffnungsantrag

1. nicht oder nicht rechtzeitig stellt oder

2. nicht richtig stellt.

(5) Handelt der Täter in den Fällen des Absatzes 4 fahrlässig, ist die Strafe Freiheitsstrafe bis zu einem Jahr oder Geldstrafe.

applies for the representatives belonging to a body of the members authorized to represent the company or to the liquidators; this does not apply if another company, of which one personally liable member is a natural person, belongs to the personally liable members.

(2) With respect to a company within the meaning of Subsection 1, Sentence 2, Subsection 1 applies accordingly if the representatives belonging to a body of the members authorized to represent the company are themselves companies, of which no personally liable member is a natural person, or if the affiliation of companies persists in such a manner.

(3) In the case of the leadershiplessness of a company with limited liability, also each member, and in the case of the leadershiplessness of a stock corporation or of a cooperative society, also each member of the supervisory board, is obligated to file the petition, unless this person had no knowledge of the illiquidity and the over-indebtedness or of the leadershiplessness.

(4) A person who, contrary to Subsection 1, Sentence 1, also in connection with Sentence 2 or Subsection 2 or Subsection 3,

1. does not file, or does not file on time, or

2. does not correctly file

an initiating petition, will be punished with a term of imprisonment of up to three years or with a fine.

(5) If, in the cases of Subsection 4, the offender acts negligently, then the punishment will be a term of imprisonment of up to one year or a fine.

(6) Im Falle des Absatzes 4 Nummer 2, auch in Verbindung mit Absatz 5, ist die Tat nur strafbar, wenn der Eröffnungsantrag rechtskräftig als unzulässig zurückgewiesen wurde.

[...]

§ 16 Eröffnungsgrund

Die Eröffnung des Insolvenzverfahrens setzt voraus, daß ein Eröffnungsgrund gegeben ist.

§ 17 Zahlungsunfähigkeit

(1) Allgemeiner Eröffnungsgrund ist die Zahlungsunfähigkeit.

(2) Der Schuldner ist zahlungsunfähig, wenn er nicht in der Lage ist, die fälligen Zahlungspflichten zu erfüllen. Zahlungsunfähigkeit ist in der Regel anzunehmen, wenn der Schuldner seine Zahlungen eingestellt hat.

§ 18 Drohende Zahlungsunfähigkeit

(1) Beantragt der Schuldner die Eröffnung des Insolvenzverfahrens, so ist auch die drohende Zahlungsunfähigkeit Eröffnungsgrund.

(2) Der Schuldner droht zahlungsunfähig zu werden, wenn er voraussichtlich nicht in der Lage sein wird, die bestehenden Zahlungspflichten im Zeitpunkt der Fälligkeit zu erfüllen.

(3) Wird bei einer juristischen Person oder einer Gesellschaft ohne Rechtspersönlichkeit der Antrag nicht von allen Mitgliedern des Vertretungsorgans, allen persönlich haftenden Gesellschaftern oder allen Abwicklern gestellt, so ist Absatz 1 nur anzuwenden, wenn der oder die Antragsteller zur Vertretung der juristischen Person oder der Gesellschaft berechtigt sind.

(6) In the case of Subsection 4, No. 2, also in connection with Subsection 5, the offense is only punishable if the initiating petition was finally rejected as impermissible.

[...]

§ 16 Reasons for Initiation

The initiation of the insolvency proceeding requires that a reason for initiation exists.

§ 17 Illiquidity

(1) The general reason for initiation is illiquidity.

(2) The debtor is illiquid if he is not able to fulfill the payment obligations as they become due. As a rule, illiquidity is to be assumed if the debtor has ceased his payments.

§ 18 Imminent Illiquidity

(1) If the debtor files the petition for the initiation of an insolvency proceeding, then imminent illiquidity is also a reason for initiation.

(2) The debtor is imminently illiquid if it is expected that he will not be able to fulfill the existing payment obligations when they become due.

(3) If, with respect to a legal person or a company without legal personality, the petition is not filed by all members of the representative body, by all personally liable members, or by all liquidators, then Subsection 1 is only to be applied if the petitioner(s) are entitled to represent the legal person or the company.

§ 19 Überschuldung

(1) Bei einer juristischen Person ist auch die Überschuldung Eröffnungsgrund.

(2) Überschuldung liegt vor, wenn das Vermögen des Schuldners die bestehenden Verbindlichkeiten nicht mehr deckt, es sei denn, die Fortführung des Unternehmens ist nach den Umständen überwiegend wahrscheinlich. Forderungen auf Rückgewähr von Gesellschafterdarlehen oder aus Rechtshandlungen, die einem solchen Darlehen wirtschaftlich entsprechen, für die gemäß § 39 Abs. 2 zwischen Gläubiger und Schuldner der Nachrang im Insolvenzverfahren hinter den in § 39 Abs. 1 Nr. 1 bis 5 bezeichneten Forderungen vereinbart worden ist, sind nicht bei den Verbindlichkeiten nach Satz 1 zu berücksichtigen.

(3) Ist bei einer Gesellschaft ohne Rechtspersönlichkeit kein persönlich haftender Gesellschafter eine natürliche Person, so gelten die Absätze 1 und 2 entsprechend. Dies gilt nicht, wenn zu den persönlich haftenden Gesellschaftern eine andere Gesellschaft gehört, bei der ein persönlich haftender Gesellschafter eine natürliche Person ist.

§ 19 Over-indebtedness

(1) Over-indebtedness is also a reason for initiation with respect to a legal person.

(2) Over-indebtedness exists if the assets of the debtor no longer cover the existing liabilities, unless the continuation of the business is, according to the circumstances, more likely than not. Claims to repayment of member loans or from legal acts that are economically equivalent to such a loan, for which the subordination in the insolvency proceeding behind the claims designated in § 39(1), No. 1 to 5 has been agreed to between the creditor and the debtor according to § 39(2), are not to be considered as liabilities in the sense of Sentence 1.

(3) If, in a company without legal personality, no personally liable member is a natural person, then Subsections 1 and 2 apply accordingly. This does not apply if another company, of which one personally liable member is a natural person, belongs to the personally liable members.

§ 26 Abweisung mangels Masse

(1) Das Insolvenzgericht weist den Antrag auf Eröffnung des Insolvenzverfahrens ab, wenn das Vermögen des Schuldners voraussichtlich nicht ausreichen wird, um die Kosten des Verfahrens zu decken. [...]

[...]

(4) Zur Leistung eines Vorschusses nach Absatz 1 Satz 2 ist jede Person verpflichtet, die entgegen den Vorschriften des Insolvenz- oder Gesellschaftsrechts pflichtwidrig und schuldhaft keinen Antrag auf Eröffnung des Insolvenzverfahrens gestellt hat. Ist streitig, ob die

§ 26 Refusal for Lack of Funds

(1) The insolvency court shall refuse the petition to initiate the insolvency proceeding if the assets of the debtor are expected to be insufficient to cover the costs of the proceeding. [...]

[...]

(4) Each person that, contrary to the provisions of insolvency or company law, in breach of duty and culpably did not file a petition for the initiation of insolvency proceedings, is obligated to make an advance payment under Subsection 1, Sentence 2. If whether the person

Person pflichtwidrig und schuldhaft gehandelt hat, so trifft sie die Beweislast. Die Zahlung des Vorschusses kann der vorläufige Insolvenzverwalter sowie jede Person verlangen, die einen begründeten Vermögensanspruch gegen den Schuldner hat.

acted in breach of duty and culpably is in dispute, then the person bears the burden of proof. The advance payment can be demanded by the preliminary insolvency receiver and each person that has a justified claim to the assets against the debtor.

§ 31 Handels-, Genossenschafts-, Partnerschafts- und Vereinsregister

Ist der Schuldner im Handels-, Genossenschafts-, Partnerschafts- oder Vereinsregister eingetragen, so hat die Geschäftsstelle des Insolvenzgerichts dem Registergericht zu übermitteln:

1. im Falle der Eröffnung des Insolvenzverfahrens eine Ausfertigung des Eröffnungsbeschlusses;

2. im Falle der Abweisung des Eröffnungsantrags mangels Masse eine Ausfertigung des abweisenden Beschlusses, wenn der Schuldner eine juristische Person oder eine Gesellschaft ohne Rechtspersönlichkeit ist, die durch die Abweisung mangels Masse aufgelöst wird.

§ 31 Commercial Register, Cooperative Society Register, Partnership Register, and Association Register

If the debtor is entered in the commercial register (*Handelsregister*), cooperative society register (*Genossenschaftsregister*), partnership register (*Partnerschaftsregister*), or association register (*Vereinsregister*), then the clerk of the insolvency court shall deliver to the court of registry:

1. in the case of initiation of an insolvency proceeding, an official copy of the order for the initiation;

2. in the case of the refusal of the petition for initiation for lack of funds, an official copy of the order of refusal, if the debtor is a legal person or a company without legal personality that is dissolved by the refusal for lack of funds.

Zweiter Abschnitt. Insolvenzmasse. Einteilung der Gläubiger

§ 38 Begriff der Insolvenzgläubiger

Die Insolvenzmasse dient zur Befriedigung der persönlichen Gläubiger, die einen zur Zeit der Eröffnung des Insolvenzverfahrens begründeten Vermögensanspruch gegen den Schuldner haben (Insolvenzgläubiger).

§ 39 Nachrangige Insolvenzgläubiger

(1) Im Rang nach den übrigen Forderungen der Insolvenzgläubiger werden in

Chapter 2. Insolvency Estate. Classification of Creditors

§ 38 Definition of the Insolvency Creditors

The insolvency estate serves to satisfy the personal creditors that have claims to the assets against the debtor established at the time of the initiation of the insolvency proceeding (insolvency creditors).

§ 39 Subordinated Insolvency Creditors

(1) In priority after the other claims of the insolvency creditors, the following

folgender Rangfolge, bei gleichem Rang nach dem Verhältnis ihrer Beträge, berichtigt:

[...]

5. nach Maßgabe der Absätze 4 und 5 Forderungen auf Rückgewähr eines Gesellschafterdarlehens oder Forderungen aus Rechtshandlungen, die einem solchen Darlehen wirtschaftlich entsprechen.

[...]

(4) Absatz 1 Nr. 5 gilt für Gesellschaften, die weder eine natürliche Person noch eine Gesellschaft als persönlich haftenden Gesellschafter haben, bei der ein persönlich haftender Gesellschafter eine natürliche Person ist. Erwirbt ein Gläubiger bei drohender oder eingetretener Zahlungsunfähigkeit der Gesellschaft oder bei Überschuldung Anteile zum Zweck ihrer Sanierung, führt dies bis zur nachhaltigen Sanierung nicht zur Anwendung von Absatz 1 Nr. 5 auf seine Forderungen aus bestehenden oder neu gewährten Darlehen oder auf Forderungen aus Rechtshandlungen, die einem solchen Darlehen wirtschaftlich entsprechen.

(5) Absatz 1 Nr. 5 gilt nicht für den nicht geschäftsführenden Gesellschafter einer Gesellschaft im Sinne des Absatzes 4 Satz 1, der mit 10 Prozent oder weniger am Haftkapital beteiligt ist.

§ 44a Gesicherte Darlehen

In dem Insolvenzverfahren über das Vermögen einer Gesellschaft kann ein Gläubiger nach Maßgabe des § 39 Abs. 1 Nr. 5 für eine Forderung auf Rückgewähr eines Darlehens oder für eine gleichgestellte Forderung, für die ein Gesellschafter eine Sicherheit bestellt oder für die er sich verbürgt hat, nur anteilsmäßige Befriedigung aus der Insolvenzmasse verlangen, soweit er bei der Inanspruchnahme der Sicherheit oder des Bürgen ausgefallen ist.

claims will be satisfied in the following order of priority and, if within the same level of priority, in proportion to their amounts:

[...]

5. in compliance with Subsections 4 and 5, claims to repayment of a member loan or claims arising from legal acts that are economically equivalent to such a loan.

[...]

(4) Subsection 1, No. 5 applies to companies that have, as a personally liable member, neither a natural person nor a company of which a natural person is a personally liable member. If a creditor acquires, upon imminent or occurred illiquidity of the company, or upon overindebtedness, equity interests for the purpose of the company's restructuring, then this does not lead to the application of Subsection 1, No. 5 with regard to the creditor's claims from an existing or newly granted loan, or to claims from legal acts that are economically equivalent to such a loan, until the sustainable restructuring.

(5) Subsection 1, No. 5 does not apply to the member of a company within the meaning of Subsection 4, Sentence 1 who is not a managing director and who holds 10 percent or less of the equity.

§ 44a Secured Loans

In the insolvency proceeding concerning the assets of a company, a creditor, in compliance with § 39(1), No. 5, may, for a claim to repayment of a loan or for an equivalent claim, for which a member has provided a security or a guarantee, only demand proportionate satisfaction from the insolvency estate insofar as the creditor remained unsatisfied when laying claim to the security or the guarantee.

Dritter Teil. Wirkungen der Eröffnung des Insolvenzverfahrens

Dritter Abschnitt. Insolvenzanfechtung

§ 129 Grundsatz

(1) Rechtshandlungen, die vor der Eröffnung des Insolvenzverfahrens vorgenommen worden sind und die Insolvenzgläubiger benachteiligen, kann der Insolvenzverwalter nach Maßgabe der §§ 130 bis 146 anfechten.

(2) Eine Unterlassung steht einer Rechtshandlung gleich.

§ 135 Gesellschafterdarlehen

(1) Anfechtbar ist eine Rechtshandlung, die für die Forderung eines Gesellschafters auf Rückgewähr eines Darlehens im Sinne des § 39 Abs. 1 Nr. 5 oder für eine gleichgestellte Forderung

1. Sicherung gewährt hat, wenn die Handlung in den letzten zehn Jahren vor dem Antrag auf Eröffnung des Insolvenzverfahrens oder nach diesem Antrag vorgenommen worden ist, oder

2. Befriedigung gewährt hat, wenn die Handlung im letzten Jahr vor dem Eröffnungsantrag oder nach diesem Antrag vorgenommen worden ist.

(2) Anfechtbar ist eine Rechtshandlung, mit der eine Gesellschaft einem Dritten für eine Forderung auf Rückgewähr eines Darlehens innerhalb der in Absatz 1 Nr. 2 genannten Fristen Befriedigung gewährt hat, wenn ein Gesellschafter für die Forderung eine Sicherheit bestellt hatte oder als Bürge haftete; dies gilt sinngemäß für Leistungen auf Forderungen, die einem Darlehen wirtschaftlich entsprechen.

Part 3. Effect of Initiation of Insolvency Proceedings

Chapter 3. Insolvency Avoidance

§ 129 Basic Principle

(1) The insolvency receiver may avoid legal acts that have been performed before the initiation of the insolvency proceeding and that are a detriment to the insolvency creditors, in compliance with §§ 130 to 146.

(2) An omission is equivalent to a legal act.

§ 135 Member Loans

(1) A legal act that, for the claim of a member to repayment of a loan within the meaning of § 39(1), No. 5, or for an equivalent claim,

1. granted security, if the act was performed during the ten years prior to the petition for the initiation of the insolvency proceeding, or after this petition, or

2. granted satisfaction, if the act was performed during the last year prior to the petition for initiation, or after this petition,

is avoidable.

(2) A legal act with which a company granted, within the periods stated in Subsection 1, No. 2, satisfaction to a third party for a claim to repayment of a loan is avoidable if a member had provided security for the claim or was liable as a guarantor; this applies for payments of claims that are economically equivalent to a loan accordingly.

(3) Wurde dem Schuldner von einem Gesellschafter ein Gegenstand zum Gebrauch oder zur Ausübung überlassen, so kann der Aussonderungsanspruch während der Dauer des Insolvenzverfahrens, höchstens aber für eine Zeit von einem Jahr ab der Eröffnung des Insolvenzverfahrens nicht geltend gemacht werden, wenn der Gegenstand für die Fortführung des Unternehmens des Schuldners von erheblicher Bedeutung ist. Für den Gebrauch oder die Ausübung des Gegenstandes gebührt dem Gesellschafter ein Ausgleich; bei der Berechnung ist der Durchschnitt der im letzten Jahr vor Verfahrenseröffnung geleisteten Vergütung in Ansatz zu bringen, bei kürzerer Dauer der Überlassung ist der Durchschnitt während dieses Zeitraums maßgebend.

(3) If an item or a right was relinquished by a member to the debtor for use or exercise, then the right to separation may not be exercised for the duration of the insolvency proceeding, but, at the most, for the period of one year from the initiation of the insolvency proceeding, if the item is of substantial importance for the continuation of the business of the debtor. The member is entitled to compensation for the use or the exercise of the item or right; for the calculation of the compensation, the average payments rendered in the last year before the initiation of the proceeding is to be taken as the basis while, for a shorter duration, the average for this period of time is applicable.

(4) § 39 Abs. 4 und 5 gilt entsprechend.

(4) § 39(4) and (5) applies accordingly.

§ 143 Rechtsfolgen

§ 143 Legal Consequences

(1) Was durch die anfechtbare Handlung aus dem Vermögen des Schuldners veräußert, weggegeben oder aufgegeben ist, muß zur Insolvenzmasse zurückgewährt werden. Die Vorschriften über die Rechtsfolgen einer ungerechtfertigten Bereicherung, bei der dem Empfänger der Mangel des rechtlichen Grundes bekannt ist, gelten entsprechend. […]

(1) Whatever from the assets of the debtor is distributed, given away, or abandoned through the avoidable act must be returned to the insolvency estate. The provisions on the legal consequences of an unjust enrichment when the lack of legal basis is known to the recipient apply accordingly. […]

(2) [...]

(2) [...]

(3) Im Fall der Anfechtung nach § 135 Abs. 2 hat der Gesellschafter, der die Sicherheit bestellt hatte oder als Bürge haftete, die dem Dritten gewährte Leistung zur Insolvenzmasse zu erstatten. Die Verpflichtung besteht nur bis zur Höhe des Betrags, mit dem der Gesellschafter als Bürge haftete oder der dem Wert der von ihm bestellten Sicherheit im Zeitpunkt der Rückgewähr des Darlehens oder der Leistung auf die gleichgestellte Forderung entspricht. Der Gesellschafter wird von der Verpflichtung frei, wenn er

(3) In the case of an avoidance according to § 135(2), the member that had provided the security or was liable as guarantor must reimburse the insolvency estate for the payment made to the third party. The obligation only exists up to the amount for which the member was liable as guarantor or up to the value of the security provided by him at the point in time of the repayment of the loan or of the payment of the equivalent claim. The member will be free of the obligation if he places the item or right that served as

die Gegenstände, die dem Gläubiger als Sicherheit gedient hatten, der Insolvenzmasse zur Verfügung stellt.

security to the creditor at the disposal of the insolvency estate.

Sechster Teil. Insolvenzplan

Part 6. Insolvency Plan

§ 217 Grundsatz

Die Befriedigung der absonderungsberechtigten Gläubiger und der Insolvenzgläubiger, die Verwertung der Insolvenzmasse und deren Verteilung an die Beteiligten sowie die Verfahrensabwicklung und die Haftung des Schuldners nach der Beendigung des Insolvenzverfahrens können in einem Insolvenzplan abweichend von den Vorschriften dieses Gesetzes geregelt werden. Ist der Schuldner keine natürliche Person, so können auch die Anteils- oder Mitgliedschaftsrechte der am Schuldner beteiligten Personen in den Plan einbezogen werden.

§ 217 Basic Principle

The satisfaction of the creditors entitled to separate satisfaction and of the insolvency creditors, the disposal of the insolvency estate and its distribution to the participating parties, as well as the conduct of the proceedings and the liability of the debtor after the termination of the insolvency proceeding, may be governed by an insolvency plan deviating from the provisions of this Act. If the debtor is not a natural person, then the interest rights or membership rights of the persons holding participation interests in the debtor can be included in the plan.

§ 219 Gliederung des Plans

Der Insolvenzplan besteht aus dem darstellenden Teil und dem gestaltenden Teil. Ihm sind die in den §§ 229 und 230 genannten Anlagen beizufügen.

§ 219 Structure of the Plan

The insolvency plan consists of the descriptive part and the structuring part. The appendices specified in §§ 229 and 230 are to be appended to it.

§ 220 Darstellender Teil

(1) Im darstellenden Teil des Insolvenzplans wird beschrieben, welche Maßnahmen nach der Eröffnung des Insolvenzverfahrens getroffen worden sind oder noch getroffen werden sollen, um die Grundlagen für die geplante Gestaltung der Rechte der Beteiligten zu schaffen.

(2) Der darstellende Teil soll alle sonstigen Angaben zu den Grundlagen und den Auswirkungen des Plans enthalten, die für die Entscheidung der Beteiligten über die Zustimmung zum Plan und für dessen gerichtliche Bestätigung erheblich sind.

§ 220 Descriptive Part

(1) Which measures have been taken following the initiation of the insolvency proceedings or shall still be taken to achieve the basis for the planned structuring of the rights of the parties are described in the descriptive part of the insolvency plan.

(2) The descriptive part shall contain all other information on the basis and the consequences of the plan that are material to the decision of the parties to consent to the plan and for its confirmation by the court.

§ 221 Gestaltender Teil

Im gestaltenden Teil des Insolvenzplans wird festgelegt, wie die Rechtsstellung der Beteiligten durch den Plan geändert werden soll. Der Insolvenzverwalter kann durch den Plan bevollmächtigt werden, die zur Umsetzung notwendigen Maßnahmen zu ergreifen und offensichtliche Fehler des Plans zu berichtigen.

§ 221 Structuring Part

How the legal positions of the parties will be changed by the plan is determined in the structuring part of the insolvency plan. The insolvency receiver may be authorized in the plan to take measures necessary for implementation and to correct obvious errors of the plan.

§ 225a Rechte der Anteilsinhaber

(1) Die Anteils- oder Mitgliedschaftsrechte der am Schuldner beteiligten Personen bleiben vom Insolvenzplan unberührt, es sei denn, dass der Plan etwas anderes bestimmt.

(2) Im gestaltenden Teil des Plans kann vorgesehen werden, dass Forderungen von Gläubigern in Anteils- oder Mitgliedschaftsrechte am Schuldner umgewandelt werden. Eine Umwandlung gegen den Willen der betroffenen Gläubiger ist ausgeschlossen. Insbesondere kann der Plan eine Kapitalherabsetzung oder -erhöhung, die Leistung von Sacheinlagen, den Ausschluss von Bezugsrechten oder die Zahlung von Abfindungen an ausscheidende Anteilsinhaber vorsehen.

(3) Im Plan kann jede Regelung getroffen werden, die gesellschaftsrechtlich zulässig ist, insbesondere die Fortsetzung einer aufgelösten Gesellschaft oder die Übertragung von Anteils- oder Mitgliedschaftsrechten.

[…]

§ 225a Rights of Interestholders

(1) The interest rights or membership rights of the persons holding participation interests in the debtor remain unaffected by the insolvency plan, unless the plan provides otherwise.

(2) In the structuring part of the plan, it can be provided that claims of creditors are converted into interest rights or membership rights. A conversion against the will of the creditors concerned is prohibited. In particular, the plan can provide for a capital reduction or capital increase, the rendering of in-kind contributions, the exclusion of subscription rights, or the payment of compensation to exiting interestholders.

(3) Any provision can be made in the plan that is permissible under company law, particularly the continuation of a dissolved company or the transfer of interest rights or membership rights.

[…]

§ 238a Stimmrecht der Anteilsinhaber

(1) Das Stimmrecht der Anteilsinhaber des Schuldners bestimmt sich allein nach deren Beteiligung am gezeichneten Kapital oder Vermögen des Schuldners. Stimmrechtsbeschränkungen, Sonder- oder Mehrstimmrechte bleiben außer Betracht.

[…]

§ 238a Voting Rights of the Interestholders

(1) The voting rights of the interestholders of the debtor are solely determined by their participation in the capital subscribed or assets of the debtor. Limitations on voting rights, special or multiple voting rights are not considered.

[…]

Siebter Teil. Koordinierung der Verfahren von Schuldnern, die derselben Unternehmensgruppe angehören

§ 269a Zusammenarbeit der Insolvenzverwalter

Die Insolvenzverwalter gruppenangehöriger Schuldner sind untereinander zur Unterrichtung und Zusammenarbeit verpflichtet, soweit hierdurch nicht die Interessen der Beteiligten des Verfahrens beeinträchtigt werden, für das sie bestellt sind. Insbesondere haben sie auf Anforderung unverzüglich alle Informationen mitzuteilen, die für das andere Verfahren von Bedeutung sein können.

§ 269b Zusammenarbeit der Gerichte

Werden die Insolvenzverfahren über das Vermögen von gruppenangehörigen Schuldnern bei verschiedenen Insolvenzgerichten geführt, sind die Gerichte zur Zusammenarbeit und insbesondere zum Austausch der Informationen verpflichtet, die für das andere Verfahren von Bedeutung sein können. [...]

§ 269c Zusammenarbeit der Gläubigerausschüsse

(1) Auf Antrag eines Gläubigerausschusses, der in einem Verfahren über das Vermögen eines gruppenangehörigen Schuldners bestellt ist, kann das Gericht des Gruppen-Gerichtsstands nach Anhörung der anderen Gläubigerausschüsse einen Gruppen-Gläubigerausschuss einsetzen. Jeder Gläubigerausschuss oder vorläufige Gläubigerausschuss eines gruppenangehörigen Schuldners, der nicht von offensichtlich untergeordneter Bedeutung für die gesamte Unternehmensgruppe ist, stellt ein Mitglied des Gruppen-Gläubigerausschusses. Ein weiteres Mitglied dieses Ausschusses wird aus dem

Part 7. Coordination of the Proceedings of Debtors that Belong to the Same Group of Undertakings

§ 269a Cooperation of the Insolvency Receivers

The insolvency receivers of debtors belonging to the group are obligated to share information and cooperate, insofar as this does not prejudice the interests of the participants in the proceedings for which they were appointed. In particular, they must disclose without undue delay all information that may be of importance to the other proceeding upon request.

§ 269b Cooperation of the Courts

If the insolvency proceedings involving the assets of debtors belonging to the group are pending in different insolvency courts, then the courts are obligated to cooperate and, in particular, to exchange information that may be of importance to the other proceeding. [...]

§ 269c Cooperation of the Creditor Committees

(1) Upon petition of a creditor committee that has been appointed in a proceeding involving the assets of a debtor belonging to the group, the court with group jurisdiction, after hearing the other creditor committees, may appoint a creditor committee for the group. Each creditor committee or preliminary creditor committee of a debtor belonging to the group that is not obviously of subordinate importance for the entire group of undertakings appoints a member of the creditor committee for the group. An additional member of this committee will be appointed from the group of the repre-

Kreis der Vertreter der Arbeitnehmer bestimmt.

(2) Der Gruppen-Gläubigerausschuss unterstützt die Insolvenzverwalter und die Gläubigerausschüsse in den einzelnen Verfahren, um eine abgestimmte Abwicklung dieser Verfahren zu erleichtern.

[...]

§ 269d Koordinationsgericht

(1) Wird über die Vermögen von gruppenangehörigen Schuldnern die Eröffnung von Insolvenzverfahren beantragt oder wurden solche Verfahren eröffnet, kann das für die Eröffnung von Gruppen-Folgeverfahren zuständige Gericht (Koordinationsgericht) auf Antrag ein Koordinationsverfahren einleiten.

[...]

§ 269e Verfahrenskoordinator

(1) Das Koordinationsgericht bestellt eine von den gruppenangehörigen Schuldnern und deren Gläubigern unabhängige Person zum Verfahrenskoordinator. Die zu bestellende Person soll von den Insolvenzverwaltern und Sachwaltern der gruppenangehörigen Schuldner unabhängig sein. Die Bestellung eines gruppenangehörigen Schuldners ist ausgeschlossen.

[...]

§ 269f Aufgaben und Rechtsstellung des Verfahrenskoordinators

(1) Der Verfahrenskoordinator hat für eine abgestimmte Abwicklung der Verfahren über die gruppenangehörigen Schuldner zu sorgen, soweit dies im Interesse der Gläubiger liegt. Zu diesem Zweck kann er insbesondere einen Koordinationsplan vorlegen.

[...]

sentatives of the employees.

(2) The creditor committee for the group supports the insolvency receivers and the creditor committees in the individual proceedings in order to facilitate a coordinated conduct of these proceedings.

[...]

§ 269d Coordinating Court

(1) If the initiation of insolvency proceedings involving the assets of debtors belonging to the group has been petitioned, or if such proceedings were initiated, then upon petition the court competent for the initiation of group follow-on proceedings (coordinating court) may commence a coordination proceeding.

[...]

§ 269e Coordinator of the Proceedings

(1) The coordinating court appoints a person as coordinator of the proceedings that is independent of the debtors belonging to the group and their creditors. The person to be appointed shall be independent of the insolvency receivers and trustees of the debtors belonging to the group. The appointment of a debtor belonging to the group is prohibited.

[...]

§ 269f Responsibilities and Legal Status of the Coordinator of the Proceedings

(1) The coordinator of the proceedings has to ensure a coordinated conduct of the proceedings involving the debtors belonging to the group, insofar as this is in the interest of the creditors. In particular, he can submit a coordination plan for this purpose.

[...]

Achter Teil. Eigenverwaltung

§ 270 Voraussetzungen

(1) Der Schuldner ist berechtigt, unter der Aufsicht eines Sachwalters die Insolvenzmasse zu verwalten und über sie zu verfügen, wenn das Insolvenzgericht in dem Beschluß über die Eröffnung des Insolvenzverfahrens die Eigenverwaltung anordnet. [...]

§ 270b Vorbereitung einer Sanierung

(1) Hat der Schuldner den Eröffnungsantrag bei drohender Zahlungsunfähigkeit oder Überschuldung gestellt und die Eigenverwaltung beantragt und ist die angestrebte Sanierung nicht offensichtlich aussichtslos, so bestimmt das Insolvenzgericht auf Antrag des Schuldners eine Frist zur Vorlage eines Insolvenzplans. Die Frist darf höchstens drei Monate betragen. Der Schuldner hat mit dem Antrag eine mit Gründen versehene Bescheinigung eines in Insolvenzsachen erfahrenen Steuerberaters, Wirtschaftsprüfers oder Rechtsanwalts oder einer Person mit vergleichbarer Qualifikation vorzulegen, aus der sich ergibt, dass drohende Zahlungsunfähigkeit oder Überschuldung, aber keine Zahlungsunfähigkeit vorliegt und die angestrebte Sanierung nicht offensichtlich aussichtslos ist.

[...]

Part 8. Self-Administration

§ 270 Requirements

(1) The debtor is entitled, under the supervision of a trustee, to administer and direct the insolvency estate if the insolvency court orders self-administration in the resolution on the initiation of the insolvency proceedings. [...]

§ 270b Preparation for Restructuring

(1) If the debtor filed the initiating petition upon imminent illiquidity or over-indebtedness and petitioned for self-administration, and if the restructuring sought is not obviously futile, then the court may determine, upon petition of the debtor, a period for submission of an insolvency plan. The period may not be longer than three months. The debtor must submit with the petition a reasoned attestation of a tax advisor, an auditor or a lawyer, or a person with a comparable qualification, who is experienced in insolvency matters, that imminent illiquidity or over-indebtedness, but not illiquidity, exists, and that the restructuring sought is not obviously futile.

[...]

Chapter 3. Glossary

Act on the Modernization of GmbH Law and on the Combating of Abuses (*Gesetz zur Modernisierung des GmbH-Rechts und zur Bekämpfung von Missbräuchen*). — This reform act of 2008 (abbreviated with MoMiG) established far-reaching changes of the GmbH law, especially with regard to the incorporation of a GmbH and its financial organization. It attempted to make the GmbH more attractive to businesses, especially relative to foreign limited liability companies, and to enhance creditor protection. It also introduced the entrepreneurial company (limited liability) (*Unternehmergesellschaft (haftungsbeschränkt)*).

Action for a declaration of voidness (*Nichtigkeitsklage*). — The action for a declaration of voidness is similar to the action for rescission. It is used, however, in cases where a resolution of the members of a GmbH is obviously and profoundly defective, i.e., where a severe violation of the law or of the articles of association is to be observed. In such cases, the resolution is automatically void. However, before its voidness is regarded as binding for all members as well as the managing directors, it is necessary for a court to declare the resolution void.

Action for rescission (*Anfechtungsklage*). — Although the action for rescission is mentioned several times in the GmbH Act, the GmbH Act itself does not contain provisions regulating the action for rescission. Instead, the courts apply the relevant provisions of the Stock Corporation Act (*Aktiengesetz*) accordingly. As a general rule, a member is entitled to file a lawsuit on the ground that the resolution of a meeting of the members of a GmbH violated either a statutory provision or a provision of the articles of association, i.e., that the resolution is defective (but not so severely defective as in the case of the action for a declaration of voidness). Thus, the action for rescission is an action to set aside a resolution of the members: The member's lawsuit leads to a judicial review with the aim of declaring the resolution of the meeting of the members to be void. The action for rescission must be filed within a certain period of time (generally within one month) after the adoption of a resolution.

Additional contribution (*Nachschuss*). — Additional contributions are contributions that members render in addition to the initial contributions. The equity of the GmbH becomes greater if additional contributions are rendered. However, additional contributions do not lead to an increase of the capital stock (as provided in the articles of association) and do not effect the par value of the membership interests. In principle, members are not obligated to make additional contributions, and it is not possible to introduce such an obligation upon a member against his will through an amendment of the articles of association. With the consent of every member, however, the articles of association may provide for contributions in addition to the initial contribution. The obligation to make additional contributions may be unlimited or limited to a certain amount. In the first case, members have the possibility to release themselves from the duty to make the additional contribution if they place the membership interest at the disposal of the company for satisfaction from the membership interest. Additional contributions do not have a significant practical importance; member loans are a much more frequently used means of financing the GmbH.

Affiliation agreement (*Unternehmensvertrag*). — A group of companies (*Konzern*) can be established by affiliation agreements. Through such agreements a legal entity subjects its governance to another company (control agreement), or obligates itself to transfer its entire profit to another company (profit transfer agreement).

Amortization (*Einziehung/Amortisation*). — See "redemption of membership interests".

Articles of association (*Gesellschaftsvertrag/Satzung*). — A GmbH cannot be founded without articles of association. In most instances, the GmbH Act uses the term "*Gesellschaftsvertrag*"; however, the term "*Satzung*", which is in practice and also in the GmbH Act itself sometimes arbitrarily used as well, can be regarded as a synonym. In either case, the articles of association can be regarded as the constitution of the GmbH. They govern the internal organization of the company and also contain provisions concerning the company's relationship to third parties. There is a statutorily prescribed minimum content of the articles of association, which in practice are often accompanied by further provisions. The articles of association may also deviate from (most of) the provisions of the GmbH Act. In general, the articles of association are the only founding document. German company law does not explicitly recognize additional corporate statutes such as by-laws. To what extent contractual side-agreements (*schuldrechtliche Nebenabreden*), which are frequently used in practice, are of a binding character is subject to a controversial debate in Germany.

Body (*Organ*). — Both forms of legal entities, partnerships (*Personengesellschaften*) as well as incorporated legal entities (*Kapitalgesellschaften*), need natural persons in order to form a will and to make decisions as well as to be led and to be supervised. To label these individuals and their function in the company, German legal doctrine uses the term "body" of a legal entity. It distinguishes between decision-making bodies, executive or management bodies, and supervisory bodies. Contrary to partnerships, in which the members are automatically regarded as the bodies, incorporated legal entities' bodies need to be appointed. As a consequence, only an incorporated legal entity can be leadershipless. The mandatory bodies of a GmbH are the members/the meeting of the members and the managing director(s). In addition, GmbHs may have a supervisory board.

Business purpose (*Unternehmensgegenstand*). — The business purpose defines by what means the company purpose should be achieved. It is therefore the more narrow term than "company purpose". German law does not adhere to an ultra vires doctrine. Consequently, the power of representation of the managing directors is not restricted to actions that are consistent with the purpose of the business.

Called-in capital (*eingefordertes Kapital*). — See "capital subscribed".

Capital maintenance (*Kapitalerhaltung*). — To a large extent, German company law focuses on the protection of creditors. It attempts to achieve this goal by the so-called legal capital system with minimum capital stock requirements and capital maintenance rules. The capital maintenance rules are designed to exclude the capital stock from distributions to members of the GmbH. Therefore, they aim to ensure that at least assets with a value corresponding to the capital stock amount are available for the distribution to creditors in the case of insolvency.

Capital stock (*Stammkapital*). — The capital stock is the sum of the par values of all membership interests. Consequently, it represents the equity of the GmbH at its incorporation date and is thus listed in the liability side of a balance sheet. The capital maintenance system refers to the capital stock amount that needs to be denominated in whole euros and that needs to be stated in the articles of association. Capital increases and capital decreases change the capital stock amount.

Capital subscribed (*gezeichnetes Kapital*). — In its parts pertaining to balance sheets, the Commercial Code (*Handelsgesetzbuch*) does not refer to the term capital stock or capital stock amount as it is used in the GmbH Act but rather to the generic term "capital subscribed". In general, the GmbH's capital subscribed equals the capital stock amount as provided for in the articles of association. Since a reform in 2009, the Commercial Code (*Handelsgesetzbuch*) provides for special disclosure rules if not all contributions to the company have been rendered or at least been called in. In such cases, contributions that have not been rendered may only be entered on the asset side of the balance sheet if they have been called in. The (total) amount of the capital subscribed and, separately thereof, the amount of the capital subscribed which has not yet been called in, are to be stated on the liabilities side of the balance sheet, as a sub-category of equity. Only the difference between the two amounts (i.e., the amount of the capital subscribed less the amount of the contributions not yet called-in) may be entered in the liability side of the balance sheet. This item has to be labelled as "called-in capital".

Co-determination (*Mitbestimmung*). — Co-determination appears to be a German particularity. In practice and as far as GmbHs are concerned, the Act on the One-Third Participation of Employees on the Supervisory Board (*Gesetz über die Drittelbeteiligung der Arbeitnehmer im Aufsichtsrat*) and the Act on the Co-Determination of Employees (*Gesetz über die Mitbestimmung der Arbeitnehmer*) form the most important acts of co-determination laws. These acts become applicable if a GmbH has more than 500 or 2,000 employees, respectively. In such an instance, a GmbH needs to have a supervisory board, and one-third or fifty percent, respectively, of the members of the supervisory board are elected by the employees (rather than by the meeting of the members).

Coercive fine (*Zwangsgeld*). — A coercive fine is not a criminal sanction, i.e., it is not a fine in the sense of criminal law. It is rather used if a person does not voluntarily fulfill his duties as they are incumbent upon him. Thus, coercive fines have the purpose to force someone to do something.

Commercial company (*Handelsgesellschaft*). — Commercial companies are all incorporated legal entities as well as all forms of partnerships recognized by the Commercial Code (*Handelsgesetzbuch*) (but not, e.g., the civil partnership, political parties, and incorporated associations/clubs). Every GmbH is a commercial company, regardless of its size, the frequency and extent of its business, or its system of accounting, etc. Consequently (see "merchant") the provisions of the Commercial Code (*Handelsgesetzbuch*) are automatically applicable to all GmbHs.

Commercial register (*Handelsregister*). — The commercial register (*Handelsregister*) is a public (and electronically run) register that provides information about facts and legal relationships of merchants, partnerships and companies. With regard to GmbHs, the typical information that can be found in the commercial register (*Handelsregister*) is, inter alia, the company name, the registered office, the capital stock amount, the business purpose, the name(s) of the managing director(s), the rules concerning the representation of the GmbH, etc. Each legal entity which is registered in the commercial register (*Handelsregister*) is given a number (e.g., HRB 75325). In Germany, the commercial register (*Handelsregister*) is run by the court of registry.

The administration of the commercial register (*Handelsregister*) is governed by the Commercial Register Regulation (*Handelsregisterverordnung*).

Company bulletin (*Gesellschaftsblatt*). — Certain publications are, due to the provisions of the GmbH Act or of the articles of association, mandatory for the GmbH. In such cases, the publication must be effected in the company bulletin. The Federal Gazette (*Bundesanzeiger*) must serve as one of the company bulletins. It can be accessed under www.bundesanzeiger.de. The articles of association may designate other public newspapers or electronic information media as a company bulletin, but such a provision does not release the company from the obligation to publish mandatory publications in the Federal Gazette (*Bundesanzeiger*).

Company in formation (*Vorgesellschaft*). — The GmbH as such does not exist before its entry in the commercial register (*Handelsregister*). However, as soon as the articles of association are signed by all members (in notarial form), the GmbH exists as a company in formation. The GmbH Act is applicable to the company in formation, provided that the provision in question does not necessitate the entry of the GmbH in the commercial register (*Handelsregister*). Consequently, contracts can already be entered into and claims can already be established in the company's name. Prior to the entry in the commercial register (*Handelsregister*), however, the "acting person" and the incorporating members of the GmbH face a risk of liability. The company in formation has to be differentiated from a mere pre-formation company which is regularly a (commercial) partnership with the common purpose to found the GmbH.

Company name (*Firma*). — The provisions governing the company name can be found in §§ 17 et seq. of the Commercial Code (*Handelsgesetzbuch*). The company name is the name under which the GmbH does business. It is to be used in court proceedings of the GmbH. While a GmbH can basically choose any name, description, abbreviation, etc., as its company name, it is mandatory to add the designation "*Gesellschaft mit beschränkter Haftung*", which means "company with limited liability", or a generally understood abbreviation of this designation, most often the abbreviation "*GmbH*". Special requirements exist for GmbHs that are formed with a capital stock of less than 25,000 euros (the so-called entrepreneurial company (limited liability) (*Unternehmergesellschaft (haftungsbeschränkt)*)).

Company purpose (*Gesellschaftszweck*). — The company purpose indicates the purpose for which the GmbH is founded. GmbHs may have any statutorily permissible company purpose – may it be for-profit or not-for-profit. It is therefore not permissible to incorporate a GmbH with a purpose that is against the law or against public policy. In addition, certain businesses (such as specialized banks, insurance companies, etc.) cannot be run by a GmbH. Typically, but not necessarily, the company purpose corresponds with the business purpose. However, company purpose is the broader of the two terms.

Company with limited liability (*Gesellschaft mit beschränkter Haftung*). — The company with limited liability (*Gesellschaft mit beschränkter Haftung*) is one of the legal entities available under German law. It is abbreviated with "*GmbH*" and it is governed by the GmbH Act. It shares the core structural characteristics typical for an incorporated legal entity (*Kapitalgesellschaft*) and is classified as a legal person (*juristische Person*).

Contribution (*Einlage*). — The GmbH Act permits two kinds of contributions: cash contributions and in-kind contributions; in the latter case, a report on the incorporation using in-kind contributions must be prepared and appended to the company's registration for entry in the commercial register (*Handelsregister*). The obligation of members to render contributions arises in the incorporation process and as part of a capital increase.

Control agreement (*Beherrschungsvertrag*). — See "affiliation agreement".

Court of registry (*Registergericht*). — In Germany, the commercial register (*Handelsregister*) is run by a local court, i.e., by the court of registry, not by private institutions or separate administrative agencies. Entries into the commercial register (*Handelsregister*) are checked by judges. The competent court is the local court for the place of the registered office of the GmbH.

Declaration of intent (*Willenserklärung*). — A declaration of intent is one of the key elements of German private law. It is a person's expression of his will that is designed to achieve a legal consequence (in private law), e.g. to accept an offer and to form a contract, to terminate a lease, etc. With regard to GmbHs, declarations of intent can only be expressed by, or delivered to, persons who have the power to represent the company. Managing directors (and liquidators) have this power automatically as bodies of the GmbH; it can also be given to other persons. Special rules apply for persons who are only authorized to take delivery of declarations of intent (§ 10(2) of the GmbH Act). In the case of leadershiplessness, every member is empowered to take delivery of declarations of intent.

Delayed filing for insolvency (*Insolvenzverschleppung*). — The managing directors of a GmbH (and, under certain circumstances, other persons as well, see "leadershiplessness") have, under penalty of law, the duty to file a petition for the initiation of an insolvency proceeding without undue delay if the GmbH is either illiquid or over-indebted. A failure to comply with this duty has two consequences: First, the managing directors have to compensate the company for payments that were made while the company was illiquid or over-indebted. Second, creditors of the GmbH may hold the managing directors liable if they suffer a loss due to the delayed filing for insolvency.

Deregistration (*Löschung*). — The GmbH Act distinguishes between the dissolution, the liquidation and the deregistration of a GmbH. The deregistration is the last event that occurs. Upon the entry of the deregistration in the commercial register (*Handelsregister*), the company ceases to exist. The deregistration can be the end of a liquidation process. However, the deregistration can also occur automatically, i.e., without the need of further actions on behalf of the company. If, for example, the company lacks assets, the deregistration takes place simultaneously with the dissolution. In such an instance, there is no need for a liquidation process.

Dissolution (*Auflösung*). — The GmbH Act provides numerous reasons for the dissolution of the GmbH. The dissolution must be registered for entry in the commercial register (*Handelsregister*). Dissolution does not mean that the GmbH has already ceased to exist. Rather, dissolution initiates the liquidation process, provided that there are distributable assets. After the dissolution, the GmbH can only conduct business necessary for liquidating the company. Until all assets have been distributed in the liquidation process, the GmbH remains a legal entity. See also "deregistration" and "liquidation".

Entrepreneurial company (limited liability) (*Unternehmergesellschaft (haftungsbeschränkt)*). — The entrepreneurial company (limited liability) (*Unternehmergesellschaft (haftungsbeschränkt)*) was introduced via the 2008 reform of the

GmbH Act. It does not require a minimum capital stock amount of 25,000 euros. The entrepreneurial company (limited liability) (*Unternehmergesellschaft (haftungsbeschränkt)*) is intended for small businesses and start-ups. It is not another legal form, but rather a GmbH with a special company name: § 5a of the GmbH Act states that "*Unternehmergesellschaft (haftungsbeschränkt)*" or "*UG (haftungsbeschränkt)*" needs to be part of the company name. By the necessities of using this cumbersome company name and of building up the statutory reserve, the GmbH Act sets incentives to raise the capital stock to or above the threshold of 25,000 euros in order to be able (but not obligated) to change the designation "*Unternehmergesellschaft (haftungsbeschränkt)*" to "*Gesellschaft mit beschränkter Haftung*" (or the relevant abbreviations, respectively). Thereby, § 5a of the GmbH Act illustrates that the entrepreneurial company (limited liability) (*Unternehmergesellschaft (haftungsbeschränkt)*) is not designed to govern a business on a permanent basis.

Executive (*Geschäftsleiter*). — Executive bodies of different incorporated legal entities are labelled with varying terms. "Executive" is the generic term for the persons belonging to executive bodies. For example, the members of the management board are the executives of a stock corporation, and the managing directors are the executives of a GmbH.

Federal Gazette (*Bundesanzeiger*). — The Federal Gazette (*Bundesanzeiger*) is the medium through which mandatory publications by the company may be effected (see "Company bulletin"). On www.bundesanzeiger.de publications, announcements as well as other legally relevant information concerning a GmbH can be searched and accessed at no charge and without registration.

Forfeiture (*Kaduzierung*). — In the case of a delayed payment of a cash contribution after it is called in, a member may be forced to forfeit the membership interest he accepted and with regard to which he is in default. If certain criteria are met, the defaulting member can be declared in forfeiture of his membership interest without being compensated. This harsh consequence is intended to serve as a means of motivating the member to render contributions as prescribed.

Group of companies (*Konzern*). — Germany is one of the few jurisdictions that provide for special statutory rules concerning groups of companies. These rules range from provisions in the Stock Corporation Act (*Aktiengesetz*), the majority of which are, by way of analogy, applicable to GmbHs as well, to provisions in the Commercial Code (*Handelsgesetzbuch*) pertaining to balance sheets, and to provisions in the numerous taxation acts. The German terminology in the context of the law of groups of companies (*Konzernrecht*) uses female versions of expressions describing the degree of kinship, for example "daughter company" (rather than "subsidiary"), and refers to the term "undertaking" (*Unternehmen*) (rather than "company").

Illiquidity (*Zahlungsunfähigkeit*). — Illiquidity is defined in § 17 of the Insolvency Code (*Insolvenzordnung*) as the debtor's inability to fulfill his payment obligations as they become due. See also "insolvency".

Imminent illiquidity (*drohende Zahlungsunfähigkeit*). — As defined in § 18 of the Insolvency Code (*Insolvenzordnung*), the debtor is imminently illiquid if he is not expected to be able to fulfill the existing payment obligations when they become due. See also "insolvency".

Initial contribution (*Stammeinlage*). — The initial contribution corresponds to the par value of the respective membership interest that a member accepts in exchange for his initial contribution. In practice, the terms "par value of the membership interest" and "initial contribution" are used as synonyms. Thus, the initial contribution only represents the amount of the contribution obligation, which a member accepts upon the incorporation of the company.

In-kind contribution (*Sacheinlange*). — The GmbH Act allows the members to render either cash contributions or in-kind contributions. In-kind contributions can only be rendered through a transfer of, e.g., real property, rights and goods (but not by carrying out services). However, even then, the value of the contributed assets is uncertain. This is the reason for the rather strict provisions of the GmbH Act, which aim to ensure that the assets actually have the respective value and that the GmbH actually receives the assets as part of the capital stock. Obeying the statutory provisions concerning in-kind contributions is oftentimes rather costly and tedious (see also "report on the formation using in-kind contributions").

Insolvency (*Insolvenz*). — Under German law, all insolvency proceedings are governed by the Insolvency Code (*Insolvenzordnung*). There are distinct statutes neither for personal bankruptcy and corporate insolvency nor for liquidation and reorganization procedures. With regard to GmbHs, § 15 of the Insolvency Code (*Insolvenzordnung*) states that insolvency proceedings can be initiated in the cases of illiquidity, imminent illiquidity, or over-indebtedness of the company. According to § 15a of the Insolvency Code (*Insolvenzordnung*), the managing directors (and, under certain circumstances, other persons as well, see "leadershiplessness") must file for insolvency if the company is illiquid or over-indebted (see also "delayed filing for insolvency").

Insolvency Code (*Insolvenzordnung*). — The Insolvency Code (*Insolvenzordnung*) is abbreviated as "InsO".

Insolvency plan (*Insolvenzplan*). — The insolvency plan is a special insolvency procedure (set out in §§ 217 et seq. of the Insolvency Code (*Insolvenzordnung*)) for the reorganization of an insolvent estate, especially for the reorganization of insolvent companies and partnerships.

Insolvency proceeding(s) (*Insolvenzverfahren*). — See "insolvency".

Insolvency receiver (*Insolvenzverwalter*). — If the insolvency proceeding is initiated with regard to a GmbH, normally an insolvency receiver basically takes over the position of the managing director(s) (but see "self-administration procedure" (*Eigenverwaltung*)). The insolvency receiver then manages the insolvent estate and therefore represents the GmbH in and out of court. A managing director will nevertheless remain in office, but most of his tasks and responsibilities are in the hands of the insolvency receiver. The insolvency receiver is chosen and appointed by the insolvency court. Typically, a preliminary insolvency receiver (*vorläufiger Insolvenzverwalter*) is appointed for the period between the filing for insolvency and the initiation of the insolvency proceeding. The powers of a preliminary insolvency receiver are determined by the insolvency court.

Leadershiplessness (*Führungslosigkeit*). — "Leadershiplessness" as defined in § 35(1) of the GmbH Act is a state in which the company has no managing director. The concept of leadershiplessness was introduced by the reform of the GmbH Act in 2008. It is designed to prevent the abuse of the corporate form GmbH with regard to two situations. First, it needs to be guaranteed that, at every point in time, declarations of intent can be delivered to the company and that documents can be served on the company. Second, the leadershiplessness concept has also consequences with regard to the right and, even more importantly, the duty to file for insolvency of the GmbH. According to § 15(1) of the Insolvency Code (*Insolvenzordnung*), every member of the GmbH is entitled to file for insolvency on behalf of the company in the case of leadershiplessness. Likewise, according to § 15a(3) of the Insolvency Code (*Insolvenzordnung*), every member of the GmbH has the duty to file for insolvency under penalty of law if the GmbH is leadershipless and either illiquid or over-indebted.

Liquidation (*Liquidation*). — After the dissolution of the GmbH, the liquidation process begins. Once the liquidation process is initiated, current transactions must be terminated, but the obligations of the dissolved company must nonetheless be fulfilled. The liquidators must collect on the claims of the company, convert the assets of the company to cash, and satisfy the company's creditors. Finally, the remaining assets of the company are distributed among the members in proportion to their membership interests. Normally, the liquidation is carried out by the managing directors or, alternatively, by external liquidators. If the company is dissolved due to the initiation of an insolvency proceeding, it is part of the tasks of the insolvency receiver to liquidate the company. See also "deregistration" and "dissolution".

List of members (*Gesellschafterliste*). — The list of members (*Gesellschafterliste*), sometimes also referred to as the list the members (*Liste der Gesellschafter*) in the GmbH Act, is, along with the articles of association, one of the most important documents of the GmbH. In relation to the company, someone is only considered to be entitled to a membership interest if he is entered in the list of members as recorded in the commercial register (*Handelsregister*). The list of members must be drafted by the managing directors, and the managing directors must file the list of members with the commercial register (*Handelsregister*) without undue delay whenever members leave or join the GmbH or change the extent of their participation; in certain situations, it is the duty of a notary (*Notar*) involved in the transfer of membership interests to sign the list and file it with the commercial register (*Handelsregister*) instead of the managing directors. The list of members forms the basis for the acquisition of a membership interest in good faith. It must also state the respective percentage of participation in the capital stock represented by the respective par value of the membership interests of all members.

Managing director (*Geschäftsführer*). — Under the GmbH Act, "Geschäftsführer" is a technical term. The managing director is a body of the GmbH. His internal powers (i.e., his power to manage the affairs of the company) and his external powers (i.e., his power to represent the company in and out of court) derive from his position in the GmbH. A GmbH must have at least one managing director; otherwise the GmbH is leadershipless (§ 35(1), Sentence 2 of the GmbH Act). There may also be other representatives of the GmbH. However, these persons are not "bodies" of the company; instead, they have been mandated and have been given power of attorney on a contractual basis. Statutory duties (such as the duty to file for insolvency) are only imposed on managing directors, not on other managers. Managing directors are bound by the resolutions of (the meeting of) the members. Although possible, it is rather unusual in Germany to have a board of managing directors with a CEO structure, as common in jurisdictions with a one-tier system of corporate governance. In addition, the position of a managing director of a GmbH has to be distinguished from the position of a member of the management board of a stock corporation.

Meeting of the members (*Gesellschafterversammlung*). — The members are the most authoritative instance of the GmbH. The resolutions of the members are adopted in meetings of the members (which are convened by the managing directors) or by means of circulating the proposed resolution (with votes in textual form), by the majority of the votes cast. The members have an all-embracing competence, i.e., they may decide on any management matter. Resolutions of the members are binding for the managing directors (unless they are illegal).

Member (*Gesellschafter*). — The GmbH Act uses the generic term "member" rather than other terms such as "shareholder". A GmbH can have one or more members; it is also possible to incorporate a GmbH with only one member. Natural persons as well as other legal entities (e.g., stock corporations, commercial partnerships, GmbHs, etc.) can be members of a GmbH. The same holds true for legal entities incorporated in foreign jurisdictions (to the extent that they are recognized by German international company law).

Member loan (*Gesellschafterdarlehen*). — Member loans are loans given by members to the company. They are a popular means of financing the GmbH because loans are much less formalistic and more flexible than the increase of capital. However, the law provides restrictions concerning the repayment of member loans. While the possibility to repay member loans is not limited by the capital maintenance rules of the GmbH Act, the consequences of repayments of member loans are governed instead by provisions of the Insolvency Code (*Insolvenzordnung*). If the member loan has been repaid to the member in the year preceding the date on which the petition for the initiation of an insolvency proceeding has been filed, the member has to refund the amount received.

Membership interest (*Geschäftsanteil*). — The membership interest represents the rights and duties arising from the status of being a member of the GmbH. Each membership interest has a par value that must be denominated in whole euros. Only a person that holds at least one membership interest is a member of a GmbH. The term membership interest is closely linked with the term "initial contribution". A member of a GmbH enjoys three categories of membership rights: financial rights (e.g., the right to receive a certain fraction of the annual profit), participation rights (e.g., the right to participate and to vote in meetings of the members) and protection rights (*Schutzrechte*) (e.g., the right to file actions for rescission). All these rights are bundled in the membership interest. The proportion of the rights associated with the membership interests to one another is determined by the par values of the membership interests. The membership interest is an instrument that is transferable but, contrary to the shares of a stock corporation, not tradable on the stock exchange. Membership interests may not be issued in bearer form, i.e. the members do not receive certificates representing their membership interests. For the transfer of membership interests by members, a contract entered into in notarial form is required. It is possible to effectively acquire a membership interest in good faith from an unentitled person.

Merchant (*Kaufmann*). — The Commercial Code (*Handelsgesetzbuch*) refers to the term "merchant" with regard to its applicability. Most of the provisions of the Commercial Code (*Handelsgesetzbuch*) are applicable to merchants only. While the decision whether a natural person (or a partnership) qualifies as a "merchant" in the meaning of the Commercial Code (*Handelsgesetzbuch*) is oftentimes difficult and contingent on the size and amplitude of business and on the system of accounting, such problems of differentiation do not exist with regard to GmbHs. According to § 13(3) of the GmbH Act, every GmbH is regarded as a commercial company and thus as a merchant within the meaning of the Commercial Code (*Handelsgesetzbuch*) (see also "commercial company").

Minimum capital stock (*Mindeststammkapital*). — German GmbH law adheres to the minimum capital stock principle. Traditionally, this principle was regarded as an important element of the creditor protection mechanisms. These days, the prevailing view on the minimum capital stock requirement is rather different: It is accepted that the threshold of 25,000 euros cannot guarantee a sound capitalization of a business. However, the minimum capital stock serves as a signal of seriousness of the incorporators of a GmbH, as they have to contribute at least this minimum capital stock amount in order to establish a GmbH. Since 2008, it is possible to incorporate a GmbH as an entrepreneurial company (limited liability) (*Unternehmergesellschaft (haftungsbeschränkt)*) with a capital stock that is below the minimum capital stock amount of 25,000 euros (thus, in extreme cases, even with a capital stock of one euro). In such a case, the designation "*Unternehmergesellschaft (haftungsbeschränkt)*" or the abbreviation "*UG (haftungsbeschränkt)*" needs to be part of the company name.

Model Protocol (*Musterprotokoll*). — The incorporation of a GmbH through a simplified procedure by the use of a model protocol was one of the inventions of the 2008 reform act. Two types of a model protocol can be found in the appendix to the GmbH Act.

Notarial form (*notarielle Form*). — Numerous legal acts necessitate "notarial form" and thus the involvement of a notary (*Notar*). According to the GmbH Act, the articles of association require notarial form. That means that the articles of association must be, in the presence of the notary (*Notar*), read out to the founding members, approved and signed by them as well by the notary (*Notar*). Furthermore, resolutions of the members amending the articles of association must be certified by a notary (*Notar*), and for the transfer of membership interests, a contract in notarial form is necessary.

Notary (*Notar*). — The notary (*Notar*) in Germany, not to be confused with, e.g., an American notary, is a highly qualified lawyer who obtained a special legal education, in addition to his law degrees. He is the holder of a very reputed public office and is appointed by the state. A notary (*Notar*) authenticates and certifies documents (such as contracts and declarations of intent) and provides independent legal advice. Contrary to practicing lawyers, however, he is bound to impartiality.

Notes (*Anhang*). — The notes form part of the annual financial statements of an incorporated legal entity. The notes are designed to explain the balance sheet and the profit and loss statement. Only the additional information provided in the notes gives a true picture of the financial situation of a GmbH.

On its own accord (*von Amts wegen*). — In general, administrative agencies tend not to take action unless someone files the appropriate petition. In some instances, however, they may act on their own accord, i.e., without any petition.

Over-indebtedness (*Überschuldung*). — According to § 19 of the Insolvency Code (*Insolvenzordnung*), over-indebtedness exists if the assets of the debtor no longer cover the existing liabilities, unless the continuation of the business is, according to the circumstances, more likely than not. This "double-stage assessment" definition emphasizes the prognosis as to whether the company will survive and fulfill its obligations in the near future.

Par value (*Nennbetrag*). — German GmbH law adheres to the principle that a par value needs to be determined for each membership interest. Different membership interests may have different par values, which must be denominated in whole euros. The total of the par values of all membership interests determines the capital stock amount of the GmbH, i.e., the total sum must equal the company's capital stock. While German stock corporation law has introduced a special form of a no-par-value share (namely a kind of share (*Stückaktie*) that has no par value, but is still linked to the capital stock amount) in 1998, the German GmbH law still does not recognize a concept of no-par value membership interests.

Profit transfer agreement (*Gewinnabführungsvertrag*). — See "affiliation agreement".

Prokurist (*Prokurist*). — A Prokurist is a representative of the GmbH who is authorized to act on behalf of the company by contract; he is registered in the commercial register (*Handelsregister*). The scope of his power of representation is defined in the Commercial Code (*Handelsgesetzbuch*). Any contractual modification of the (broad) scope of his power of representation is not effective with regard to third parties.

Purpose of the business (*Gegenstand des Unternehmens*). — See "business purpose".

Redemption of membership interests (*Einziehung von Geschäftsanteilen*). — In former times, the redemption of membership interests was called "amortization". Through a redemption, a membership interest ceases to exist. The member loses all rights associated with the respective membership interest. However, the capital stock amount is not affected by a redemption, as the redemption changes the par value of the remaining membership interests. Alternatively, a new membership interest may be issued. For practical purposes, only the compulsory redemption is of importance. It requires a resolution of the members in addition to a reason clearly specified in the articles of association at a point in time prior to the acceptance of the membership interest by the member concerned.

Report on the incorporation using in-kind contributions (*Sachgründungsbericht*). — In-kind contributions are a permissible means of financing the GmbH. As GmbH law follows the principle of effective raising of capital and the effective rendering of contributions, it has to prevent the overvaluation of in-kind contributions. Such an overvaluation would have the consequence that, in effect, not as much capital is paid in with regard to membership interests as stated in the articles of association. Thus, the objects of in-kind contributions as well as the par value of the membership interests for which the in-kind contributions are to be rendered, must be determined in the articles of association. In addition, the members must present the facts that are material to the adequacy of any rendering of in-kind contributions and must make the valuations of the objects of in-kind contributions plausible. This information is given in the report on the incorporation using in-kind contributions. The report needs to be in writing and to be signed by all members personally. It is primarily addressed to the court of registry. The court of registry has to refuse the entry of the GmbH in the commercial register (*Handelsregister*) if in-kind contributions have been overvalued.

Representative belonging to a body (*organschaftlicher Vertreter*). — Numerous persons may be authorized to represent a GmbH. Statutory representatives, for example, are authorized by law, whereas Prokurists and authorized signatories have been given such authority by contract. Representatives belonging to a body fall in neither of these categories. Their power to represent the GmbH derives automatically from their holding of a position in one of the (representative) bodies of the GmbH.

Self-administration procedure (*Eigenverwaltung*). — The Insolvency Code (*Insolvenzordnung*) recognizes a "debtor-in-possession" approach to insolvency proceedings, as it allows insolvent GmbHs to administer and direct the insolvency estate themselves under the supervision of a trustee (*Sachwalter*) (rather than under the command of an insolvency receiver (*Insolvenzverwalter*)) if certain conditions are fulfilled. Since the Act on the Further Facilitation of Corporate Reorganization (*Gesetz zur weiteren Erleichterung der Sanierung von Unternehmen, ESUG*) came into force in 2012, self-administration procedures have become more common.

Supervisory board (*Aufsichtsrat*). — The so-called two-tier system of corporate governance is one of the key characteristics of German stock corporation law. In addition to a management board, every stock corporation must have a supervisory board. Slightly simplifying, one might say that the supervisory board has, in an institutionalized and in a more clearly defined way, the task that non-executive directors have in jurisdictions with the unitary board system (one-tier system of corporate governance). The supervisory board is not a mandatory body of a GmbH. However, the articles of association may provide for a supervisory board. Alternatively, co-determination law makes a supervisory board mandatory for the GmbH if certain conditions regarding the company's size are fulfilled. If a supervisory board is appointed, numerous provisions of the Stock Corporation Act (*Aktiengesetz*) are to be applied to GmbHs.

Textual form (*Textform*). — The Civil Code (*Bürgerliches Gesetzbuch*) differentiates between written form, electronic form and textual form in §§ 126 to 126b of the Civil Code (*Bürgerliches Gesetzbuch*). While "written form" necessitates an actual printing (or hand-writing) and the "electronic form" requires a qualified digital signature, the "textual form" has the least preconditions. E-mails, (simple) copies and scanned documents, for example, are documents in "textual form".

Transformation Act (*Umwandlungsgesetz*). — A legal entity such as a GmbH can be transformed into a different legal form or de-merged or merged into another entity under the provisions of the Transformation Act (*Umwandlungsgesetz*). When this Act came into force in 1995, it was the legislature's intention to enable a change of corporate form without the necessity to first liquidate an existing entity and then to create a new one. The Transformation Act (*Umwandlungsgesetz*) contains provisions concerning mergers (*Verschmelzungen*), de-mergers (*Spaltungen*) and changes of the legal form of an entity (*Formwechsel*) and thereby enables the members, inter alia, to change the legal form of a business from a GmbH to a stock corporation, to a commercial partnership, etc., or vice-versa without going through costly and complex liquidation procedures. In a comparable way, mergers and de-mergers are facilitated. The Transformation Act (*Umwandlungsgesetz*) is abbreviated as "UmwG" and is accompanied by the Transformation Tax Act (*Umwandlungssteuergesetz*) which allows transformations to take place in a tax-advantaged way.

Transparency register (*Transparenzregister*). — The (ultimate) beneficial owners of, inter alia, GmbHs have to be reported to the transparency register (unless this information can electronically be retrieved from the commercial register (*Handelsregister*)). The registration of the beneficial owners aims at preventing money laundering. The transparency register (*Transparenzregister*) was introduced in 2017 and is governed by the Money Laundering Act (*Geldwäschegesetz*) and the Regulation on the Inspection of the Transparency Register (*Transparenzregistereinsichtnahmeverordnung*).

Undisclosed in-kind contribution (*verdeckte Sacheinlage*). — Oftentimes members try to circumvent the strict rules applicable to in-kind contributions in order to save time and money. A typical example for such an attempt would look as follows: The formation of the GmbH (or an increase of capital stock) is carried out by cash contributions, but the company immediately uses the cash for payments to the members in exchange for goods. This is called an undisclosed in-kind contribution. According to traditional case law, such an undisclosed in-kind contribution did not release the members from their obligation to render their cash contribution. To a good extent, this view was confirmed by the 2008 reform of the GmbH Act. Today, however, § 19(4) of the GmbH Act allows the deduction of the value of the asset already provided from the still-existent obligation to render a cash contribution. This means that the transaction(s) is/are reviewed from an economic perspective rather than in a formalistic way.

Chapter 4. List of Vocabulary

A

Abänderung des Gesellschaftsvertrags	amendment of the articles of association
abhängiges Unternehmen	controlled undertaking
abberufen (einen Geschäftsführer)	to dismiss (a managing director)
Abschlussprüfer	auditor
Absonderungsrecht	right to separate satisfaction
Abstimmung	voting
Abtretung (eines Geschäftsanteils)	transfer (of a membership interest)
Abtretungsvertrag	transfer contract
Aktiengesetz	Stock Corporation Act
Aktionär	shareholder
Aktivposten	asset item
Aktivseite (der Bilanz)	asset side (of the balance sheet)
Amortisation	amortization
Amtsgericht	local court
Änderung des Gesellschaftsvertrags	amendment of the articles of association
Auflösung (der Gesellschaft)	dissolution (of the company)
Anfechtungsklage	action for rescission
Anhang	notes (to the financial statements)
Anlagevermögen	non-current assets
Anmeldung	registration
(zur Eintragung im Handelsregister)	(for entry in the commercial register (*Handelsregister*))
Anschaffungskosten	acquisition costs
Auflösung (von Rücklagen)	release (of reserves)
Aufsichtsrat	supervisory board
Aufsichtsratsmitglied	member of the supervisory board
ausgeschlossener Gesellschafter ...	excluded member
Außengesellschaft	disclosed partnership
Aussonderungsrecht	right to separation

B

Bareinlage	cash contribution
beglaubigen	to authenticate
Beherrschungsvertrag	control agreement
bekannt machen	to publish
Bekanntmachung	publication
Beschluss (der Gesellschafter)	resolution (of the members)
Beschlussfassung	adoption of a resolution
Bestätigungsvermerk	audit opinion
bestellen (einen Geschäftsführer)	to appoint (a managing director)

Beteiligung	participation
Betrag des Mindeststammkapitals	minimum capital stock amount
Betrag des Stammkapitals	capital stock amount
Betriebsgeheimnis	trade secret
Beweislast	burden of proof
BGB-Gesellschaft	civil partnership
Bilanz	balance sheet
Bilanzgewinn	unappropriated profit
Bilanzstichtag	reference date of the balance sheet
Buchführung	accounting
Bundesanzeiger	Federal Gazette
Bundesgerichtshof	Federal Court of Justice
Bundesgesetzblatt	Federal Law Bulletin
Bundeszentralregistergesetz	Federal Central Register Act
Bürgerliches Gesetzbuch	Civil Code

D

Drittelbeteiligungsgesetz	One-Third Participation Act
drohende Zahlungsunfähigkeit	imminent illiquidity

E

eigene Geschäftsanteile (der Gesellschaft)	(the company's) own membership interests
Eigenkapital	equity
eigenkapitalersetzende Gesellschafterdarlehen	member loans in lieu of equity
Eigenverwaltung	self-administration procedure
einfordern (von Einlagen)	to call in (contributions)
eingeforderter Nachschuss	called-in additional contribution
Einlage	contribution
Einlageverpflichtung	contribution obligation
einstweilige Verfügung	interim injunction
Eintragung (in das Handelsregister)	entry (in the commercial register (*Handelsregister*))
Einzahlungen	payments
Einziehung (Amortisation)	redemption (amortization)
Einziehung (von Geschäftsanteilen)	redemption (of membership interests)
Entlastung	discharge
Ergebnisverwendung	appropriation of the profit or loss
Ergebnisverwendungsbeschluss ...	resolution on the appropriation of the profit or loss
Eröffnungsbilanz	opening balance sheet
Errichtung	founding
Erwerb (eines Geschäftsanteils) ...	acquisition (of a membership interest)
Erwerber (eines Geschäftsanteils)	acquirer (of a membership interest)
existenzgefährdender Eingriff	infringement endangering the survival of the company by extraction of indispensable financial resources

F

Fehlbetrag	deficit
Feststellung (des Jahresabschlusses)	adoption (of the annual financial statements)
Firma	company name
Formwechsel	change of legal form
Fortführungsprognose	continuation prognosis
Führungslosigkeit	leadershiplessness

G

Gegenleistungsanspruch	claim to consideration
Gegenstand des Unternehmens	purpose of the business
Geldeinlage	cash contribution
genehmigtes Kapital	authorized capital
Genossenschaft	cooperative society
Genossenschaftsregister	cooperative society register
Gesamtschuldner	joint and several debtor(s)
Geschäftsanschrift	business address
Geschäftsanteil	membership interest
Geschäftsbetrieb	business operation(s)
Geschäftsbrief	business letter
Geschäftsführer	managing director
Geschäftsführung	management
Geschäftsgeheimnis	business secret
Geschäftsjahr	fiscal year
Geschäftsleiter	executive
Geschäftsverbindung	business relationship
Gesellschaft	company
Gesellschaft bürgerlichen Rechts	civil partnership
Gesellschaft mit beschränkter Haftung	company with limited liability
Gesellschaft ohne Rechtspersönlichkeit	company without legal personality
Gesellschafter	member
Gesellschafterbeschluss	resolution of the members
Gesellschafterdarlehen	member loan
Gesellschafterliste	list of members
Gesellschafterversammlung	meeting of the members
Gesellschaftsblatt	company bulletin
Gesellschaftsvertrag	articles of association
Gesellschaftszweck	company purpose
Gesetz über das Verfahren in Familiensachen und in den Angelegenheiten der freiwilligen Gerichtsbarkeit (FamFG)	Act on Proceedings in Family Matters and in Matters of Non-contentious Jurisdiction

Gesetz über die Drittelbeteiligung der Arbeitnehmer im Aufsichtsrat (DrittelbG)	Act on the One-Third Participation of Employees on the Supervisory Board
Gesetz über die Mitbestimmung der Arbeitnehmer (MitbestG)	Act on the Co-Determination of Employees
Gesetz über Ordnungswidrigkeiten (OWiG)	Administrative Offenses Act
Gesetz zur Modernisierung des GmbH-Rechts und zur Bekämpfung von Missbräuchen (MoMiG)	Act on the Modernization of GmbH Law and on the Combating of Abuses
Gesetz zur weiteren Erleichterung der Sanierung von Unternehmen (ESUG)	Act on the Further Facilitation of Corporate Reorganization
Gesetz zur Erleichterung der Bewältigung von Konzerninsolvenzen	Act on the Facilitation of the Handling of the Insolvency of Groups of Companies
gesetzliche Rücklage	statutory reserve
Gewerbesteuer	trade tax
Gewinn	profit
Gewinn- und Verlustrechnung	profit and loss statement
Gewinnabführungsvertrag	profit transfer agreement
Gewinnausschüttung	distribution of profits
Gewinnrücklage	retained earnings
Gewinnverteilung	profit distribution
Gewinnvortrag	profit carried forward
gezeichnetes Kapital	capital subscribed
Gründung	incorporation
Gründungsaufwand	incorporation expenses
gutgläubiger Erwerb	acquisition in good faith

H

Handelsbücher	accounting books
Handelsgesellschaft	commercial company
Handelsgesetzbuch	Commercial Code
Handelsregister	commercial register
Handelsregisterverordnung	Commercial Register Regulation
Handlungsbevollmächtigter	authorized signatory
herrschendes Unternehmen	controlling undertaking
hin- und herzahlen	to pay back and forth

I

Innengesellschaft	undisclosed partnership
Insolvenz	insolvency

Insolvenzantrag	petition for the initiation of an insolvency proceeding
Insolvenzgericht	insolvency court
Insolvenzordnung	Insolvency Code
Insolvenzplan	insolvency plan
Insolvenzverfahren	insolvency proceeding(s)
Insolvenzverschleppung	delayed filing for insolvency
Insolvenzverwalter	insolvency receiver

J

Jahresabschluss	annual financial statements
Jahresbilanz	annual balance sheet
Jahresergebnis	annual profit or loss
Jahresfehlbetrag	annual deficit
Jahresüberschuss	annual net profit
juristische Person	legal person

K

Kaduzierung	forfeiture
Kapitaleinlage	capital contribution
Kapitalerhaltungsregeln	capital maintenance rules
Kapitalerhöhung	capital increase
Kapitalerhöhung aus Gesellschaftsmitteln	capital increase from company funds
Kapitalgesellschaft	incorporated legal entity
Kapitalherabsetzung	capital reduction
Kapitalrücklage	capital reserve
Kaufmann	merchant
Kommanditgesellschaft	limited commercial partnership
Kommanditgesellschaft auf Aktien	partnership limited by shares
Kommanditist	limited partner
Komplementär	general partner
Konzern	group of companies
Konzernabschluss	consolidated financial statements
Konzernlagebericht	group management report
Körperschaftsteuer	corporate tax
Kreditwesengesetz	Banking Act

L

Lagebericht	management report
Landgericht	district court
Liquidation	liquidation
Liquidator	liquidator
Liste der Gesellschafter	list of the members
Löschung (der Gesellschaft)	deregistration (of the company)

M

Masselosigkeit	lack of funds
Mehrheitsgesellschafter	majority member

Minderheitsgesellschafter	minority member
Mindestbetrag des Stammkapitals	minimum capital stock amount
Mindeststammkapital	minimum capital stock
Mitberechtigter	co-entitled person
Mitberechtigung	co-entitlement
Mitbestimmungsgesetz	Co-Determination Act
Musterprotokoll	model protocol

N

Nachschuss	additional contribution
Nachschusspflicht	duty to make additional contributions
Nennbetrag	par value
Nichtberechtigter	unentitled person
Nichtigkeitsklage	action for a declaration of voidness
Notar	notary
notarielle Form	notarial form
Notgeschäftsführer	temporary managing director

O

Offene Handelsgesellschaft	commercial partnership
Offenlegung	publication
Ordnungswidrigkeit	administrative offense

P

Passivposten	liability item
Passivseite (der Bilanz)	liability side (of the balance sheet)
Personengesellschaft	partnership
Personenhandelsgesellschaft	commercial partnership
Prokurist	Prokurist (no translation)
Prüfer	auditor(s)
Prüfung	audit
Publizitätsgesetz	Public Disclosure Act

R

Rechnungslegungsstandards	accounting standards
Rechtsform	legal form
Rechtsgeschäft	legal transaction
Rechtshandlung	legal act
Rechtskraft	res judicata
Rechtsvorgänger	predecessor in interest
Registergericht	court of registry
Rückgewähranspruch	claim to repayment
Rücklage	reserve
Rücklage bilden	to accumulate a reserve
Rücklagenauflösung	release of reserves

S

Sacheinlage	in-kind contribution
Sachgründungsbericht	report on the incorporation using in-kind contributions

Sachwalter	trustee
Satzung	articles of association
Satzungsänderung	amendment of the articles of association
Sitz der Gesellschaft	registered office of the company
Sorgfalt (eines ordentlichen Geschäftsmanns)	care (of a prudent businessman)
Spaltung	demerger
Sperrjahr	restrictive year
Stammeinlage	initial contribution
Stammkapital	capital stock
Stellvertreter (des Geschäftsführers)	deputy (of the managing director)
Strafgesetzbuch	Criminal Code

T

Textform	textual form
Transparenz- und Publizitätsgesetz	Transparency and Public Disclosure Act
Transparenzregister	transparency register

U

Übernahme (eines Geschäftsanteils)	acceptance (of a membership interest)
Übernahmeerklärung	declaration of acceptance
übernehmen (einen Geschäftsanteil)	to accept (a membership interest)
Überschuldung	over-indebtedness
Übertragung (eines Geschäftsanteils)	transfer (of a membership interest)
Umsatzsteuer	value added tax
Umlaufvermögen	current assets
umwandeln (von Rücklagen)	to convert (reserves)
Umwandlungsgesetz	Transformation Act
Umwandlungssteuergesetz	Transformation Tax Act
uneingeschränkter Bestätigungsvermerk	unqualified audit opinion
Unternehmensgegenstand	business purpose
Unternehmensvertrag	affiliation agreement
Unternehmergesellschaft (haftungsbeschränkt)	entrepreneurial company (limited liability)

V

Veräußerer (eines Geschäftsanteils)	transferor (of a membership interest)
verbundene Unternehmen	affiliated undertakings
verdeckte Sacheinlage	undisclosed in-kind contribution
verjähren	to become time-barred
Verjährung	statute of limitation
Verlust	loss
Verlustdeckungshaftung	liability for the covering of losses
Verlustvortrag	loss carried forward
Vermögensgegenstand	asset
Vermögenslosigkeit	lack of assets
Versicherungsaufsichtsgesetz	Insurance Supervision Act
Verschmelzung	merger

Vertretungsbefugnis	power of representation
Verwaltungsbehörde	administrative agency
Verzugszinsen	default interest
vollwertig	nominally and economically equal in value
Vorbelastungshaftung	liability for pre-entry charges
Vorgesellschaft	company in formation
Vorgründungsgesellschaft	pre-formation company
Vorstand	management board

W

Wertaufholung	reversal of impairments
Widerspruch (auf der Gesellschafterliste)	notice of pendency (on the list of members)
Willenserklärung	declaration of intent

Z

Zahlungsaufforderung	request for payment
Zahlungsunfähigkeit	illiquidity
Zweigniederlassung	branch office

Index

The numbers next to the terms listed below indicate the paragraph number of Chapter 1 in which the reader can find an explanation of the respective term.